THE TWILIGHT OF SOCIAL CONSERVATISM

The Twilight of Social Conservatism

American Culture Wars in the Obama Era

John Dombrink

NEW YORK UNIVERSITY PRESS

New York and London

NEW YORK UNIVERSITY PRESS
New York and London
www.nyupress.org

References to Internet websites (URLs) were accurate at the time of writing. Neither the author nor New York University Press is responsible for URLs that may have expired or changed since the manuscript was prepared.

Library of Congress Cataloging-in-Publication Data
Dombrink, John.
The twilight of social conservatism : American culture wars in the Obama era /
John Dombrink.
pages cm   Includes bibliographical references and index.
ISBN 978-0-8147-3812-2 (pb : alk. paper) — ISBN 978-0-8147-9517-0 (cl : alk. paper)
1. Social values—United States. 2. Culture conflict—United States.
3. Conservatism—United States. 4. Politics and culture—United States.
5. United States—Politics and government. 6. Christianity and culture—United States.
I. Title.
HN90.M6D653   2015
306.0973—dc23   2015009277

New York University Press books are printed on acid-free paper, and their binding materials are chosen for strength and durability. We strive to use environmentally responsible suppliers and materials to the greatest extent possible in publishing our books.

Manufactured in the United States of America

10 9 8 7 6 5 4 3 2 1

Also available as an ebook

For Maya, Paul, and Kara

For Mary Ann and Clete, Patsy and Jeff, Kathleen and John,
and their families

Focus group participants told us that they don't want national or federal focus on abortion or social issues. Republicans ultimately lose.

—Republican pollster/consultant Frank Luntz, November 13, 2012

The Bible Belt is collapsing. It's bad for the country, but good for the church . . . We are no longer the moral majority. We are a prophetic minority.

—Southern Baptist leader Rev. Russell Moore, 2013

CONTENTS

ACKNOWLEDGMENTS

I was very fortunate during the preparation of this book to have the assistance and insights of many people at varying stages. I am deeply grateful to the interest of two colleagues at the University of California, Irvine—Carroll Seron and Val Jenness, themselves impressive sociolegal scholars—who took the time to attend presentations of parts of this book and offer guidance. At a distance, Arlene Skolnick also engaged me in discussion on these issues and offered her perspective and reading references.

I benefited greatly from opportunities to present portions of this work as it was being explored or completed. I am grateful to colleagues Alan Wolfe and Erik Owens (Boston College), Diane Winston (University of Southern California), Roger Magnusson (University of Sydney), Paul Babie (University of Adelaide), Johnny Nhan and Pat Kinkade (Texas Christian University), and Frederick Gagnon (University of Quebec at Montreal). At preliminary French and English sites of an expansion of this work, I am very thankful to Maurice Punch, Joel Joffe, Waheed Alli, Alain Bauer, Liora Israel, Jennifer Merchant, François de Chantal, and many others who provided assistance. I was also able to present versions of these chapters in different settings and am thankful to those who hosted me: Jack Baugh, Adrian Windsor, Christine Trost, Toni Dwyer, Julia Hume, Collette Chattopadhyay, and Scott and Laurie Dubchansky.

Colleagues, both at UCI and elsewhere, were very helpful in offering ideas on the nature of the project and other support. For that I am grateful to Jim Meeker, Henry Pontell, Simon Cole, William C. Thompson, Cheryl Maxson, Charis Kubrin, Ron Huff, Susan Turner, Susan Coutin, George Tita, Tony Smith, Anthony McGann, William Schonfeld, Ron Weitzer, Jerry Skolnick, Mark Kleiman, Barbara Owen, Richard Flory, William N. Thompson, Dan Hillyard, Jim Gray, and Mark Poster. I was very fortunate to have Gil Geis involved in the development of my work in this area. At NYU Press, Ilene Kalish was always supportive and interested in the project from its earliest plans and throughout drafts, and Caelyn Cobb and Aiden Amos provided important assistance, as did Dorothea Stillman Halliday, Betsy Steve, and skilled copyeditor Jennifer Dropkin at the end of the process. The anonymous reviewers offered very helpful advice.

I am thankful for the insight of UCI doctoral students in Criminology, Law & Society who were teaching assistants or students in related courses during the preparation of this book: Harry Mersmann, Laura Bringer, Natasha Pushkarna, Jasmine Montgomery, Jenny West-Fagan, Marisa Omori, Gavin Lee, Luis Rodriguez, Matt Fritz-Mauer, Sofia Laguna, Matt Renner, and Anna Raup-Kounovsky. I also appreciate the diligence of UCI undergraduate students who served as research assistants at various points during the project: Matt Alecock, Jason Giang, Ryan Jebreil, Tony Cabrera, Jonathan Huang, Diana Sun, Alexander Shin, and Adam Tornquist.

In the Department of Criminology, Law & Society, many people made my pursuit of this effort much easier. I am thankful to Margaret Wyvill, Lynette Vaz, Nate Gapasin, Robin Weirich, Mary Underwood, Ashley Vikander, Mickey Shaw, Jennifer Lane (and Robert Boyd, John Salinas, and Eric Carter), and especially Leslie Noel. The Criminology Outreach Program teams, and the many excellent mentors and coordinators, and teachers and mock trial judges, provided valuable support during this time. I am thankful to the many UCI Criminology Outreach Program mentors and Bob Sterling, Jackie Washington, Ellen Febonio, Peg Encheff, and their teacher colleagues as well as Esteban Rodriguez, Irma Hernandez, Sal Sarmiento, and Roy Delgado.

I am thankful to the many individuals who gave me insights or support in various conversations and ongoing efforts: B. J. Beu, Phil and Sharon Garrison, Paul and Jan L'Esperance, Greg Trimarche, Brenda Yecke, Julie Phillips, Jeff Amos and Todd Brooks, Bill Peterson, Andrew Reikes, Steve Kawata, Parmis Khatibi, Emilie Chow, Christopher Kroner, JoAnna Schoon, Joanne Culverhouse, Steve Sogo, Joan Politeo, Tom Donoghue, Chris Green, Hoss Tabrizi, Ed Ornelas, Bob Armstrong, Juan Lara, Kirk Andrews, Roger Kempler, Gasper Patrico, Michael Hass, Tad Heitmann, Roger Stewart, Juan Carlos Gallego, Michael Bourne, Tom Vickers, Lyda Hill, Kathy Jones, Tommy Kemp, Keiko Sakamoto, Chris Weaver, Jane DuBois, Bobby Lovell, Mary Ann Gaido, Larry Agran,

Sam Gilmore and Wendy Goldberg, Kathy and Bahram Esfahani, Cecilia Dunne, Eileen Dunne, Brian Dunne and Zhang Peng, Annie Dunne and Tony Cerami, and Brian and Gloria Dunne.

This book is dedicated to the sisters with whom I was lucky to grew up and have enjoyed as adults and who were my early teachers and supporters (and wonderful role models themselves) and their partners and families. And every day, I am thankful for the support and creative example of my partner Maya Dunne and her stellar work on philanthropy, social justice, and food and health policy; our son Paul (who offered creative insights in many ways from Boston and Austin, provided musical background, and did important work on footnotes and missing data); and our daughter Kara (impressive in her scholarship, soccer, backpacking, and many endeavors and her well-crafted essays on the computer in the adjacent room).

Introduction

I was a college senior at a Catholic university when *Roe v. Wade* was decided by the U.S. Supreme Court in January 1973. It was an unusual day, in that former president Lyndon Johnson passed away that same day after a heart attack at his ranch in Texas. That meant that the Supreme Court's historic 7–2 ruling could not be the lead headline in the *New York Times* the next day (though it was a large secondary headline).

While several states had begun liberalizing their abortion laws in the late 1960s, including Governor Ronald Reagan's California in 1967, some described the decision in *Roe* as a "bolt out of the blue." While critics and increasingly mobilized opponents strategized the fastest ways to reverse the decision in *Roe*, they could not succeed in eventually passing a constitutional amendment to define that life begins at conception. But they were able to limit federal funding and insert abortion politics into our national political discussion in a way that has lasted for the last three decades.

By 1980, as I was finishing my doctoral studies at Berkeley and completing a dissertation on the legalization of casino gambling, that quiet terrain was changing dramatically. The "Moral Majority," founded by the Baptist minister Jerry Falwell, was pushing back on what they viewed as the unfolding moral decline in American society. There were places like my parish and neighborhood, where the older adults—probably Franklin Roosevelt Democrats—were less enamored in the 1970s with the changes of the 1960s and the McGovern Democrats and had found that the newly reformed Democratic Party didn't necessarily represent their values. They fit the concept of the "Reagan Democrat." Ronald Reagan, elected president in 1980 in part because of these voters, would then make the triumvirate of social conservatism, economic conservatism, and foreign policy conservatism the underpinning of his transformative presidency. Today, all Republican candidates and conventions make a point of honoring him and his role in their political development in their statements.

The election of Bill Clinton in 1992 convinced me and others that the Reagan era was limited, through it was not fading quietly. For example, Republican primary challenger Pat Buchanan, speaking at the 1992 Republican National Convention, thundered a full-throated naming of a culture war going on in America, "a religious war going on in our country for the soul of America. It is a cultural war, as critical to the kind of nation we will one day be as was the Cold War itself" (Buchanan 1992). George W. Bush's two terms as president did later rely upon a strong social conservative message, with defunding of stem cell research, pushes for state defense of marriage acts, and support of an attempt to pass a federal constitutional amendment against same-sex marriage.

By 2007, when I co-wrote, with Daniel Hillyard, *Sin No More*, a book about legislated morality in America, I was convinced that the strength of American social conservatism—the Moral Majority, the Christian Coalition, the Traditional Values Coalition, and increasingly the Catholic bishops—was waning. I did not go as far as those who thought that Barack Obama had, with his 2008 election, ended the culture war. Still, the idea that his victory had demonstrated the diminishing power of the "Reagan Democrats" was worth exploring. The tea party emergence in 2009 and the anger and resentment they tapped into—while ostensibly about the role of government—revived opposition with a Buchanan-like fervor. Its strident anti-Obama tone was bracing in its graphic displays of anger and resistance and its racial animus. That very engaged contestation inspired this book examining the contours of the culture wars in the Obama era.

On that day in 1973, I would not have predicted the advent of same-sex marriage and its acceptance—even California had not started a path of legal reform. I might have been optimistic about drug law reform, but it would take decades for those early stirrings to find a high level of societal support. But I also wouldn't have thought that the reproductive rights issue would be so continuingly a source of friction in American society and that the American political structure would be so integrally tied to those issues. Throughout this book, I argue that the high point of that culture war era and its underpinnings has now passed. The vitality of socially conservative ideas—against same-sex-marriage, against reproductive rights, protecting the primacy of conservative religious doctrine—has faded. This book seeks to chronicle that shift.

What This Book Is Not

This book is not a political science text that looks at the theories of electoral participation, though it references at time ideas and data from such studies. Nor is a treatise on the details of running a campaign—identifying themes, raising money, producing and airing ads (some of them "attack ads"), performing in debates and question-and-answer sessions, speaking to large gatherings of voters or debates—though some have come into play in the analysis of the 2012 election in the furtherance of issues involved in the American culture war and the backlash of the Obama years.

Nor is this a book deeply about Barack Obama. Certainly, since it deals with the time of his first term and his reelection, he is naturally deeply intertwined with the analysis of the various issues considered within the book. And he certainly looms over this time period. Later, when historians consider the efficacy of various presidents and their administrations, they will place Obama and his work among his counterparts and consider his accomplishments and shortcomings. For now, it is probably safe to consider, as the book does, these years as the "Obama era." In many ways, others might compete. It could be the "Steve Jobs era" or the "smartphone era." With Amazon founder Jeff Bezos buying the *Washington Post* in 2013 with 1% of his net worth, it arguable could be considered the "Internet commerce era." Or the "YouTube era." Or the "legal marijuana era." Or even the "Kobe and Lebron era."

And there are many ways in which Obama did not change the contours of politics or of the presidency. Critics of his on the left have found him too safe, too willing to continue the policies of his predecessor and the Bush administration, especially in foreign policy, where the drone attacks he sanctioned and the use of force abroad was to them at odds with the posture he had adopted in running for president in 2008 (the best to contrast himself with then-Senator Hillary Clinton). They have faulted his healthcare plan—derisively called "Obamacare" by his opponents, discussed in Chapters 2, 6, and 7—as being too corporate, as hewing too much to the desires of the insurance industry and the pharmaceutical industry, and for not supporting a single-payer, government-centered health system as in England or other Western industrialized countries. The fact that a similar plan was adopted first in the United

States by the Commonwealth of Massachusetts when Mitt Romney was governor (an issue of paternity that would trouble him throughout the 2012 Republican primary season and blunt much of the critique that tea party adherents and conservatives brought against Obama from 2009 forward), added an unusual twist to the proceedings. In a country that has a unique and indelible stain of racial animus in its history, including its Civil War, the election of the first African American president made these years a meaningful time in an altogether different way.

Nonetheless, the book does tread carefully around the issue of whether American electoral politics can be used as a measure of societal status and change. To place too great an emphasis on it is to potentially get lost in the "inside baseball" of political campaigns, the ebbs and flows of ad purchases, fundraising, debates, "gotcha" moments, and the news media. For many, though, the symbolism of the 2008 election, the ups and downs of American political consciousness since then, and Obama 2012 reelection, has been an extended referendum on the shift away from social conservatism in American society. This book seeks to map that terrain.

Genesis

As mentioned earlier, the genesis for this book came at the end of my previous work, *Sin No More* (Dombrink and Hillyard 2007). That book had argued that the image of America presented by strategists like Karl Rove—who presaged that the 2004 re-election of George W. Bush as president would hopefully lead to another several decades of conservative rule in America—was of an America as a "center-right" country. Daniel Hillyard and I had argued that Americans were in fact more moderate than so depicted and that underneath the surface of an ongoing culture war backlash was in fact an America moving toward normalization and liberalization of a range of personal morality laws and attitudes, from same-sex marriage to stem cell research and assisted suicide. That book was formulated before Barack Obama's ascent to the head of the Democratic Party and the presidency. There were two mentions of his policy and speeches in *Sin No More*: one to his well-considered 2004 Democratic convention speech on bipartisanship and anti-polarization, and another to his comments on faith and politics (relevant especially since he offered a renewed Democratic Party openness to and explicit mention of religion in its campaigns and policies). But the growth and shifts of the same cultural trends during his administration, between 2009 and 2014, in many cases driven by his policies, necessitates further examination.

Overview

This book examines the ongoing contests and shifting political and social landscape of America in the Obama era as it applies to the core elements of the "culture war" and to a central American disjuncture: the liberalization of American society on many measures, at the same time of the enormous conservative pushback that continues, and the polarization that still characterizes us in 2015.

Chapter 1, "Liberalization and Backlash in the Obama Era," establishes the basis for the book's assessment of the state of American conservatism in the Obama era. It takes as its central point this paradox between the growing liberalization of some features of American society (such as same-sex marriage) and growing conservatism at the same time (e.g., the tea party). This chapter establishes this paradox as the central tension in the book and provides the roadmap for the following chapters. I examine the progress of the vitality of the social conservative approach in a decidedly different era—the time of the repeal of the "Don't Ask, Don't Tell" military policy, the expansion of same-sex marriage, and the enactment of historic healthcare reform. At the same time, I focus on the percentage of Americans self-identifying as conservative that has inched up in the Gallup polls to a new high. Yet Barack Obama was reelected president in 2012. The subsequent chapters will further explore and analyze this paradox and offer predictions for success or failure in the various contests for value dominance.

Chapter 2, "Anger and Resentment Anew: Tea Parties and the Obama Backlash," focuses on the engines and contours of the "Obama backlash" and the expressions of the tea party movement, with its cries that "America is being taken from us" and attempts to reimpose "normal people values." I document a new culture war resistance ("birthers," "deathers," "Tenthers" [those who believe that, following the Tenth Amendment, all powers not specifically assigned to the federal government should be the province of the states], "truthers," and tea party activists) and identify polarization and hyper-partisanship as the themes of discourse, and even governing, but I conclude that this backlash is not rooted in the morality issues of the prior culture war. These two chapters present, review, and analyze data regarding attitudes and issue framing during the years 2008–2014, which are the focus of the book.

The following three chapters together present an argument as to why social conservatism will no longer have the profile and effect that it had during the height of the Moral Majority and social conservative years. Chapter 3, "Marriage Equality: America and the New Normal," traces the steady and dramatic changes in American attitudes toward, and legal reform of, marriage equality. This is analyzed as an example of the "de-wedging" of one of the key "wedge issues" utilized by the social and religious conservatives from 1980 onward, that of gay rights generally and same-sex marriage specifically. I use as a touchpoint one analyst's observation: "It's hard to imagine a significant issue in which the center of gravity is shifting faster than gay marriage in this country."

Chapter 4, "After Falwell: Shifts and Continuities in the Culture War and the Role of Religion in America," analyzes the role of religion, especially its conservative manifestations in contemporary American society. It buttresses the arguments presented in Chapter 3, especially the moderation of American religiosity and the diminution of the power of social conservatives to shape American politics and policy. This chapter supports the notion of an increasingly tolerant America. Contrary to Chapter 2, this chapter argues that the backlash of the 2008–2013 period is not being driven by religious conservatism. With the maturation and drift of its members, even the evangelical movement has grown to more resemble the profile and positions of more mainstream religious denominations in America.

Instead, the chapter argues that the moderating impulses within American religion have become dominant. With the growth of those claiming no religious denomination (the seculars, or the "nones")—especially among the millennial generation—the effects on the policies and issues discussed in this book are and will continue to be substantial.

Chapter 5, "'Vota Tus Valores': The Culture War in a Diversifying America," poses a provocative demographic question: What will be the effect of the growing ethnic diversity of the United States on legal consideration of the personal morality issues discussed in this book? Will a growing "Latinoization" of the American population continue in a liberalized direction, or will cultural conservatism give rise to a slowdown in the granting of personal rights through the extension of personal autonomy? Will a religiously observant Latino population follow the precepts of their church leaders and embrace conservative pro-life measures on reproductive rights and same-sex marriage? Or will the collision of different demographic impulses—youthful Latino voters trending one way, their elders another—produce a muted effect for the short term and a convergent liberalism in the long term?

What Chapter 6, "Campaign 2012: Of Plutocrats, Rape, and the 'Ascendant Majority,'" offers is severalfold: First, I offer an analysis of how the backlash of the tea party movement, so prominent in 2009 and 2010, played out in the reality of a 2012 presidential campaign. Second, I highlight the planned and unplanned, inadvertent and unwise, use of culture war issues and symbols—issues that had traditionally excited the social conservative religious base, stolen away "Reagan Democrats," and caused problems in national elections—and what this portends for future American sociopolitical development.

In the same way that Chapter 1 begins with the implications of the election of Barack Obama as American president on November 4, 2008, Chapter 7, "Whither the Culture War? The 'Unwedging' of Old Frames," concludes by looking at his re-election four years later, on November 6, 2012. I present data on the impact of the millennial generation and the rise of the progressive "ascendant majority" (and issues such as contraception); the suggestion of strategic plans and "rebranding" of the Republican Party, and the internecine struggles that has produced; an analysis of the role of polarization in the body politic; and the conclusion, which analyzes these elements and predicts the complications of populism (including "libertarian populism"), the reduced salience and role of social conservatives, and the end, finally, of the potency and relevance of "Reagan Democrats."

Overall, in this book I argue that the "wedge issues" that have been successful in American politics are losing their power. This "unwedging" is what characterizes America in 2015, especially amid the effect of the rising importance of the millennial generation—a decidedly more secular and progressive generation on these issues. Even marijuana legalization has (re-)emerged as an issue. It seems improbable that these wedge issues will soon regain their potency. As one religious conservative leader recently wrote, such shifts in American society suggest that likeminded religious-based social conservatives should now view themselves as a "prophetic minority," rather than a "Moral Majority" (Russell Moore 2013).

1

Liberalization and Backlash in the Obama Era

There are some who question the scale of our ambitions,
who suggest that our system cannot tolerate too many big
plans. . . . What the cynics fail to understand is that the
ground has shifted beneath them, that the stale political arguments that have consumed us for so long, no longer apply.
—President Barack Obama, January 2009 inaugural speech

The single most important thing we want to achieve is for
President Obama to be a one-term president.
—U.S. Senate Minority Leader Mitch McConnell (R-
Kentucky), October 2010

When Barack Obama was elected president of the United States in
November 2008, it was indeed a historic moment for a country that
had fought a civil war almost 150 years before over issues that included
the right of plantation owners to own African slaves as their property.
Obama's victory was impressive by several standards. Just four years after
President George W. Bush's political advisor Karl Rove had proclaimed
that the 2004 Bush reelection demonstrated that America was a "center-
right" country, and that those election results would insure many years
of conservative and Republican rule, the country had turned instead
to a different direction, in a remarkable manner. Though he prevailed
by a popular vote of 53%-46%, Obama had won in the critical electoral
vote by a much larger margin and had succeeded in states that had been
out of the Democratic column for some time—such as Indiana, North
Carolina, and Virginia. He had even prevailed in Florida, the site of the
2000 election dead heat between Bush and Democratic candidate and
vice president Al Gore.

Barack Obama had achieved a greater percentage of the total vote than
had any Democratic candidate since Lyndon Johnson in 1964. Demo-

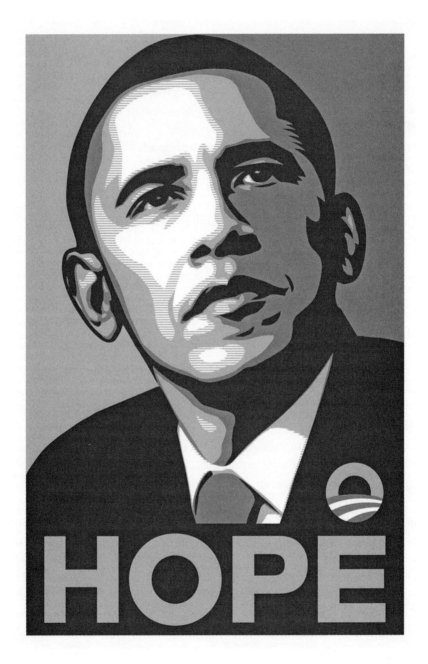

Figure 1.1. This iconic poster represented the momentum behind Barack Obama in the 2008 election.

crats also won control of the U.S. Senate and the House of Representatives, giving Obama an opportunity, at least in his first two years, to set an agenda and push for passage of significant legislation. To some, the Obama election represented more than the ascent of a progressive Democratic vision. To them, the newly elected president—who himself had famously emerged on the national scene with a 2004 Democratic convention speech that spoke of a "red America where we have gay friends, and a blue America where we worship an awesome God" (*Washington Post* 2004)—represented a sea change in another direction: the promise to be a post-partisan president who could move beyond the hyper-partisanship that had been characterizing American politics from the time of Richard Nixon and the Vietnam war. Soon after the 2008 American presidential election, some social scientists and political analysts concluded that the contours of the election and its outcome had signaled an end to the polarization and culture wars that had typified American politics for the prior three decades. To them, demographic changes would be forcing the demise of the culture wars, broadly defined. To others, the moderating of religious groups was having a similar effect. In both cases, it was thought that electoral defeat would have the effect of minimizing and defusing the contestation of the culture war issues—especially the long-standing "wedge issues" of religion, gay rights, and reproductive rights.

As social conservatives came to grips with the 2008 electoral defeats, there were those among them who argued the opposite. They emphasized the greater salience of culture war issues as a way of reviving their role and maintaining the thrust of those wars. To some, such a focus could be the seeds for the conservative movement's "intellectual rebirth." To those leaders, social conservative voices in the national debate "won't be silenced." This book provides an analysis and assessment of the meaning and implication of those changes. In particular, it chronicles the conservative resurgence of 2009 and 2010 and the midterm elections rolling back the Democratic majority in the House of Representatives. It examines the successful—though never comfortable—Obama re-election in a very contested 2012 campaign.

In a previous work, *Sin No More* (Dombrink and Hillyard 2007), I had argued that, despite conservative rhetoric, the tide was turning on the core legal and moral issues of the American culture war, with all moving toward normalization in American society—but not always easily. Daniel Hillyard and I challenged the dominant interpretation of the 2004 election as showing a social conservative America, what Karl Rove has called a "center-right" country. In continuation, this book reports on research extending that analysis into the 2008–2014 period. This book poses the question, Which is the best explanation of the current trends in American society on issues related to political division? It concludes with the assertion that we are witnessing the decline of social conservatism as a vital force in the shaping of American political and social thought.

I present competing analyses. Is the best depiction of America on issues that the culture war celebrated, on which social and religious conservatives mobilized, one of growing toleration? Does the coming to maturity of the "millennial generation" of American youth predict a growing normalization and legalization of gay rights and same-sex marriage? Chapter 6 shows these values competing/colliding in the 2012 presidential election. Or is the portrait of contemporary America to be found in the anger and resentment and challenge to the Obama presidency represented by the "tea parties," "birthers," "deathers," "Tenthers," and the congressmen who yelled "You lie!" at the president during a speech in Congress and "Baby killer!" as a colleague announced that he would end his focus on pro-life issues and support the Obama healthcare plan in March 2010? Which is the near American future? Is the consistent theme the increasing moderation on some issues, as was argued in *Sin No More*? Or is today's key story one of backlash and growing polarization? And is it possibly a combination of both?

Birthers, Deathers, Tenthers, and Tea Parties: Polarization and Hyper-partisanship

When one can easily find Internet images in 2009 onward of Barack Obama in the pose of Nikolai Lenin, or with a bust of Karl Marx in the Oval Office, or shown in the startling pose of Heath Ledger's Joker character from *The Dark Knight* (Nolan 2008), or Photoshopped in a traditional racialized pose shining the shoes of Sarah Palin, or depicted as Adolf Hitler in "Dreams from My Führer"—a parody of Obama's 1995 memoir, *Dreams from My Father*—it is difficult to remember that there was indeed a post-election "honeymoon period" for him, like those that most newly elected presidents enjoy. It is also hard to recollect that there was a parallel "wandering in the desert" moment for the Republican

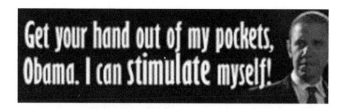

Figure 1.2. Anti-Obama Internet ad.

Party, which was torn between pragmatists and moderates and conservatives who felt that Senator John McCain had lost the presidential election in 2008 precisely because he did not represent the full-throated conservatism that the Reagan years had established as a growing force in American politics. Obama, who had been celebrated for bring a potential post-racial, post-partisan and post–Baby Boomer president, was soon on the road to a vilification that has been unique, given the era of the 24/7 news cycle and unprecedented social media.

During the building of the Obama backlash, the images of opposition were striking and severe: "Hey Barack, go stimulate yourself"; "Just another bum, looking for change"; "I'll keep my faith, guns, freedom, and money . . . you keep the change"; "Dreams of my Führer" (with the image of Obama as Hitler); "Obama is what you get when you allow illegals, idiots, and welfare recipients to vote"; "Why so socialist?"; "Yes we will!" (with Obama in foreground and images of Marx, Lenin, and Mao in background); "Obama for President: because this time socialism is going to work" (with the image done in style of an Obama 2008 campaign sign).

These events had been taking place in the opposite direction of what several political analysts thought might take place (or hoped would occur). Peter Beinart had supported this line of analysis, writing soon after the 2008 election:

> When it comes to culture, Obama doesn't have a public agenda; he has a public anti-agenda. He wants to remove culture from the political debate. . . . Barack Obama was more successful than John Kerry in reaching out to moderate white evangelicals in part because he struck them as more authentically Christian. That's the foundation on which Obama now seeks to build. (Beinart 2009)

At the same time Beinart was expressing hopes for a post-partisan Obama administration, some social conservatives like Gary Bauer (and eventually Rush Limbaugh) were exhorting their followers not to give in, not to compromise, and to draw a line in the sand for conservatism:

> Within hours of Senator Barack Obama's election, those on the Left, in the media and even some in our ranks began making demands for conservatives to cooperate with the new administration in the early months of his presidency. I reject those demands.
>
> It won't be easy, but more Americans still describe themselves as conservative than as liberal, and they are looking for leadership, not more sellouts. (Bauer 2008)

Bauer would later add:

> It has again become fashionable to declare the end of the culture wars, the highly charged political debates about religion, abortion, homosexuality, race and related issues. But . . . the culture wars are as highly charged as ever. They will endure until the issues that provoked them are resolved. (Bauer 2009b)

Soon after the Obama election, some progressive analysts were considering the "end of conservatism" and the twilight of Reaganism, the guiding philosophy of Republican candidates for almost 30 years. Rush Limbaugh exhorted conservative followers of his show and American conservatism to take up the fight and see resistance as the proper path to the rebirth of a conservative presence or dominance (Limbaugh 2009). In a notable February 2009 speech at the Conservative Political Action Conference, Limbaugh, delivering his "anti-state-of-the-union address" only one month after the Obama inauguration, was clear in his analysis: "Obama is dangerously wrong":

> President Obama is so busy trying to foment and create anger in a created atmosphere of crisis, he is so busy fueling the emotions of class envy that he's forgotten it's not his money that he's spending. In fact, the money he's spending is not ours. He's spending wealth that has yet to be created. And that is not sustainable. It will not work.

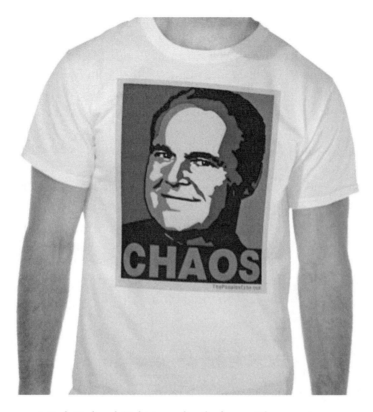

Figure 1.3. A Rush Limbaugh T-shirt parodies the famous Obama poster.

On the left side when you get into this collectivism socialism stuff, these people on the left, the Democrats and liberals today claim that they are pained by the inequities and the inequalities in our society. And they believe that these inequities and inequalities descend from the selfishness and the greed of the achievers. And so they tell the people who are on different income quintiles, whatever lists, they say it's not that you're not working hard enough, you could have what they have, perhaps, if you applied it. They're stealing it from you.

Spending a nation into generational debt is not an act of compassion. All politicians, including President Obama, are temporary stewards of this nation. It is not their task to remake the founding of this country. It is not their task to tear it apart and rebuild it in their image. (Limbaugh 2009)

"Hell no?" asked Rush Limbaugh in his August 14, 2010, broadcast. "Damn no! We're the party of Damn no! We're the party of 'Hell No!' We're the party that's going to save the United States of America!" (Bromwich 2010). Limbaugh had updated the claim of leading 1960s conservative William F. Buckley, who wrote that his *National Review* "stands athwart history, yelling Stop!" (Buckley 1955).

In arguing against the need for an inclusive "big tent" approach in launching a coalition that would bring the Republican Party back to power, former Arkansas governor, Southern Baptist minister, and 2008 Republican presidential candidate Mike Huckabee was clearly with Limbaugh: no big tents. Huckabee hinted at the purity required for a conservative resurgence: "However wrongheaded Democrats might be, they tell you exactly what they're going to do. The real threat to the Republican Party is something we saw a lot of this past election cycle: libertarianism masked as conservatism." (Huckabee 2008). This challenge to those who would propose a reduced emphasis on social conservative topics was direct.

Obama as Socialist

One common charge from the tea parties and Republican opponents was that President Obama had taken a decidedly socialist path to bringing the American economy back in the time of economic turmoil. A 2010 Harris Poll found that 67% of Republican respondents felt that Barack Obama was a socialist. This translated to 40% of the American public.

To the historian Rick Perlstein, these charges were similar to those that had confronted Democratic presidents promoting government as a response to economic concerns, including Franklin Roosevelt and Lyndon Johnson. In the context of this "genealogy," he argued that the threat of the "enemy within" America was a common theme (Perlstein 2010). To another observer, "Tea party activists seem to live in information silos that reinforce their beliefs. To an alarming extent the frame of Obama bringing socialism to America include[s] allegations that Obama and his allies are part of a vast left-wing conspiracy" (Berlet 2009). To another:

> Something very much like the tea party movement has fluoresced every time a Democrat wins the presidency, and the nature of the fluorescence always follows many of the same broad contours: a reverence for the Consti-

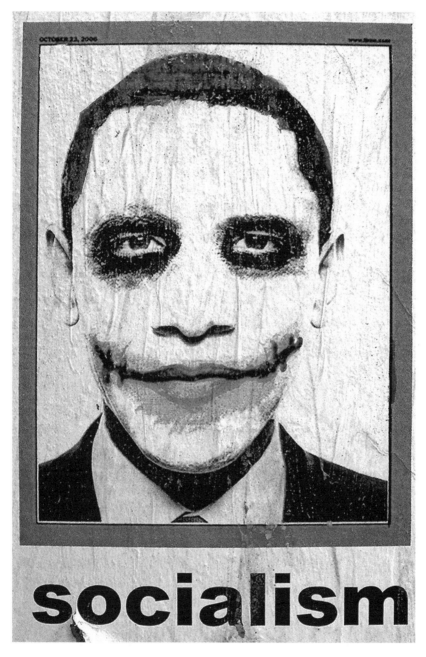

Figure 1.4. A popular anti-Obama ad mixing his portrait with makeup reminiscent of
Batman's Joker (Nolan 2008).

tution, a supposedly spontaneous uprising of formerly non-political middle-class activists, a preoccupation with socialism and the expanding tyranny of big government, a bitterness toward an underclass viewed as unwilling to work, and a weakness for outlandish conspiracy theories. (Drum 2010)

The polarization and hyperpartisanship that had escalated in Washington, D.C. (and the nation) became vibrant in 2009 when the Obama administration proposed its healthcare reform proposal, and the Democratic-controlled House of Representatives and Senate began deliberations on a potentially radical restructuring of an important American concern.

Lone among its industrial counterparts, America had persisted without a government-funded national healthcare system and had promulgated a market-driven system that left as many as 44 million of its citizens without healthcare coverage. As had happened with the Clinton administration in 1993 (although its efforts did not succeed), the features of the Obama reform—creation of a risk pool for uninsured Americans, reduction in Medicare payments, abolishment of the role of preexisting conditions—was dwarfed by the perception that the reform was a "typical" Democratic "giveaway" program of fiscal support, albeit this time benefiting millions of Americans.

"Normal People Values"

In 2008, Republican congresswoman and conservative leader Michele Bachmann had said about Sarah Palin and her family, then under attack, that "they stand for normal people and normal people values, and we say amen to that" (Posner 2008). This theme relates back to the heart of the culture war struggles—the Obama administration represented a foreign presence that was portrayed as a challenge to "traditional American values." In April 2009, Republican strategist Karl Rove exhorted: "Mr. President, stop apologizing for our country." It was in this context that some of the 46% of voters who had preferred John McCain to Barack Obama began to be attracted to the 2009 charges that Obama was not born an American, that his Hawaiian birth certificate was missing or fraudulent. To these "birthers," the legitimacy of the Obama administration was to be called into question by a basic fact of "standing"—he was

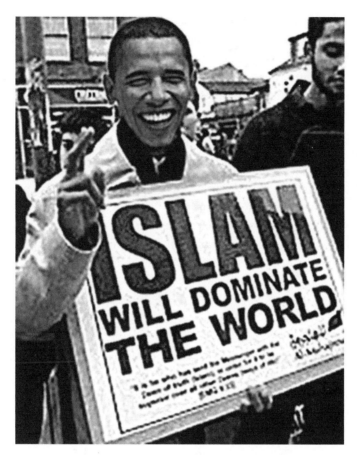

Figure 1.5. A Photoshopped portrait of Obama holding a sign that reads "Islam will dominate the world."

not eligible to be president of the United States. While this may appear to be a marginal claim, polls reported that at least 45% of American Republicans reported agreeing that Obama's citizenship was indeed dubious.

Another avenue of foreignness was Obama's religiosity. In the 2008 campaign, the Obama strategists paid particular attention to righting the perception that Democratic Party was not "religion-friendly," that there was a "God gap" in the eyes of voters. A staged discussion/debate in 2008 with the progressive evangelical reverend Jim Wallis (author of *God's Politics*; Wallis 2005) among Democratic aspirants John Edwards, Hillary Clinton, and Obama was a substantial and nuanced discussion of faith in politics (Sager 2010). The irony was that for once, the Republican Party was led by a person, John McCain, who was relatively undemonstrative in his religiosity and had lost favor among conservative religious groups after his 2000 criticism of Rev. Jerry Falwell and Rev. Pat Robertson as "agents of intolerance." (CNN 2000).

Obama's religious lineage had indeed been one of the vectors upon which criticism of him as anti-American had flourished in the 2008 campaign, when his longtime United Church of Christ pastor had been videotaped urging that instead of "God Bless America," a more appropriate sentiment should be "God Damn America" for all the injustice, racial and otherwise, that the county had promoted. Following the belief in Obama as a non-U.S.-born citizen came charges of his religiosity: that he was indeed a Muslim. These issues had been floated in the 2008 campaign, as one might expect with a candidate with the name Barack Hussein Obama. What was remarkable was that even in 2010, 57% of Republicans told pollsters that they believed President Obama to be a Muslim (Harris Poll 2010).

In using the words "normal people values," Bachmann used a term that deeply resonates with the effort of Richard Nixon to find support for his party and program and Vietnam war policy among the "Silent Majority" of his 1969–1974 presidency:

> So tonight, to you, the great silent majority of my fellow Americans, I ask for your support. I pledged in my campaign for the Presidency to end the war in a way that we could win the peace. (Nixon 1969)

Nixon would later send his vice president Spiro Agnew to speak on behalf of the usefulness of a "positive polarization." Agnew became the "hatchet man" for attacks on those whom the Nixon administration believed were tearing the country apart (Perlstein 2008). A blogger for a conservative political website made the connection between the two forces in 2010:

> Nixon was right on the money. The Silent Majority was an accurate description of honest people who generally lived in the suburbs, small towns and in rural areas all over the nation, who carried their own freight, who paid their taxes, who were self-reliant, and who expected or wanted little or nothing from the government except to be left alone.

Ultimately Nixon was way ahead of his time. Way, way ahead. Or perhaps more accurately, he was timeless. He would feel totally vindicated today. Because he was talking about people like the newly vocal Tea Party movement who have decided that enough is enough, that they are over-taxed, that their government is failing them and is wasting their hard-earned money, and is harming their futures and their children's futures through corruption and greed. (*Red State* 2010)

To critics, Obama also represented the type of elite values that Thomas Frank had written about in *What's the Matter with Kansas?*—"Volvo drivers" and "latte drinkers" who considered the Midwest a "fly-over area" and devalued the life of making things and growing things just as they valued the world of finance that had gone so wrong by 2008 (Frank 2004). The more unemployment continued with little alleviation, occurring at the time that the Obama administration was focused on healthcare reform (which was a lengthy, bitter, divisive, and complicated fight), the longer they allowed themselves to be open to the criticism that they were out of touch with the American people.

Realignment?

Some political analysts and social scientists predicted that the 2008 election of Barack Obama signaled the shift in American politics to an era of "post-partisanship" and an end to the "culture wars" that had helped define contested American politics and political discourse for 30 years. A mature, industrialized, democratic society, it was argued, would move beyond the "wedge issues" and misplaced moral grievances of an often anxious polity and address more central economic and social concerns. Several analyses even suggested that the era of Reagan conservatism, represented by the ascendance of forces aligned with the 1980s presidency of Ronald Reagan, had been brought to an end by the Obama election. From the vantage point of 2010, that sentiment seemed overly optimistic, underestimating the capacity of resistance from the American conservative movement, itself changing shape as times have dictated.

The well-respected social scientist and public intellectual Alan Wolfe wrote soon after the election: "Obama defeated the politics of polarization in the general election—and he did so convincingly" (Wolfe 2009). The Democratic strategist Ruy Teixeira saw the same phenomenon unfolding, writing that "one likely shift is an end to the so-called culture wars that have marked American politics for the last several decades, with acrimonious disputes about family and religious values, feminism, gay liberation and race" (Teixeira 2009). The political analyst John Judis similarly cited demographic trends, tying them to structural and ideological shifts:

> [Obama's] election is the culmination of a Democratic realignment that began in the 1990s, was delayed by September 11, and resumed with the 2006 election. This realignment is predicated on a change in political demography and geography. Groups that had been disproportionately Republican have become disproportionately Democratic, and red states like Virginia have turned blue. Underlying these changes has been a shift in the nation's "fundamentals"—in the structure of society and industry, and in the way Americans think of their families, jobs and government. (Judis 2008)

The 2008 campaign season had been a lengthy one, with new technologies offering blog posting and articles throughout a competitive campaign season, with the twists and turns of a campaign featuring the party of a poorly considered president and the possibility of the first woman or first African American major party nominee. While economic conditions overshadowed culture war issues, which played a smaller part in the framing of that election, compared to 2004, issues such as abortion and gay rights continued to be rallying issues for social conservatives, especially once Alaska governor Sarah Palin was selected as the Republican vice presidential candidate.

The election of Senator Barack Obama as president in November 2008, buoyed by a strong electoral vote count, was greeted with many suggestions that the results indicated a turn of America from a conservative or center-right direction, which had started with the election of Ronald Reagan as president in 1980. How did America arrive at a moment when major media were questioning the "end of conservatism," the "twilight of Reaganism," and the "end of the culture war"?

Religion and Realignment

In his last media interview before his death in 2007 at the age of 73, Rev. Jerry Falwell, the founder of the Moral Majority group in the United States in the late 1970s, and a prime leader of the social and religious conservative movement in the United States, refused to retract his 2001 statement that the events of September 11 that year were in part retribution for America's embrace of abortion and homosexuality. Falwell's leadership had coincided with the ascendance of American fundamentalist and evangelical Christians from a form of disengaged—essentially world-rejecting—piety to an engaged stance with public policy and the law. The 2004 voter turnout among self-described white evangelical Protestants—78% of it going to support the re-election of President George W. Bush—represented a great success for Bush advisor Karl Rove and those who had argued for the engagement of that crucial part of the electorate.

The death of Falwell came at a crossroads for social conservatives and the culture wars they energized in the United States. Comments from those who were his allies softened his edges—saying he was biblically conservative but not mean. Dr. James Dobson remembered him as pivotal in the awakening of the evangelical community, saying: "I don't know anyone who had a greater impact on the evangelical movement" (CNN 2007a). To supporters, Falwell wasn't afraid of political correctness—for which, in their opinion, he got skewered by the media. To them, there was an effort to marginalize him because he had such political influence. The continuing influence of the groups that Falwell had started and supported was a major topic of the day's commentary. One libertarian newspaper termed the movement that Falwell left "past its peak," reiterating the classic libertarian position that "morality cannot be improved through the intervention of the state" (*Orange County Register* 2007). The *Los Angeles Times* wrote that the wall separating church and state in America was "porous long before Jerry Falwell started chipping away at it" (*Los Angeles Times* 2007). To leading social conservative Gary Bauer, progressive notice of Falwell's passing was offensive:

> . . . the outright hatred that has been on display at leftwing web sites and media outlets. From the Democratic Underground to the Daily Kos, self-

described leftists and so-called "progressives" have celebrated the news of Rev. Falwell's death. In San Francisco, a group danced on a "mock-up" of his grave. Outspoken atheist Christopher Hitchens told CNN's Anderson Cooper, "I think it's a pity there isn't a hell for him to go to." Radical homosexual rights groups spewed their hatred at the news, with many blaming Rev. Falwell for the AIDS epidemic, rather than the unsafe practices still prevalent in their community. For folks who pride themselves on "tolerance," they should be ashamed. (Bauer 2007)

With the death of Rev. Falwell, and the aging and deaths of some of the other leaders of the religious right in the United States, public attention was focused on an issue that social scientists and scholars of religion had been approaching—the decline of the size and influence of religious social conservatives in American law, politics, and culture. While there are some who question whether the "religious right" at its highest point indeed could claim as many members as some would have, the 2004 election—even after adjusting for poll faults—was taken as data that Karl Rove's notion of a conservative rule for a generation, based in no small part on religious votes, was within reach.

The Declining Salience of Same-Sex Marriage as a Useful Wedge Issue

In 2004, same-sex marriage was a rallying point for social conservatives and those remobilizing for the re-election of President George W. Bush. It had been demonstrated that a Defense of Marriage Act (DOMA) on a state's ballot created a more robust conservative turnout—and worked as a device to categorize candidates and polarize voters in many American states, not only those which would be considered most conservative. By 2010, 37 states had passed some form of a DOMA (some more than once), and in only one example—Arizona in 2006—had a state failed to do so (and two years later, Arizona did pass an equivalent measure). Given this, it was not surprising that the voters of Maine (2009) repealed a legislatively passed same-sex marriage law and the voters of California, using the initiative process as well, rejected a state supreme court ruling permitting same-sex marriage (a result that would be overturned by the U.S. Supreme Court in 2013).

This chapter briefly discusses this in the context of considering same-sex marriage as a "normalization" that has begun to occur in the United States. To date, there are 37 American states that permit same-sex marriage. Of these, Massachusetts was first, with a 2003 state supreme court ruling. To those who had captured the progressive deliberation of the state of Vermont in adopting the first civil unions for same-sex couples, it would be little surprise to find that it was one of the first five states and the only one to pass the law legislatively (without a subsequent repeal). Connecticut and New Hampshire make political sense, but Iowa stood out as a heartland state, while New York and New England states were more predictable. Of course, California took the long path, over five years from the state supreme court decision to the U.S. Supreme Court decision overturning the repeal of that earlier state decision.

In *Sin No More*, Hillyard and I assessed the contours of the culture war in the 2000–2007 period, with significant analysis of the role of social conservatives and the religious right on issues especially within the purview of the legal system: gay rights, abortion, assisted suicide, and stem cell research (Dombrink and Hillyard 2007). By 2006, polls found that same-sex marriage was already cooling off as a salient political issue for Americans (by 2015, this change would be much commented on because of its dramatic and rapid change). This change continued a trend that had begun with the emergence of a gay rights movement focused on the decriminalization of sodomy issues in the 1970s and the lobbying for and passage of anti-discrimination measures based on sexual orientation that followed later that decade. This issue has a demonstrably demographic dimension. As younger cohorts of Americans—including evangelicals—assert a decidedly more tolerant or expansive view toward same-sex marriage, it no longer can serve as an effective underpinning of a culture war campaign or electoral strategy.

McCain advisor Steve Schmidt, soon after the 2008 defeat, gave a speech in which he declared that his party's attachment to the opposition to same-sex marriage was an issue that would cause problems as these cohorts aged (Seelye 2009). To him, future Republican focus on personal morality issues was a poor strategic choice. In the repositioning and finger pointing occurring after the 2008 defeat, social conservative positions were under attack for contributing to the defeat. Conservative *New York Times* columnist Ross Douthat admitted that same-sex marriage was a demographic inevitability, a point that even conservative siren Rush Limbaugh would concede by 2012 (Frassica 2009). Frank Rich, admittedly then a progressive columnist for the *New York Times*, argued that "antigay animus" had become an issue that would repel voters, rather than attract them, in the future (Rich 2010). Thus was set in motion a cultural shift in attitudes toward marriage equality—and gay rights generally—that continues to grow, with over 50% of the American public now signaling their support for marriage equality in various national polls.

Conclusion: The Future of the American Culture Wars

When Richard Nixon oversaw the mobilization of socially conservative Americans to speak against the scruffy protestors and who were speaking and acting on behalf of civil rights, anti-war efforts, drug law changes, gender role understanding, and emerging rights issues, he used Vice President Spiro Agnew to speak on behalf of the usefulness of a "positive polarization." Agnew became, as many vice presidents before and after (some, like him, relegated to a lower shelf on American political history), the "hatchet man" for attacks on those who the Nixon administration believed were tearing the country apart. Nixon's enemies list, and the fear, even paranoia, toward those who opposed him, of course led to his slow descent through the Watergate scandal and eventual resignation (Clines 1996; Perlstein 2008). Nixon used these techniques a decade before American conservatism came to rely upon the social and religious conservatives brought forward by Rev. Jerry Falwell and others, through the Moral Majority, the Christian Coalition, and other such organized groups. But they relied upon the same focus on anger and resentment that can be used to characterize the contemporary anti-Obama movement, be they decentralized "tea parties," the even less organized anti-government protestors, or the institutionally organized and well funded Super-PACs (political action committees) that have supplanted the Republican National Committee.

Some have pointed out that the tea party movement—despite the anger and resentment expressed by it—does not express deep concern about prior key issues of social conservatives, the way same-sex marriage, for example, does. Poll results have generated a discussion about a central defining characteristic of the "tea party" organizations. Are they essentially libertarian, as many were made out to be in their early ascendance and focus on fiscal issues of taxation and spending? Or are they "Christianist," integrally connected to the same Christian conservatives who have served as a major organizing force for the American Republican Party and conservative causes since the emergence of Rev. Falwell and the Moral Majority in the late 1970s? (Sullivan 2010). Democratic analyst and strategist Ed Kilgore wrote soon after the Obama election that "the critical plurality of Americans are happy to declare a truce in the culture wars as long as progressives don't behave like conquering secularist radicals" (Kilgore 2009). Those like Kilgore, or others who had argued that a "truce" in the culture wars was imminent (Porter 2010), seemed overly optimistic by 2010. Former vice president and presidential candidate Walter Mondale, the elder Democratic statesman who had himself been pummeled electorally in the 1984 Reagan re-election, summed up a different view succinctly: "In my opinion, Obama had a few false presumptions. One was the idea that we were in a post-partisan era" (Mayer 2010).

To sociologist Paul Starr, the events of 2009 and the backlash election of 2010 were part of a long-evolving tapestry of movement and backlash that has typified the last 20 years of American politics, which also explains the persistence of the culture wars:

> Both conservatives and liberals have been looking for a decisive victory in the great political contest of our times. Periodically, one side advances its cause and dares to believe that it has achieved a definitive political realignment, but its advances turn out to mobilize the opposition more than its own supporters. In the great tug-of-war of the past 20 years, there has been no conclusive move in either direction. (Starr 2010)

While Starr might be right in asserting the closeness of American divisions, he may also be accused of downplaying the depth of American divisions. At the same time, we are cautioned by how the Republican House victory in 2010 unleashed very conservative programs (such as the proposed "Ryan budget") and resistance (especially to the Affordable Care Act [ACA], or "Obamacare."). At the same time, losses—such as those in November 2012—also have been generative of conservative pushback, but in a conflicted and very fluid Republican environment.

As Chapter 2 demonstrates, the culture war helped spark the backlash against Obama in the height of the tea party emergence of 2009 and 2010, even as the tea party movement itself didn't address social conservative issues as much as it expressed an anti-government agenda. But events since that time—especially as they developed from the passage of the Affordable Care Act and on through the 2012 campaign season—suggest that the culture war "wedge issues" that have been successful for over 30 years in politics are losing their edge. This "unwedging" is what characterizes America in 2015, especially amid the effect of the rising importance of the millennial generation and a more ethnically diverse America. This book tells the story of those shifts and realignments. For now, Chapter 2 captures the vehemence and policy implications of the backlash against President Obama in the early tea party period of 2009 and 2010.

2

Anger and Resentment Anew

Tea Parties and the Obama Backlash

We've come to take our government back.
—U.S. Senator-elect Rand Paul (R-Kentucky), November 2,
2010

The America I know and love is not one in which my parents
or my baby with Down Syndrome will have to stand in front
of Obama's "death panel" so his bureaucrats can decide,
based on a subjective judgment of their "level of productiv-
ity in society," whether they are worthy of health care. Such a
system is downright evil.
—Sarah Palin, 2010

Assembling the Tea Party

The images of angry Americans, usually white and often older, dressed
as colonial-era patriots and staging mock insurgencies (or staging symbolic gestures for a real insurgency), came to dominate the American
political landscape and strategists' attention from 2009 forward. Who
were these people, and what were the bases and implications of the
social movement they had ignited? Was it a populist burst, pushing
back against the perceptions of class and corporate favoritism in the
bailout of Wall Street and the American automotive industry? Was it
a churlish assembling of anti-tax activists, who continued to follow a
Reagan-era belief in the importance of limited government (and indeed,
had been disquieted by the more profligate conservatism and foreign
interventionism of George W. Bush)? Or was it largely an "anti-Obama"
movement, driven by opposition to whatever policies he and his party in
power in two houses of Congress proposed, a movement upset with the

rapidity of change that characterized the Obama (and Bush) responses to the economic maladies of 2008? Was it a movement that had a clear understanding of budgets and federal policies, or did it veer from vitriolic attack to simplistic solutions, as some of its critics charged? Or was it at its heart a movement triggered by racism and bigotry? As the tea party phenomenon grew, so did attempts by traditional bodies to make sense of it. Beyond the political parties' reactions, the national media tried to determine what the phenomenon consisted of:

> The fierce animosity that Tea Party supporters harbor toward Washington and President Obama in particular is rooted in deep pessimism about the direction of the country and the conviction that the policies of the Obama administration are disproportionately directed at helping the poor rather than the middle class or the rich, according to the latest *New York Times/CBS News* poll. (Zernike and Thee-Brenan 2010)

To foreign policy expert Walter Russell Mead, the tea partiers represent something more substantial than some of the dismissive evaluations of their genesis or concerns:

> The Tea Partiers represent something very old in American life and in some ways they want a return to traditional American values, but the traditional American value that inspires them the most is the value of revolutionary change. The Tea Party movement is the latest upsurge of an American populism that has sometimes sided with the left and sometimes with the right, but which over and over again has upended American elites, restructured our society and forced through the deep political, cultural and institutional changes that from time to time the country needs and which the ruling elites cannot or will not deliver. (Mead 2010)

Democratic strategist Mark Mellman, writing several months before the 2010 midterm elections at which the tea party effect would be substantial, suggested that the public's attitudes in 2010 could be summarized as "anti-politics; anti-incumbent; anti-establishment; and (I am sorry to say) anti-Democratic" (Mellman 2010). Writing also in May 2010, *Washington Post* political reporter Dan Balz offered a different sense, that of the broad swath of critique coming toward Washington from among many populations in the country:

> Their victories speak to the broadest trend shaping the political climate, which is voter anger. Voters have lost faith in their politicians, whom they see as a privileged class that has lost touch with the concerns of Main Street. But in today's ideologically polarized environment, left and right are joined only by their disgust with the status quo. (Balz 2010)

To other pollsters, tea party activists are "mostly social conservatives, not libertarians on social issues. Nearly two-thirds (63%) say abortion should be illegal in all or most cases, and less than 1-in-5 (18%) support allowing gay and lesbian couples to marry" (Rasmussen and Schoen 2010). To social conservative activist Gary Bauer, defending the views and priorities of the tea party "patriots" was paramount, given the pressures the "liberal media" to portray them as bigots or "know-nothings":

> The Tea Party patriots overwhelmingly identify as Independents. Some are disaffected Republicans. Some are Democrats. They tend to be middle class and patriotic. They know that higher taxes are not the solution but part of the problem. They are deeply committed to following the Constitution, and they worry about Big Government becoming a threat to our liberty. These are all mainstream values, yet there is a constant effort by cultural elites to demonize these good Americans with false charges of racism, extremism, etc. (Bauer 2010a)

To conservative analyst David Harsanyi, the tea partiers were a welcome movement, not "Christianist" but socially conservative without making that aspect of their beliefs the most salient issue for them right now:

> And though tea party supporters are more conservative than the average voter on social issues, as well—particularly abortion, according to a separate Gallup Poll—The *New York Times* reports that 8 in 10 tea party activists believe the movement should focus on economic issues rather than cultural ones. How long have we been hearing from moderate, sensible, worldly Republican types that if only—if only—the right found

God on economic issues and lost God on the social ones, there would be an expansion of appeal and support? Apparently, they were right. (Harsanyi 2010)

Political scientist Michael Kazin, a leading expert on the role and shape of populist movements in American history, described the Tea Partiers as being like traditional populists in that they see themselves as "the virtuous common people against the immoral elites" (*KOSU News* 2010). Another scholar observed that "the Tea Party movement is interesting in that there is a combination of localism, nativism and populism that we've seen at various points in America. It's coalescing at a time when the government is growing to an unprecedented size" (Liptak 2010).

These observations fit with the assessment of the tea party phenomenon as an "againster" movement—the issues of what it agrees upon were often more confused. One snarky comment was "If you were to make a Venn Diagram of the issues Tea Party members care about, and the issues Tea Party members are confused about, you'd only see one circle" (Benen 2010). The issues that drove this observation would include the sight of many older-aged tea partiers protesting government debt expansion and perceived fiscal profligacy (in the healthcare and bailout mode) while at the same time shouting to "keep your hands off Medicare."

Many accounts have focused on events in early 2009 as a major catalyst for the tea party movement in the United States (Zernike 2010: 131). On February 19, 2009, CNBC business reporter Rick Santelli denounced the Obama-backed congressional support for homeowners in foreclosure as "promoting bad behavior" and raised the possibility of a "Chicago tea party" (CNBC 2009). While this event was an important contributor to the growing resentment that followed, and was represented in the various "tea party" manifestations, we also have to consider what sort of backlash was being constructed before that date. Certainly that there was immediate response to the Obama election, as was previously discussed in Chapter 1. Movement conservatives like Gary Bauer and Rush Limbaugh were early and constant in their exhortations for conservatives to push back against the Obama administration and not take the "bait" of bipartisanship. Some analysts would be prescient in their late 2008 observations that a President Obama would be much used as a target, a sense of threat and urgency, and a fund-raising and organizing focus for conservatives. That observation has characterized the last six years.

This chapter examines the roots of the anti-Obama backlash of 2009 forward. It largely follows the construction and amplification of the tea party, the major development of that time. At some point, it also foreshadows the detailed political activity that occurred as part of the 2012 presidential campaign. The chapter seeks to identify the nature and terrain of that "againster" phenomenon and how it has shaped American politics and society. The chapter serves as a counterweight to Chapter 1 in that it identifies the scope of the vociferous backlash against the Obama presidency from its earliest months.

Interpreting the Meaning of the Tea Partiers

In one variant of analysis of the tea party phenomenon, it is seen as historically specific, driven by issues about taxation and the role and size of government following the major economic shocks of 2008. In this way, it is resonant of the campaign of independent presidential candidate H. Ross Perot, who garnered 19% of the presidential vote in 1992. That campaign was also seen as a critique of existing president George H. W. Bush and his administration, and the subsequent three-way contest was a reflection of the inability of the mainstream Republican party to keep Perot from poaching supporters from their party. In contrast to this, there are those like historian Rick Perlstein, who see the tea party as but a more recent manifestation of an "againster" phenomenon that has arisen whenever progressive forces, and governments, have reached sufficient power to change the status quo (Perlstein 2010). Additionally, Kevin Drum titles his version of this theory that of "new whine in old bottles" (Drum 2010). To Drum and Perlstein, the central tea party tenet that that Barack Obama "doesn't love America" is only the most recent manifestation of a theme that has been used against Democratic candidates (and presidents) stretching at least back to Franklin Roosevelt.

In the variety of analyses, "pushbacks," and critiques of the tea party phenomenon, there has been one strand that has emphasized taking the protestors—at least their more mainstream variants (difficult given their decentralized nature)—at face value and not underestimating their potential. Former Clinton administration official William Galston, part of the leadership of the *Democratic Strategist* publications, presents one version of this approach. Commenting on a Pew poll on Americans identification of themselves and placement of their beliefs vis-à-vis the Republicans, the Democrats, and the tea party, Galston pointed out that more Americans were beginning in 2010 to see themselves as further from the Democratic Party versions and visions and that

> voters now place themselves much closer to the Republican Party than to the Democratic Party on this left-right continuum. Indeed, the ideological gap between the Democratic Party and the mean voter is about three times as large as the separation between that voter and the Republican Party. And, startlingly, the electorate places itself a bit closer to the Tea Party movement (which is well to the right of the Republican Party) than to the Democratic Party. (Galston 2010c)

Soon after the 2010 midterm elections, political analyst David Gergen urged a similar view—in response to a critique by a journalist of the "wrongheadedness" of the tea party, which was often portrayed as misled, racist, or both: "I flatly reject the idea that Tea Partiers are crazy. They had some eccentric candidates, there's no question about that. But I think they represent a broad swath of the American electorate that elites dismiss to their peril" (Wenner and Bates 2010). Pollster Peter Hart, a much-relied upon Democratic pollster, offered a similar view: "I agree with David. When two out of five people who voted last night say they consider themselves supporters of the Tea Party, we make a huge mistake to suggest that they are some sort of small fringe group and do not represent anybody else" (Wenner and Bates 2010).

Gergen and Hart had been responding in part to a post-2010 election response by the journalist Matt Taibbi (of *Rolling Stone*), who had emphasized the more extreme nature of the tea party elements: "To me, the main thing about the Tea Party is that they're just crazy. If somebody is able to bridge the gap with those voters, it seems to me they will have to be a little bit crazy too. That's part of the Tea Party's litmus test: 'How far will you go?'" (Wenner and Bates 2010). Another perspective views the tea party activists as often unknowing "fronts" for the usual corporate powers. For instance, satirist Bill Maher ridiculed the handwritten signs to "keep your government hands off my Medicare."

Political journalist Taibbi is a major proponent of this position:

> If you want to understand why America is such a paradise for high-class thieves, just look at the way a manufactured movement like the Tea Party corrals and neutralizes public anger that otherwise should be sending pitchforks in the direction of downtown Manhattan. (Taibbi 2010)

One central point of attention and dissension that began with the rise of the party phenomenon in 2009 was the issue of whether they essentially represented a constituency of political independents, a growing force in American politics, especially given the rising level of distaste for the polarization that is engaged in by the two major political parties. In 2008, independent voters—those voters who registered but declined to state a party affiliation or who described themselves as independent—voted 52–44 for candidate Obama, and their support was viewed as crucial to his framing of issues and eventual electoral success (Nicholas 2010). In November 2010, however, this group voted Republican by a 19-point margin, emphasizing the sense of overreach and lack of attention to fiscal constraints—in large part emphasizing the healthcare reform as an example and setting off soul-searching political reflection and analysis within the Obama and Democratic circles (Kornblut 2010). Even accepting this point, analysts and political scientists have often divided the world of "Independents" into "Republican-leaning" independents, who are largely conservative in their positions, and those who are "Democratic leaning," figuring that, in the absence of a vital "independent" party, and the infrequent appearance of charismatic independent candidates, those labeled independents will eventually choose between candidates of the two major parties (Jones 2009). Often, the axes of independence are presented as less than linear or consistent, given that the libertarian impulses of many independents may cause them to reject both traditional Democratic supports for economic intervention and regulations, as well as to reject overintrusiveness on personal morality issues by conservative Republican regimes. In this view, tea partiers are essentially libertarians, caring less about abortion, same-sex marriage, and other central issues of the culture war. Even some progressive analysts have embraced this position (Michelle Goldberg 2010).

Another variant of this critique of the "tea partier as libertarian" position directly contests the proposition that the "tea party" phenomenon is largely a secular drive, drawing from the fiscal concerns of Americans rather than the same personal morality "wedge issues" that have fueled the culture wars for decades. A competing perspective holds that the "tea partiers" are largely drawn from the same reservoirs of social and fiscal conservatives that form the Republican base. Several avenues have been pursued to disentangle these beliefs and positions. Several surveys have queried those who consider themselves supporters or members of the tea party, asking about their beliefs on a range of religious and culture war issues. A 2010 *New York Times* survey—immediate considered suspect by the anti-Obama forces—suggested the alignment with traditional Republican constituencies:

> A *New York Times/CBS News* poll of backers of the emerging Tea Party movement shows that its supporters are more affluent and better educated than the general public. They tend to be white, male, and married. They are loyal Republicans, with conservative opinions on a variety of issues. And their strong opposition to the Obama administration is more rooted in political ideology than anxiety about their personal economic situation. (Zernike and Thee-Brenan 2010)

Political blogger Andrew Sullivan typified this proposition in the discussion of the tea party phenomenon when he suggested that the tea partiers were indeed they "Christianists," who largely believe in the same precepts as the religious right and other social conservatives who formed the key part of the basis of the "Reagan revolution" and the George W. Bush years:

> The . . . myth is that they are somehow unlike the Christianist right, and more tolerant and easy-going on social issues. . . . I think this is wishful thinking. My own view is that they are hard-line Christianists in a different outfit—powdered wigs, muskets and red cheeks—and are outliers on issues of modernity—racial integration, women's rights, gay equality. (Sullivan 2010)

This point was prompted by the release of a poll that showed that tea partiers were more strongly anti same-sex marriage than all seniors, a telling point to Sullivan and others, who saw the age demographic as a key impediment to marriage equality for gays and lesbians in the current time. For example, an MSNBC poll found that fully 92% of self-defined and aligned tea partiers wanted the Obama healthcare reform repealed, while 67% thought that the 2009 government stimulus was poor policy. Notably, 82% didn't support same-sex marriage at the same time that just 40% of non–tea party Republicans thought the stimulus was a bad idea.

One of the most consistent and strident charges against the tea partiers is that they represent a racist streak in American politics, one that has been exacerbated by the election of a multi-racial president in Barack Obama—that, in opposing Obama, they are more racist than not. Proponents of this position cite the many graphic depictions of anti-Obama sentiment (see Chapter 1). They note incidents like the 2007 playing of the parody song "Barack the Magic Negro" by eventual tea party supporter Rush Limbaugh, who claimed he was only following a concept presented in a newspaper's op-ed pages about the beliefs in Obama being able to deliver on his many issues (Aravosis 2007).

To many Democratic and progressive analysts, even high-ranking officials, tea party movement members suffer from false consciousness—as Thomas Frank emphasized in his book on social conservatives in Kansas (Frank 2004)—and are being manipulated by larger, wealthier institutions and sectors of society. Senate Majority leader Harry Reid (D-Nevada), contesting a 2010 Senate challenge from an avowed tea party candidate (which Reid won), held that position, telling one writer:

> I think those people have actually been manipulated by big business. . . . Power brokers, chambers of commerce from around the country—they don't want anything the Tea Party wants. They want to maintain control of government, and this was their cynical way to do that. The Tea Party might seem new, but it's not new. Toward the end of World War II, when you had Father Coughlin out there spewing his venom, you had people upset because Truman was the accidental president, just like Obama is the accidental president, and the economy was headed downhill because the war was grinding down, and you had Coughlin with eight million people listening to his poison. So this is not new. (Warren 2010)

Early on after 2008, during the rise of the anti-Obama movement, many Republican politicians were generally cautious in taking an aggressive stand against a president elected with a burst of momentum, along with his party's control of two houses of Congress. Sarah Palin and others criticized Obama for "bowing" to foreign leaders, especially in the Middle East. This critique of Obama's appeasement approach in foreign policy echoed earlier Reagan critiques of Carter and critiques of Clinton, not to mention the perceived weakness of Democratic presidential candidates on foreign policy generally. In 2011, Mitt Romney added a new subtitle to his campaign book, which became *No Apology: Believe in America* (Romney 2011). In one sense, the birther controversy can also be read this way, beyond the narrow legal and factual question. One central notion is that Obama is not "one of us." Rush Limbaugh and others have opined that Obama wants America to fail. (To be fair, it should be noted that George W. Bush, often depicted as a chimp and portrayed as stupid, endured the attacks of those like Keith Olbermann, who led an opinion segment on MSNBC in 2007, titled "Bush: Pathological Liar or Idiot-in-Chief?" [see Olbermann 2007].) Conservative journalist Charles Krauthammer coined a term, "Bush Derangement Syndrome," to refer to over-the-top fixation with criticism of Bush doctrine and policies (Krauthammer 2003). In the same vein, "Clinton derangement syndrome" has been utilized, and Ken Gormley (2010) exhaustively discusses the manifestation of it in the Special Prosecutor actions and 1998 impeachment hearings against President Clinton.

The Contributions of Sarah Palin

As 2008 Republican vice presidential candidate Sarah Palin appeared at events in 2009 and after, such as an early tea party "convention," she became an early darling of the tea party movement. After famously emerging as the vice presidential nominee, she had been utilized to energize the base of the Republican Party, a base that resonated with her pro-life profile and exhortations. But as Palin's star faded in 2008, she was left with a low approval rating among the American public, a status that persists. (Fissures between her and the McCain strategy team became prominent even as the 2008 election was winding down, and she responded to them in her "Western can-do" manner in *Going Rogue*, a bestseller that sold more than two million copies; Palin 2009.)

With the advent of the tea party phenomenon, Palin decided to ride its wave, supporting candidates from its ranks who challenged—sometimes successfully—candidates from the Republican establishment. She resigned from the Alaska governorship, ostensibly to spend more time being active politically nationally (which was difficult to do from the geographically remote state of Alaska), but certainly to also cash in on speaking engagements and some oddities of the celebrity Facebook zeitgeist—such as a combination cable television reality show and documentary series on Alaska. Why speak of Palin in a serious context? Isn't she a media creation, a focus of the moment who has already faded away as a serious candidate? Even now, analysts differ between whether her main motivation is to make money as a cultural icon, with a television reality series most notably, or to be an eventual candidate for the Republican presidential nomination (although she demurred in 2012).

Stanley Fish captured, in an anecdotal incident, some of what he considered the elite revulsion at the Palin phenomenon:

> When I walked into the Strand Bookstore in Manhattan last week, I headed straight for the bright young thing who wore an "Ask Me" button, and asked her to point me to the section of the store where I might find Sarah Palin's memoir, *Going Rogue: An American Life*. She looked at me as if I had requested a copy of "Mein Kampf" signed in blood by the author, and directed me to the nearest Barnes and Noble, where, presumably, readers of dubious taste and sensibility could find what they wanted. (Fish 2009)

In the midst of the 2009–2010 healthcare reform debate, Palin—an early an avid user of Twitter and other social media—tweeted her followers, saying: "Commonsense Conservatives & lovers of America: Don't Retreat, Instead—RELOAD!" (an exhortation that will become more relevant in a later section in this chapter). As the tea party has emerged in the last six years as a different type of movement, one focused in Reaganish style on the size and role of government, "culture warriors" like Palin (Salam 2009) have sought to yoke together disparate sides of the movement, in the manner that Reagan did in the 1980 period (Vaisse 2010). To Goldberg, one key attribute that characterizes tea partiers is their sense of "furious dispossession" (Michelle Goldberg

Figure 2.1. A common (Photoshopped) meme of Obama and Palin still circulating by the 2012 election season.

2010), the idea of "taking our country back." To historian Rick Perlstein, many of the framing images portray the state as the enemy.

It cannot be underestimated that the tea party phenomenon arrived at a time when America as a country (and as a concept?) was being challenged on the world stage. Typical of this were late-night comedian Jay Leno's jokes about Obama visiting our money in China, such as this from 2010: "Well, this week, China gave a vote of confidence in the U.S. dollar. Well, you know why? They own them all. Of course they're confident" (Leno 2010). With China looming as a new world power, there are many who feel marginalized by the economic restructuring and perhaps feel that they don't count. The late social critic Christopher Hitchens added:

> Most epochs are defined by one or another anxiety. More important, though, is the form which that anxiety takes. Millions of Americans are currently worried about two things that are, in their minds, emotionally

related. The first of these is the prospect that white people will no longer be the majority in this country, and the second is that the United States will be just one among many world powers. (Hitchens 2011)

Jonathan Alter emphasized Hitchens's first point, when he added a new epilogue to his 2010 book on President Obama's first year:

> For a large segment of Americans far inland from the coasts, Obama had become the scary face of a changing nation, the personification of all they found threatening. He represented not too little change but too much. And yet a country dominated since its founding by older, white, straight Christians now had room for African Americans, Latinos, gays, and others once considered outside the mainstream. (Alter 2011)

One evolving phenomenon may be that the real cultural divide is indeed one defined by social class, education, and employment and advancement opportunities in the contemporary and future economies. In this sense, a 2011 report on how the current economic problems are differentially felt and differentially perceived—especially as they apply to future scenarios—by social class, is illustrative. With the election of a multi-racial president in Barack Obama, the symbolic moment of 2008 has helped affirm a situation in which working-class whites—the group often profiled in discussion of culture war divisions—have demonstrably different views of the fate and future of the country:

> A mere 10 percent of whites without college degrees say they are satisfied with the nation's current economic situation. Most—56 percent—say the country's best days are in the past, and more, 61 percent, say it will be a long time before the economy begins to recover. Fully 43 percent of non-college whites say "hard work and determination are no guarantees of success," and nearly half doubt that they have enough education and skills to compete in the job market. (Cohen and Balz 2011)

And more Americans view America as in decline, being eclipsed by China, causing greater uncertainty and anxiety (Gjelten 2011).

The tea party phenomenon emerged in a similar way and manner that Reaganism offered a response to America's declining fortunes in the world and defeat in the Vietnam War. The rise of OPEC and suddenly rising gasoline prices and rationing of gasoline, with cars lining up to fill tanks every other day, typified that era, as did the situation of Americans held hostage by the emerging fundamentalist rebels of a country (Iran) many Americans couldn't find on a map. Alongside this, "againster" critiques of the ways in which Obama has engaged the world, bowing to foreign leaders and making less than a strong case for American supremacy in world affairs—a critique that has continued into his second term—form an undertone of outpouring of sentiment against him.

Although it was not a major theme in the 2010 midterm elections, one of the frames that Sarah Palin applied to the resurgent conservatism was that of the role of women. Indeed, the historian Ruth Rosen (2010) agrees that there has been a demonstrated effect of the role of women in the nascent tea party organizations. In arguing for the role of conservative women in the resurgent conservative movement, what she characterized as "mama grizzlies," Palin stressed: "You don't want to mess with moms who are rising up. If you thought pit bulls were tough, you don't want to mess with mama grizzlies." Palin reiterated this idea that part of the groundswell of the tea parties was indeed a new brand of feminism: "All across this country, women are standing up and speaking out for common sense solutions. . . . They are forming a new conservative feminist movement that will help make government work again for us" (CNN 2010). One analyst places this directly in the context of the deficit and fiscal framing:

> Palin's name for the female midterm candidates was telling: "Mama Grizzlies." . . . Something important sets today's maternal feminism apart from the earlier strain: it casts budgeting and governance as maternal issues. Palin put her fiscal conservatism in the homey rhetoric of a PTA president: "I think a whole lot of moms . . . are concerned about government handing our kids the bill." (Hymowitz 2011)

Palin herself emphasized this in her 2010 book, connecting the issue of the deficit and American debt with the issues of the American family and the future: "We're worried that we're not protecting the innocence and safety of children. And we're worried that their future opportunities are being thwarted by shortsighted political decisions being made today" (Palin 2010: xvi).

Palin, and those who support her, may feel like one of the characters in Jonathan Franzen's 2010 novel *Freedom*, who feels that the main character, Walter, fits the type of a person less concerned with her plight in these economic perilous times:

> Walter wasn't even really a neighbor, he didn't belong to the homeowners association, and the fact that he drove a Japanese hybrid, to which he'd recently applied an OBAMA bumper sticker, pointed, in her mind, toward godlessness and a callousness regarding the plight of hardworking families, like hers, who were struggling to make ends meet and raise their children to be good, loving citizens in a dangerous world. (Franzen 2010: 544)

Palin also referenced some of the economic divide analysis, which speaks to the future culture wars being eventually fought between those who are high school educated and those who are college educated: "And every parent of a high school graduate or a young soldier, sailor, airman or Marine knows the sense of pride and accomplishment that comes with raising a good and decent child" (Palin 2010: xix–xx).

Palin also folded her critique of Obama in with those who charged that, in addition to apologizing for America, he was disdainful of "American exceptionalism," arguing once before a foreign audience that he was respectful of all countries' exceptional history. While this may not have amounted to much of a 2012 angle of criticism and attack on the Obama re-election effort, it had certain resonance with conservative critics and political candidates in 2011: "We have to know what makes America exceptional today more than ever because it is under assault today more than ever" (Palin 2010: xx).

Obama and Healthcare Reform

Many progressives and other Democrats had collectively been disappointed by the failure of the Clinton administration to secure a healthcare reform bill in the first Clinton term. The failure of the 1993 effort, which was pilloried by Republicans, small businesses, and the health and insurance industries, was instrumental in the sizeable electoral defeats of the Clinton administration in the 1994 midterm elections (Skocpol 1996). By returning a Republican majority to the House of Representatives that it had not enjoyed in 40 years, Newt Gingrich and his group of hardliners found reward for their tactics of opposition and partisanship.

While abortion had not played a central role in the 2008 campaign, it would return in 2009–2010 as an issue in the healthcare reform debate. While it became apparent that there would be no Republican bipartisan "cross-aisle" support of the Affordable Care Act (ACA) measure— which some opponents came to refer to as "Obamacare"—the sense of the backlash became palpable when Congressman Joe Wilson (R-South Carolina) yelled "You lie!" at President Obama as he gave a September 2009 speech outlining his healthcare proposal to the combined houses of Congress (Hulse 2009).

In a posting labeled "Obamacare = Abortion," social conservative Gary Bauer wrote during the last weeks of the Congressional negotiations and vote-getting:

> If Obamacare becomes law, it will amount to a de facto repeal of the Hyde Amendment, which prohibits taxpayer-funding of abortions. It will be the most pro-abortion legislation to pass Congress in decades, making abortion a healthcare "right" subsidized with your hard-earned tax dollars. (Bauer 2010b)

Sarah Palin would later call Obama the "most pro-abortion president in American history" (Robbins 2010).

Even the U.S. Conference of Catholic Bishops, after initially promoting healthcare reform as part of that Church's view of social justice, backed away from the Obama plan, saying that it did not satisfy their leadership on the issue of financial support for abortion as a health option. (Conversely, later a leading group of Catholic women religious, Network, gave pro-life Democratic representatives cover to support the ACA by arguing for the healthcare reform as precisely part of the mission of their church). Then House Speaker Nancy Pelosi was besieged by pro-choice members of her caucus who felt that she was selling out a plank she had supported all her career. She was accused of trusting the most socially conservative factions within the House Democratic membership to provide the necessary last votes for passage of the Obama bill. Pro-choice organizations like NARAL were upset that a contingent of pro-life Democrats, a minority in the House caucus, were extracting de-

Figure 2.2. Tea Party political sticker circulated after the
2009 incident.

mands for the limitation on abortion funding and insurance to endure
their support got passage of the eventual bill:

> Last night we learned that Rep. Bart Stupak has reached new lows in try-
> ing to force his abortion-coverage ban into the health-care bill. He filed
> a new resolution yesterday and he and his allies are threatening to bring
> down the whole bill unless they get their way. Our allies on Capitol Hill
> are standing strong, and they need you to back them up. That's why we
> need to call on all members of Congress to reject Stupak's outrageous
> last-minute attempts to hijack health-reform legislation. (NARAL 2009)

It was in this context that a Texas Republican congressman yelled "baby
killer" at Democratic congressman Bart Stupak as Stupak announced in
a dramatic nighttime House session that he would finally support the
Obama healthcare reform plan (Sherman and Shiner 2010). Stupak had
decided to withdraw his objections on the abortion issue, given the president's promise to issue an executive statement reiterating the intended
separation of health funds and funds that could be directed to abortions.
In a remarkable year, it was a high point—-or a low point—of the political discourse that had come to typify America in the Obama era. It was
certainly no one's definition of a post-partisan moment.

How the Backlash Was Framed

Government spending is out of control, and Americans
like you have made it clear you are sick of it. Our debt is
expected to almost double by 2020 with no end in sight. The

time to take action is now. We will need your help to stop
Big Government from bankrupting America.
—Americans for Prosperity, 2010

Certainly the key themes of the 2010 election and the continuing anti-Obama sentiment were set in motion by the unprecedented infusion of federal dollars into American banking and industry. The moment may be regarded by many as the crucial bipartisan moment when American, even global, capitalism was salvaged (Alter 2010). To them, the need for a bipartisan approach to the capital and credit problems of Wall Street trumped the more parochial concerns of political parties. Amid the housing crisis and in the tail end of the presidential campaign, this approach was emphasized by those who met to structure a federal bailout, and the eventual Troubled Asset Relief Program. When that was followed by a government acquisition of a 60% ownership role in General Motors, some of the stirrings of the tea parties were generated by the perception of an overexpansive role of government. The successes of Reaganism, and its orthodoxy of less government, had taken hold over 20 years prior. By 2010, nearly 50% of respondents to a Pew poll said that they were less likely to vote for someone who had voted in favor of the bank bailout, as opposed to a much smaller percentage who would support such a politician.

William Galston, one of the contributors to the weekly *Democratic Strategist*, who served in the Clinton White House, understood the tea partiers in that context:

> There has been no place to hide from the Great Recession, and the traditional formula—get a good education and be persistent—is not reliably producing the right outcomes. The American people know that something out of the ordinary is taking place: 63 percent believe that the economy is undergoing "fundamental and lasting changes," versus only 37 percent who think it is experiencing a temporary downturn. This shift has consequences that go well beyond the economic. For many Americans, the old verities have been cast aside, with nothing to take their place. As far as they can see, they've done everything right, but their expectations have been upended and their life-plans disrupted. In these circumstances, people are bound to think that the country is on the wrong path, and they

Figure 2.3. Tea Party rally in 2009, protesting the Affordable Care Act.

are bound to feel a combination of confusion and anger toward a political system that they see as having let them down. (Galston 2010a)

Was the opposition to the Obama agenda a continuing example of false consciousness—as raised so effectively by historian Thomas Frank in *What's the Matter with Kansas?* (2004)—that led working-class evangelical Protestants to collaborate in their own economic demise by joining forces with a coalition of corporate power and social conservatives in the Republican Party? As Frank wrote, "As a formula for holding together a dominant political coalition, the backlash seems so improbable and so self-contradictory that liberal observers often have trouble believing it is actually happening" (Frank 2004: 8).

In Frank's critique, the morality war is represented by a backlash—which is a central feature of the generating power of the conservative movement around such culture war issues such as abortion, gay rights, and threats to religion—and represents false consciousness in tea partiers' belief of what essentially ails them. In this vein, close to the 2010 election, political satirist Bill Maher ended his show with a critique of tea party protestors as essentially stooges of corporate America. Whereas the faces he showed of protesters were the dominant media frame, Maher suggested instead that delving below the surface would provide us instead with Karl Rove, the conservative donor Koch bothers, and the central motor of conservative Republican establishment politics from the last decade driven by corporate concerns.

Many conservatives bristled at what they perceived as the dismissive manner in which liberal (and what Rush Limbaugh called the "drive-by media" and others have called the "lamestream media") critiques of the tea parties were proceeding. This amplified to them an earlier turning point because to them the last rites performed on the conservative movement at the time of the Obama election were precipitous and condescending. Many of them might have considered the Obama 53–46 election in 2008 an anomaly, given the nation's severe economic problems and what they perceived as a lackluster and not-fully-committed conservative candidate in John McCain. To longtime conservative writer R. Emmett Tyrell, pronouncements such as that by Sam Tanenhaus of "the end of conservatism" were an example of this hubris: "If there be justice in this world, Tanenhaus will be con-

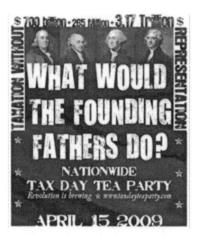

Figure 2.4. Advertisement for
National Tea Party Day in 2009.

signed to the Wilderness for the rest of his life after writing that excep-
tionally imbecilic 'The Death of Conservatism'" (Tyrell 2010).

Bush presidential advisor Karl Rove had famously argued that the
2004 reelection of George W. Bush was the beginning of a multi-year
Republican control of the federal government because America was a
"center-right country" (Dombrink and Hillyard 2007). Rove was diminished by the results of 2006 and 2008, when it appeared that the
realignment that he had forecast would not come to be. Indeed, perhaps
another realignment, perhaps considered as a "re-realignment," was taking place with the Obama victory (certainly many Democrats, liberals,
and pundits thought or hoped so). Later, with the 2010 midterm election
vote looming, Rove's groups' efforts raised over $38 million to support
the efforts of Republican candidates and attack Democratic candidates
in close congressional races. Triumphantly returning to the arena, Rove
wrote that November 2010 would be a "Democratic apocalypse," which
turned out to be one of his better predictions (Rove 2010b).

The 2010 Midterm "Shellacking"

The midterm election results of November 2, 2010, punctured whatever
hopes among Democrats and progressives that 2008 was a progressive "realigning" election and threw into question the contours of the

polarization and culture wars that had typified America since 1980. To tea party icon Rand Paul, then senator-elect from Kentucky (after defeating a Republican establishment candidate in the primary) and son of Republican congressman and former Libertarian presidential candidate Ron Paul, the lessons of the November 2010 election were clear:

> We've come to take our government back. The American people are not happy with what's going on in Washington. Tonight there is a tea party tidal wave, and we're sending a message to them. It's a message that I will carry with me on day one. It's a message of fiscal sanity, a message of limited government and balanced budgets. (Thompson and Gardner 2010)

Paul's sentiments were supported by polls then that regarded the tea party phenomenon as a positive force in the country.

> The tea party movement may well be the most powerful and potent force in America. More than half, or 54 percent, of Americans believe the tea party movement has been a good thing for the U.S. political system, our new survey revealed. Only 22 percent say that it is a bad thing, while 19 percent say it has made no difference. (Rasmussen and Schoen 2010)

To *New York Times* columnist David Brooks, the results were a combination:

> Between June and August of 2009, the working class became disillusioned with Democratic policies. Working-class voters used to move toward the Democrats in recessions; this time, they moved to the right, shifting attitudes on everything from global warming to gun control. In Tuesday's exit polls, 56 percent of voters said government does too much, while only 38 percent said it should do more. (Brooks 2010)

But early 2010 postelection polls showed that Americans were not supportive of efforts to totally repeal the Obama healthcare reform package—a position they maintained four years later—even though that was one of the rallying cries of the tea parties and of the Republican leadership.

A post-election Gallup poll found that

At the close of an eventful midterm election season that focused heavily on the Tea Party message and candidates, Americans remain broadly divided in their reactions to the Tea Party movement. . . . The national Tea Party movement itself is also relatively polarizing, with about equal percentages of Americans calling themselves supporters and opponents. (Saad 2010)

Considering this, the future remains unclear—or perhaps more certain to veer in seemingly two-year cycles from one search for a solution to its opposite. One political consultant referred to the rapidity with which change was taking place, not entirely suggesting that voters were fickle, but probably impatient: Voters "have the clicker in their hands and they have no problem hitting the next button. It's now at warp speed. You can see it in two-year cycles." (Hennessey and Oliphant 2010). In 2010, that cycle had turned in a manner that even hopeful conservatives were not easily predicting in early 2009.

From Anger to Repeal

I take my first political breath every morning with one thought in mind—repeal Obamacare. That's my motivation in life. This bill is something else. It is the crown jewel of socialism. President Obama, and I'm willing to say it, ushered in socialism under his watch . . . my opinion is we can't shut this president down fast enough.
—Republican congresswoman Michele Bachmann, February 2011, cited by Charles Johnson (2011)

The repeal of the Democratic-designed healthcare reform law, the statute deriving from the Patient Protection and Affordable Care Act (ACA) and signed into law in March 2010, was the immediate focus of the newly elected Republican wave of anti-Obama congressional representatives. An early response was the introduction aimed at that law's repeal. The two-page bill (HR2), with 182 co-sponsors, was titled, "To Repeal the Job-Killing Health Care Law and Health-Care Related Provisions in the Health Care and Education Reconciliation Act of 2010" (U.S. House of Representatives 2011). Beyond the healthcare repeal, the focus of the new Republican majority was focused on reversing some of the progressive programs they critiqued as an Obama/Reid/Pelosi overreach. Thus an early bill from the 112th Congress sought to restrict any federal funds from being used to support Planned Parenthood. House Amendment 95, attached to the HR1 bill for appropriations for the continued operation of the federal government, was passed by the House of Representatives in February 2011 and stood for a while in the way of passage by both houses of a continuing resolution to keep the federal government operating (it was eventually, and predictably, voted down along party lines in the Senate).

Conservative activist Gary Bauer offered the idea that opposition to Planned Parenthood was being done in the context of generally cutting unnecessary government funding or programs, in the same way that a highway renaming or a workshop on First Ladies' dresses might be cut, rather than imbued with any moral weight or partisan payback:

> A coalition of fiscally conservative and socially conservative groups is putting pressure on members of Congress to get serious about cutting the budget. Congress must set priorities for our limited tax dollars. We are asking congressmen to do just that, and to start by defunding Planned Parenthood, America's largest abortion business. (Bauer 2011b)

Still, Gergen warned that the reaction of the exultant Republicans with that victory in hand could offer a similar object lesson:

> The danger for the Republicans is that they will overplay their hand. We've had a pattern of newly elected people who feel they have a mandate of some sort, and then go beyond what the public really wants. Clinton got his hand slapped early on because voters thought he had overreached to the left. Then Newt Gingrich and George W. Bush got slapped for overreaching to the right. Now Obama has gotten his hand slapped for pursuing too much government. There's going to be a tendency on the part of some Republicans to sense blood in the water—Obama's wounded, let's spend the next two years taking him out. But the public is clearly looking for action on the economy, not for more politics in the sandbox. (Wenner and Bates 2010)

On another, smaller, and symbolic level, the then-new House speakership of John Boehner expressed pride that they had reversed the Pelosi-era insertion of biodegradable utensils in the House dining room, with a move toward good old-fashioned plastic forks, knives, and spoons. Alongside skepticism about the truth and import of global warming—an assault on science in general, as some have claimed—any gesture, however small, was meant to convey the pushback of the backlash against Obama and his colleagues. To fiscal conservatives, like activist Grover Norquist, the results were a clear rejection of the president, his policies, and his importance: "We crushed him. He's only half his previous size. He's an irritant. He's not scary anymore" (Smith and Tau 2011). That Obama was a limited president—to one term, a la Jimmy Carter—with a blunting of his ambitious healthcare reform and other programs, was a rallying cry for the now encouraged American conservative movement. The year ahead looked like a time when they would be ascendant and eclipse the power of the president they mocked as "The Messiah" or "The One."

The Relationship of Tea Party Activists and the Republican Party Establishment

To hopeful progressives and Democratic officials, November 2, 2010, was a dark day in what was understood to be a "shellacking" for President Obama and the Democratic party (MSNBC 2010). Longtime conservative theorist R. Emmett Tyrell emphasized how the goals of the

Figure 2.5. Tea party billboard in Iowa painting Obama as a dictator.

tea party movement dovetailed well with the conservative movement that he had helped guide over 50 years:

> Now there is a new group we have welcomed into our Big Tent, the Tea Partiers. They really do want to slash government, balance the budget, and address the entitlements that are scheduled to bankrupt the U.S. Treasury. They are the latest addition to conservatism and we welcome them. Their arrival will finally allow us to do something about the enormous deficits that face Social Security, Medicaid, and Medicare. They must keep the pressure on. We will keep the pressure on. We shall all bring the Republican Party, and the country back, to Constitutional values. (Tyrell 2010)

There was open tea party antagonism toward "establishment" Republican candidates as they contested the 2010 and 2012 primary elections. Kentucky in 2010 was a prime example. In that case, the tea party candidate Rand Paul defeated an establishment candidate, Trey Grayson, backed by U.S. Senate Minority leader Mitch McConnell. Paul went so far as to declare himself agnostic in any future vote for Majority (or Minority) Leader in the Senate—a position that McConnell wielded—if he were to be elected senator. Paul characterized Grayson as a "friend of Obama" (and thus no "friend of coal," an important issue in Kentucky, and one germane to that primary election). In Florida in 2010, tea party candidate and former state senate president Marco Rubio attacked his senatorial opponent and popular Florida governor Charlie Crist for his embrace of Obama. Crist was challenged for his support of the Obama stimulus, for which he had claimed that the Florida economy would benefit. And he was also derided for his physical embrace of Obama.

Bell wrote (2010) that he thought that a "big tent" would unite the disparate factions within the conservative backlash to Obama. And he appears to be right in the short term, as these factions united as a force against Obama. Others were not so sanguine. One political scientist explained his apprehension: "It's energized the hardcore base of Republicans who tend to share a lot of Tea Party ideas, but on the other hand, it's going to bring to the floor a split that has been in the Republican Party for quite a long time" (Keck 2010). While this coalition was certainly victorious in November 2010, it later displayed some cracks within the coalition. One example of chafing within the big tent concept was expressed by a social conservative this way:

> The leadership of the GOP has evidently decided that we are a nation of businesses, and that our wallet matters most. The only promise they will make is that they will be economic conservatives if we elect them back into power. Fiscal conservatism, it is fast becoming apparent, is the only indisputable dogma honored by the GOP leadership. You will never see GOP Chairman Steele claiming his party is a "big tent" when it comes to limiting government excess, or hear Governor Mitch Daniels say America needs a "truce" on economic issues. (Peters 2010)

By suggesting that America—and Republicans strategically—needed to de-emphasize the social issues that had formed the basis of party doctrine and outreach since the days of Reagan, Indiana governor Mitch Daniels ran into some severe criticism from some socially conservative politicians and activists, as Kilgore notes:

> Daniels's statements about dialing down the culture wars have already been vocally rejected by potential presidential rivals Mike Huckabee, John Thune, and Rick Santorum. Rush Limbaugh has said that Daniels's position reflects the interests of a Republican "ruling class" that wants to rein in social conservatives and the Tea Party movement. (Kilgore 2011)

Institutional Republicans like Richard Lugar, the Republican senator from Indiana (and the target of a successful tea party primary challenge in 2012) found the tea party critiques inchoate and not fashioned as a plan for governing:

> Mr. Lugar said at a breakfast with reporters this month that he believed that many Tea Party supporters were motivated by anger "about how things have turned out for them." They want to express themselves, but their complaints often boil down to nothing more specific, he said, than "we want this or that stopped, or there is spending, big government." "These are all, we would say, sort of large cliché titles," he said, "but they are not able to articulate all the specifics." (Zernike 2011)

Former Christian Coalition strategist and Republican party official Ralph Reed expressed concern that the social conservative issues could get lost amid a growing focus on the deficit and fiscal issues: "There is some concern that if people become too comfortable in not talking about the cultural issues, that that could ultimately curdle into a lack of interest. . . . And I understand that concern. And to some extent I share that concern" (Gardner 2011b). But Reed also expressed optimism that the two thrusts could coexist profitably: "I'm a supply-sider when it comes to politics. . . . Once they see where the supply of voters is . . . they're going to find that they have to have a broad, comprehensive message that encompasses both the cultural agenda and the economic agenda" (Burns 2011).

Even then, some mainstream conservatives like George Will were less than complimentary in their attitudes toward Palin and some of her fellow potential candidates, as 2012 approached:

> But the nominee may emerge much diminished by involvement in a process cluttered with careless, delusional, egomaniacal, spotlight-chasing candidates to whom the sensible American majority would never entrust a lemonade stand, much less nuclear weapons. (Will 2011)

For tea party activists, the struggle over whether to emphasize social issues like abortion was not an unimportant issue. Soon after the November 2010 election, Operation Rescue founder Randall Terry and other social conservative activists sent incoming House speaker Boehner a clear message that these issues were an important consideration for his leadership of the Republican Party during the upcoming Congress:

> We call on you to be a man of your word: defund Planned Parenthood, International Planned Parenthood Federation, their affiliates in the U.S., its territories, and all nations of the world. Planned Parenthood is the world's foremost child killer. Since the GOP now controls federal spending, we demand you not give one more penny of our money to this godless organization that murders babies, and corrupts youth under the guise of "sex education."
>
> *Mr. Boehner, defunding Planned Parenthood is a "non-negotiable."*
>
> If you defund Planned Parenthood, you will be remembered as a hero in time and eternity. But if you fail to act—in your words—you will not

"get a pass." We will run candidates against you and your fellow Republicans in the 2012 primaries. We will not suffer "hypocrites for life."

God have mercy on your soul if you were using murdered babies as a political stepping-stone. (Boehnerteaparty 2011)

Boehner would later enrage conservatives with his brokering of a debt limit deal in 2013 and personify the "establishment" Republicanism that many of the new tea party adherents found wanting.

The Tucson Turn

The angry "town halls" of 2009, the simultaneous rise of the "tea parties," and the decidedly partisan backlash against the Obama healthcare proposal, combined with stagnant economic conditions and disappointment among progressives on several Obama domestic and foreign policies, made the Obama agenda vulnerable in 2010. In November 2010, the Democratic Party received what Obama referred to as a "shellacking," holding onto its Senate majority but seeing the loss of over 60 House seats, ending the four-year dominance of the party in that body. So it was that American entered 2011, even with some post-election bipartisan legislative successes, with the feeling that the "Obama era" might just have reached its zenith, a two-year phenomenon that would not come close to paralleling the "Reagan Revolution." The 112th Congress, starting in January 2011, would have, at least in one house of Congress, the goal of impeding and dismantling the Obama accomplishments and agenda.

That spirit shifted on an early January Saturday in Tucson, Arizona, with the shooting at a constituent meeting of narrowly re-elected Democratic congresswoman Gabrielle Giffords and the killing of six who attended the event. The shootings opened a national dialogue and debate on the level of incivility (and the connection of the backlash to the acts of a troubled man). However indirectly connected to the political divisiveness, the violence unleashed on a moderate Democratic congresswoman—and the killing of a federal judge and a nine-year old girl, among others—caused a pause in American discourse, as the often conflicting values of civility and partisanship became discordant. Americans overwhelmingly supported the sentiments of President Obama in expressing national sadness and outrage, without his directly blaming his political opponents. Americans responded with a strong polling rebuke of the state of political dialogue.

The facts, while not the motivation and ultimate responsibility, are well-established. Twenty-two-year old Jared Loughner appeared at a "meet your congresswoman" session arranged by Democratic congresswoman Gabrielle Giffords armed with a semi-automatic handgun. He proceeded to shoot Giffords, wounding her grievously, and killed six attendees at the gathering, including federal judge John Roll and nine-year-old Christina-Taylor Green, with 31 shots in all. He was subdued at the scene. (Loughner was later found capable of standing trial, pled guilty to the charges, and was sentenced to life in prison.)

In some ways, the shooter that day could be seen as a modern-day (and real-life) incarnation of Robert DeNiro's character Travis Bickle in Martin Scorsese's 1976 film *Taxi Driver*. In that story, Bickle, after being spurned as a love interest by a campaign worker for a presidential candidate, tries to save a damsel in distress—in this case, an adolescent prostitute, Iris, played by Jodie Foster, whom he met in his cab—and he also tries to talk her out of working as a prostitute. Later he tries, and fails, to assassinate the presidential candidate. Then he returns to Iris and shoots her pimp. It is this avenging angel side of Bickle that catapults him into the role of hero in the mean streets of New York City. While the Tucson killings were the distorted work of a mentally disassociated young man, they can also be seen as a Bickle-type avenging, in which the Statue of Liberty played the Jodie Foster character. So much had been made in the prior two years of the ways in which liberty was at stake in America. The interpretation by angry town hall participants and tea party activists that the country had been taken from them and that it needed to be "taken back" certainly provided the background against which a disturbed young man could act out. As former President Bill Clinton observed soon after the shootings, "Both the hinged and the unhinged" heard the dialed-up level of anger, accusation, and partisanship that had come to characterize America by early 2011.

Tucson area (Pima County) sheriff Clarence Dupnik led quickly with a statement connecting the national anger to the shootings in his jurisdiction. At a press conference that first day, he proclaimed:

... when you look at unbalanced people, how they respond to the vitriol that comes out of certain mouths about tearing down the government. The anger, the hatred, the bigotry that goes on in this country getting to be outrageous. And unfortunately, Arizona I think has become sort of the capital. We have become the Mecca for prejudice and bigotry. (*Politico* 2011a)

(Arizona would later become a national focus point for its immigration policy, its efforts against the Affordable Care Act, and the state legislative passage of a bill permitting "conscientious objection" from florists, bakers, and the like allowing them to refuse to provide services for same-sex weddings.) While progressive commentators like MSNBC's Keith Olbermann approved of the sheriff's statements (a Facebook page was started, entitled "Clarence Dupnik Is My Hero"), conservatives like U.S. Senator Jon Kyl (R-Arizona) found fault with the connections and implications that the sheriff had drawn:

It's probably giving him too much credit to ascribe a coherent political philosophy to him. We just have to acknowledge that there are mentally unstable people in this country. Who knows what motivates them to do what they do? Then they commit terrible crimes like this. I would just note Gabrielle Giffords, a fine representative from Tucson, I think would be the first to say don't rush to judgment here. (*Face the Nation* 2011)

Given a day to reflect, Dupnik reiterated his sentiment:

I think that when the rhetoric about hatred, about mistrust of government, about paranoia of how government operates and to try to inflame the public on a daily basis, 24 hours a day, seven days a week, has impact on people especially who are unbalanced personalities to begin with. (Weigel 2011b)

When progressive blogger Markos Moulitsas of the *Daily Kos* tweeted shortly after the shootings of Congresswoman Gabrielle Giffords, "Sarah Palin: Mission Accomplished," he was accused of fanning the flames of incivility (Moulitsas 2011). But it was indeed the fortunes of the visible conservative former vice presidential candidate—who had claimed

"Don't Retreat, Instead—RELOAD!" as a guiding philosophy—that were being discussed as one of the main responses to the Tucson shooting. And it was the centrality of Palin as a representation of the backlash and tea party–generated anger that became a focus of media discussion. Indeed, Rep. Giffords had spoken out again the Palin-backed effort to identify competitive House seats for 2010 by using a "bull's-eye" on Southern Arizona and elsewhere. To Giffords, Palin had crossed the line. Gifford had herself argued, "We are on Sarah Palin's targeted list. The way that she has it depicted has the crosshairs of the gunsight over our district. When people do that, they have got to realize there are consequences to that action" (Nichols 2011).

After the shooting, Palin would explain that her marks were indeed "surveyor's marks," and she backtracked in what was perceived as an overly defensive manner at the time that a more sympathetic or broader approach would have appeared more "presidential." Still, the problem was that a politician who had made "Don't Retreat, Instead—RELOAD!" a motto for her political strategy, and who was herself pictured often in her reality show brandishing the rifles that were often used in the Alaska backcountry, had trouble explaining away the bull's-eyes. One of Palin's advisors gave an interview in which she attempted to explain away the graphics of the bull's-eyes:

> [PALIN AIDE REBECCA] MANSOUR: I just want to clarify again, and maybe it wasn't done on the record enough by us when this came out, the graphic, is just, it's basically—we never, ever, ever intended it to be gunsights. It was simply crosshairs like you see on maps.
> BRUCE: Well, it's a surveyor's symbol. It's a surveyor's symbol.
> MANSOUR: It's a surveyor's symbol. I just want to say this, Tammy, if I can. This graphic was done, not even done in-house—we had a political graphics professional who did this for us. (Weigel 2011a)

Raul Grijalva, a Democratic congressman from Arizona, and colleague of Giffords, added: "The climate has gotten so toxic in our political discourse, setting up for this kind of reaction for too long. It's unfortunate to say that. I hate to say that . . . if you're an opponent, you're a deadly enemy" (Nichols 2011). It also didn't help that the tea party–backed Republican who opposed Giffords in 2010 had held an

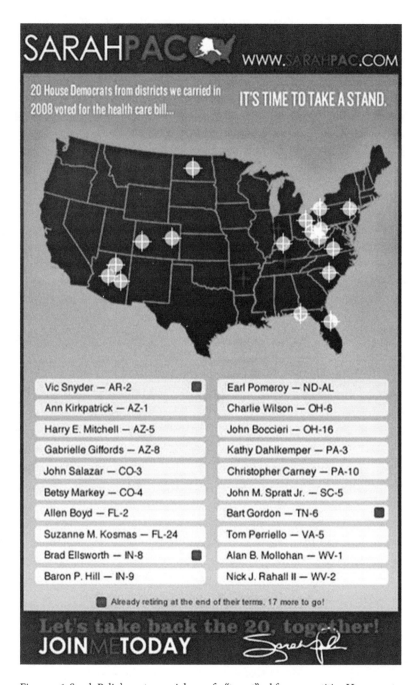

Figure 2.6. Sarah Palin's controversial use of a "target" ad for competitive House seats.

event during that campaign that offered: "Get on Target for Victory in November. Help remove Gabrielle Giffords from office. Shoot a fully automatic M16 with Jesse Kelly." A Tucson tea party leader insisted that their rhetoric wouldn't change after the Giffords shooting, since they saw the two as unrelated (McMorris-Santoro and Rayfield 2011).

While it was clear that the shootings in Tuscon would alter the national conversation on politics and the Obama presidency, some observers thought that it could offer only brief respite and perhaps even exacerbate existing polarization. As George Packer wrote in the *New Yorker*:

> This relentlessly hostile rhetoric has become standard issue on the right. . . . And it has gone almost entirely uncriticized by Republican leaders. Partisan media encourages it, while the mainstream media finds it titillating and airs it, often without comment, so that the gradual effect is to desensitize even people to whom the rhetoric is repellent. We've all grown so used to it over the past couple of years that it took the shock of an assassination attempt to show us the ugliness to which our politics has sunk. (Packer 2011)

Obama Speeches

Presiding at a ceremony honoring those killed in Tucson, at the University of Arizona on January 12, 2011, President Obama attempted to rise above the partisanship and the recent violence, connected or not connected to partisan bickering. Obama would use this incident as an opportunity to offer a more balanced, conciliatory notion of the nation's situation than the overheated rhetoric of 2009 and 2010 had permitted:

> At a time when our discourse has become so sharply polarized—at a time when we are far too eager to lay the blame for all that ails the world at the feet of those who think differently than we do—it's important for us to pause for a moment and make sure that we are talking with each other in a way that heals, not a way that wounds. (Obama 2011a)

As other presidents had done with inaugurations and important ceremonial speaking, President Obama introduced religion as a basis for understanding and healing (an important move, given that a large number of Americans still believe that he is Muslim):

Scripture tells us that there is evil in the world, and that terrible things happen for reasons that defy human understanding. In the words of Job, "when I looked for light, then came darkness." Bad things happen, and we must guard against simple explanations in the aftermath. (Obama 2011a)

Obama wound his speech around the importance of reconciliation and dialogue, speaking against the polarization and partisanship that many had decried and which the town halls and tea party movement had brought to the forefront:

What we can't do is use this tragedy as one more occasion to turn on one another. As we discuss these issues, let each of us do so with a good dose of humility. Rather than pointing fingers or assigning blame, let us use this occasion to expand our moral imaginations, to listen to each other more carefully, to sharpen our instincts for empathy, and remind ourselves of all the ways our hopes and dreams are bound together. (Obama 2011a)

Even then, partisan observations followed, like this from two conservative radio talk-show hosts—"It's a Democratic political rally," they said, referring to the memorial service in Tucson. Conservative writer and blogger Michelle Malkin called the memorial service a "bizarre pep rally" in her live blogging of the memorial, asking, "Will there be giant foam fingers and blue cotton candy, too?" (Malkin 2011).

Instead, most Americans reported that they had tired of what they saw as a dysfunctional turn toward hyper-partisanship. An ABC–*Washington Post* poll taken soon after the speech found a different America listening and reflecting. In response to a question about "the tone of the country's political discourse," 82% reported finding it negative. Fully 78% of the respondents approved of "President Obama's response to the Arizona shooting incident" (Balz and Cohen 2011).

With Sarah Palin responding in a defensive manner about her earlier mottoes and graphics and President Obama preaching reconciliation, America had moved in a short time to a plateau different from where it had been when the new year began. As one analyst observed:

In the span of a single news cycle, Republicans got a jarring reminder of two forces that could prevent them from retaking the presidency next year. At sunrise in the east on Wednesday, Sarah Palin demonstrated that she has little interest—or capacity—in moving beyond her brand of grievance-based politics. And at sundown in the west, Barack Obama reminded even his critics of his ability to rally disparate Americans around a message of reconciliation. (Martin 2011)

With the proposal in Arizona for a new "civility institute" (Tumolillo 2011), some conservatives complained that the onus for creation and maintenance of the "incivility" was laid at their feet by the mainstream media. Some conservatives complained that the newfound focus on civility held a strong liberal bias, as amplified through the mainstream media, and was designed to limit conservative critiques of Obama and the Democratic agenda at a time when the conservative movement was on the upswing, for example, "Now we can't even have strong debates?" (*John and Ken Show* 2011a). Gary Bauer wrote:

It is currently fashionable to decry the supposedly uncivil and divisive tone of our politics. Not surprisingly, conservatives are often singled out by the media for unnecessarily fomenting dissent and discord. But the divisive tone of our political rhetoric reflects legitimate divisions that exist in America over very fundamental issues—over the role of government, over America's place in the world, over what kind of future our children will have, over the definition of our most basic social institutions, and over the very meaning of life and death. (Bauer 2011a)

Within two weeks, Obama was set to deliver his annual State of the Union speech. To the man who had encountered the yell of "You lie!" during a previous speech in Congress, it was unclear that the renewed emphasis on civility—not embraced from all quarters—would transform the polarization and hyper-partisanship that was characterizing American political life of late.

Reversing what had been a trend that had seen him vilified, and his party losing seats, the bounceback from the Tucson speech continued. While cynics might describe any State of the Union speech as a series of platitudes and popular framing and promises, it was a potentially risky moment for the president, whose party had just lost so many seats in the House. His focus was on the need to retool America, to keep it competitive, to "Win the Future" (which Sarah Palin, on her Twitter account, ridiculed as "WTF?"; Barrett 2011). To analyst Joe Klein, Obama had instead managed to achieve something that was uncertain a few months earlier: "And that was the most remarkable thing about the speech: Obama completely reversed the American political calculus of the 1980s and '90s. He made the Democrats the party of optimism and the Republicans the party of root canal" (Klein 2011b). Klein was referring to the official Republican Party response to the speech, in which Representative Paul Ryan began to outline his dramatic plan for deficit reduction, a theme that would continue through the spring and presume to be a major focus of the 2012 presidential and congressional campaigns (as opposed to the congressional tea party caucus reply, in which Representative Michele Bachmann gave the entire speech looking at the wrong camera). A *CBS News* poll taken shortly after the speech found that "an overwhelming majority of Americans approved of the overall message" (*CBS News* 2011). Liberal MSNBC commentator Rachel Maddow credited the president with "wrenching the center back from the right" and "stopping the country's rightward drift" (Green 2011).

With the observation of the centennial of the birth of Ronald Reagan also in this time frame, Obama the day prior to his State of the Union speech had praised the conservative icon. In no less a mainstream outlet than *USA Today*, which compiled a series of testimonials and reflections, Obama wrote:

> But perhaps even more important than any single accomplishment was the sense of confidence and optimism President Reagan never failed to communicate to the American people. It was a spirit that transcended the most heated political arguments, and one that called each of us to believe that tomorrow will be better than today. At a time when our nation was going through an extremely difficult period, with economic hardship at home and very real threats beyond our borders, it was this positive outlook, this sense of pride, that the American people needed more than anything. (Obama 2011b)

Later, Obama would seek to emphasize that he did not see the Tucson shootings as a reason to embrace a gun control policy more stringent than that which the American public supported. While gun ownership and use have been one component of the culture wars, broadly drawn (Melzer 2010), elements of the Democratic Party and President Obama eventually decided that an assault on that issue would not be beneficial to their attempts to maintain a ruling majority in the country. Gun control advocates were dismayed that, even after other mass shootings, gun control had not successfully become a "wedge" issue in favor of the Democrats, despite their interest in moving the issue. So it was that, even after the carnage in Tucson, Obama used a newspaper there for a 2011 op-ed piece continuing to support the Second Amendment (especially since the Supreme Court had recently crystallized its support):

> Clearly, there's more we can do to prevent gun violence. But I want this to at least be the beginning of a new discussion on how we can keep America safe for all our people. I know some aren't interested in participating. Some will say that anything short of the most sweeping anti-gun legislation is a capitulation to the gun lobby. Others will predictably cast any discussion as the opening salvo in a wild-eyed scheme to take away everybody's guns. And such hyperbole will become the fodder for overheated fundraising letters. But I have more faith in the American people than that. Most gun-control advocates know that most gun owners are responsible citizens. Most gun owners know that the word "commonsense" isn't a code word for "confiscation." And none of us should be willing to remain passive in the face of violence or resigned to watching helplessly as another rampage unfolds on television. (Obama 2011c)

Still, not all forms of hyperpartisanship were dialed down. During the State of the Union address, one Republican congressman from Georgia tweeted: "Mr. President, you don't believe in the Constitution. You believe in socialism" (*Politico* 2011a). A month after Tucson, visible expressions of anger appeared prominently at the well-attended (over 10,000) annual conservative activist conference, the Conservative Political Action Conference. One news site reported:

> BUMPER SNICKERS from the Conservative Political Action Conference (CPAC)...[included]: "WILL WORK FOR AMMO." ... "KEEP HONKING— I'M RELOADING." ... "FORGET 911—DIAL .357." ... "WARNING! DRIVER ONLY CARRIES $20.00 WORTH OF AMMUNITION." (Allen 2011)

Conclusion: 2012 and Beyond

To noted sociologist Paul Starr, the events of 2009 and 2010 were part of a long-evolving tapestry of movement and backlash that has typified the last 20 years of American politics, which also explains the persistence of the culture wars:

> Both conservatives and liberals have been looking for a decisive victory in the great political contest of our times. Periodically, one side advances its cause and dares to believe that it has achieved a definitive political realignment, but its advances turn out to mobilize the opposition more than its own supporters. In the great tug-of-war of the past 20 years, there has been no conclusive move in either direction. (Starr 2010)

The idea of the victorious Obama was seen by many in 2008 and 2009 as an embrace of change and a sign that the culture war would wane (a good thing to those who foretold its demise). The backlash against the Obama administration, phrased in the angry town halls of 2009, coalescing in the tea party opposition of 2009 and 2010, and culminating in the midterm election reversals of November 2010, offered a competing narrative—a rejection of the Obama change and a chance to "take our country back." The shootings in Arizona in January 2011, at a time when the second narrative would seem to be ascendant, called that interpretation into question. However indirectly connected to the political divisiveness, the violence unleashed on a moderate Democratic congresswoman, and the killing of a federal judge and a nine-year old girl, among others, caused a pause in American discourse, as the often conflicting values of civility and partisanship became discordant. It also suggested some of the limits of the "againster" backlash that characterized the period. The events of Tucson, Obama's reaction to it, and the narrative of his 2011 State of the Union speech—reframing the national conversation—allowed him to reverse the decline in ratings and potential that the November 2010 midterms had provided. As noted before, November 2, 2010, could be seen as the crest of the tea party movement. After it, there would be divisions, there would be acknowledgment that focusing on the deficit (a Ross Perot moment, not a Jerry Falwell moment) would be the course of the moment, and there would be even calls for a "truce" on culture war issues like abortion and same-sex marriage that presidential candidate and Indiana governor Mitch Daniels proposed, with a focus on fiscal issues as paramount.

The tripartite coalitions that Ronald Reagan had successfully yoked his presidency to—economic conservatives, foreign policy conservatives, and social conservatives—has been distended in different eras. It has been at its most successful—as during the Reagan presidency itself—when all three sides were functioning together. Despite the "anti-Obama" nature of the tea party movement emergence, one putative thrust has been that it is essentially a fiscal and deficit/debt-focused movement. To the extent this is true, and not simply a way to change the framing of a now-discredited overfocus on personal morality issues, it still poses a problem for the anti-Obama coalition. At its heart, is the thrust of the current tea party moment truly the focus on government budgets, deficit, and debts? Will foot soldiers of the movement show up at polls, encourage, phone, and drive others to do so and contribute the deeply committed volunteer bases that the social conservative side has done for the Republican Party since the days of Ronald Reagan and the emergence of Jerry Falwell and the Moral Majority? The election of 2012 didn't suggest that.

The next four chapters provide analysis and arguments to challenge the contention that America is indeed moving in the conservative direction that a snapshot of the anti-Obama backlash of 2009–2010 suggested. Chapter 3 argues that the traditional basis for such culture war partisanships, the social conservative Christian Right—which had directed much of the culture war over the prior 30 years—no longer possesses the ability to frame and shape these divisions in American society. For that analysis, the chapter examines the remarkable rise of American support for marriage equality in the last decade. Chapter 4 focuses on the moderating nature of religion (and secularism) in contemporary America. Chapter 5 argues that any expectation for the social conservatism of a growing Latino community and other elements of a growing American ethnic and racial diversity is not supported. Finally, Chapter 6 offers a moment and a measure for the realization of that nascent framing power. The 2012 election ended up not delivering on the promise of removing the much-vilified Obama from office.

3

Marriage Equality

America and the New Normal

Devaluing them [gay and lesbian military] in that regard is just inconsistent with us as an institution.
—Admiral Michael Mullen, chair, Joint Chiefs of Staff, February 2010

For the first time ever, all 100 firms on *Fortune*'s Best Companies To Work For list this year have non-discrimination policies that include sexual orientation.
—James O'Toole, 2012

These people who are making a big deal out of gay marriage? I don't give a fuck about who wants to get married to anybody else! Why not?! We're making a big deal out of things we shouldn't be making a deal out of. . . . They go on and on with all this bullshit about "sanctity"—don't give me that sanctity crap! Just give everybody the chance to have the life they want.
—Clint Eastwood, movie director, actor, and primetime speaker at 2012 Republican National Convention, in *GQ*, September 2011

In August 2013, the producers of the annual Oscar telecast for the Academy of Motion Picture Arts and Sciences announced that they would bring back comedian and television talk-show host Ellen DeGeneres to be the host of the 2014 Oscar show, a position she had held before in 2007. (Weisman 2013). For the Oscar officials, the shift from the more profane Seth McFarlane, who had hosted in 2013, to the popular DeGeneres was a risk-averse development. In recent years, less than wonderfully successful shows with television late-night comedians

David Letterman or Jon Stewart, or with actor Chris Rock, or young actors James Franco and Anne Hathaway as co-hosts, had often sent the Oscar producers and planner back to the search for the perfect host who would enlarge the audience and deliver increased viewer ratings.

One Hollywood reporter for a leading trade magazine stated, "Ellen is a safe choice" (Alexander 2013). Otherwise, that Ellen was married to a female actress proved not to be much of a theme in that day's story. With over 21 million Twitter followers (making her 14th on the list of most followed according to twittercounter.com) and 2.47 million average daily viewers to her mid-day television talk show, Ellen was a prominent fixture in American popular culture. Early on in the *Los Angeles Times* story, DeGeneres was quoted from her Twitter account: "It's official: I'm hosting the #Oscars!" DeGeneres wrote, "I'd like to thank @TheAcademy, my wife Portia and, oh dear, there goes the orchestra" (Weisman 2013). DeGeneres's eponymous character had "come out" as a character on the television sitcom *Ellen* in 1997, a move that prompted ABC television to place a "parental advisory" notice on each subsequent show. That was a year after Democratic president Bill Clinton had signed the federal Defense of Marriage Act (DOMA), a law that would be overturned by the U.S. Supreme Court in June 2013 and that Clinton himself described in a 2013 *Washington Post* op-ed piece as "vestiges of . . . an unfamiliar society." (Clinton 2013). DeGeneres herself came out publicly at the same time with an appearance on Oprah Winfrey's talk show and an article in *Time* magazine. In time, she would come to be referred to as "public lesbian number one" by one feminist academic (Reed 2005).

Perhaps Ellen DeGeneres's reference to fellow actress Portia DeRossi as her wife stirred some backlash in social conservative circles or eye rolling among those for whom the glamour and excess of Hollywood is equivalent to the coarsening of America and the steady dissolution of core American family values. It would not surprise them that the same entertainment industry analyst referred to DeGeneres's choice as a host as a good opportunity for the motion picture industry to demonstrate its commitment to diversity.

At the time of the passage of the federal DOMA law in 1996, only 37% of respondents to a national poll had replied that they did "have any friends or relatives or co-workers who have told you, personally, that they are gay or lesbian"; 62 percent reported that they did not. In 1975, that number had been 24%. In 2008, it would be 57% (Harris/*USA Today*/*Los*

Figure 3.1. Ellen and Portia's high-profile romance gains mainstream acceptance.

Angeles Times poll). In 1996, only 27% of respondents to the Gallup poll responded that they thought that marriages between same-sex couples should be permitted. The scope and trajectory of change in those 17 years was dramatic.

This is the first of three chapters that together present an argument as to why social conservatism will no longer have the profile and effect that it had during the Falwell years. Chapter 3 traces the steady and dramatic changes in American attitudes toward, and in the legal reform of, marriage equality as an example of the "de-wedging" of one of the key "wedge issues" utilized by the social and religious conservatives from 1980 onward, namely the issues of homosexuality, gay rights, generally, and same-sex marriage, specifically. It uses as a touchpoint pollster Geoff Garin's 2010 observation that "it's hard to imagine a significant issue in which the center of gravity is shifting faster than gay marriage in this country" (Haberman et al. 2012).

Falwell

Shortly before his death in May 2007, Jerry Falwell, the Baptist minister who had founded the social conservative and religious political group Moral Majority in 1979 and who had been a leading voice for social conservatism in America for three decades, gave an interview to CNN. In the interview with Christiane Amanpour, not shown until after his death, Falwell was asked if he wanted to retract the comments he had made shortly after the 9/11 attacks in America, in which he had asserted,

> I really believe that the pagans, and the abortionists, and the feminists, and the gays and the lesbians who are actively trying to make that an alternative lifestyle, the ACLU, People for the American Way, all of them who have tried to secularize America. I point the finger in their face and say "you helped this happen." (Christian Broadcasting Network 2001)

He seemed to pause for a moment with Amanpour and then replied that he would not reconsider the statement, that he would let those comments stand, almost six years after the 9/11 attacks.

Figure 3.2. Jerry Falwell, once heralded as a leader of American conservative fundamentalism.

AMANPOUR (IN VOICE-OVER): And Falwell continued to connect liberal beliefs to Islamic terrorism, such as blaming the attacks of September 11th on the prevalence of abortion in America.

AMANPOUR: You know, you caused a huge amount of controversy after 9/11 when you basically said that the Lord was removing his protection from America.

FALWELL: I still believe that. I believe that a country that is—

AMANPOUR: And that America probably deserved it.

FALWELL: Here's what I said, what—no. I said that the people who are responsible must take the blame for it.

AMANPOUR: You did.

FALWELL: We were killing—

AMANPOUR:—but you went on to say what I've just said.

FALWELL: We're killing a million babies a year in this country by abortion. But I was saying then and I'm saying now, that if we, in fact, change all the rules on which this Judeo-Christian nation was built, we cannot expect the Lord to put his shield of protection around us as he has in the past.

AMANPOUR: So you still stand by that?

FALWELL: I stand right by it. (CNN 2007b)

Though Falwell had seemingly not changed in nearly six years, America had. In 2001, there were no states that allowed same-sex marriages, and the percentage of Americans who supported that legal reform in 2001 numbered only 35%. By May 2007, when he gave Amanpour the interview, that support was staring to rise to the more than 50% it is today.

The twin themes of the culture war in America, for the 30 years between the beginning of the "Moral Majority" in 1978 and the death of Falwell in 2007 (see Winters 2012a, 2012b), have been the issues of gay rights and abortion. When Falwell and others urged the largely world-denying and politically uninvolved Protestant fundamentalists to become politically involved in the late 1970s, it set forth a movement that would shape American politics and public policy for those 30 years, strong and strident in its opposition to the growing modernity of American society. Using this lens, in this chapter I examine the activities of the 2008–2014 period for the extent to which the culture war, as it is understood, has become loosened from the moorings of these two subjects.

"Don't Ask, Don't Tell": Early Shifts

Since 1993, the United States had employed a unique policy, crafted as a compromise by then newly elected president Bill Clinton, that would

Figure 3.3. Joint Chiefs of Staff Admiral Mike Mullen, who supported the end of the "Don't Ask, Don't Tell" policy in the U.S. military.

stop far short of allowing openly gay and lesbian soldiers to serve in the military. The "Don't Ask, Don't Tell" (DADT) policy had served as a middle ground between outright acceptance and the previous policy of discharge. As time went by, however, it seemed less consistent with national values in the area of sexual orientation, which had changed steadily. Admiral Michael Mullen, then the chair of the American Joint Chief of Staffs, had articulated in 2010 that "devaluing them [gay and lesbian military] in that regard is just inconsistent with us as an institution." Appearing alongside Defense Secretary Robert Gates, who articulated the Obama administration's position on DADT, Mullen explained to the Senate Armed Service Committee, while explaining that the Joint Chiefs would await congressional direction on DADT and would devise a plan for implementing the policy, that "it is my personal belief that allowing gays and lesbians to serve openly would be the right thing to do. No matter how I look at this issue, I cannot escape being troubled by the fact that we have in place a policy which forces young men and women to lie about who they are in order to defend their fellow citizens" (Joint Chiefs of Staff 2010).

In President Clinton's defense, the executive order he signed in 1993 that became known as "Don't Ask, Don't Tell" was a compromise position between the hopes of gay and lesbian advocates and those of military officials who did not want an open military, in a sexual orientation sense. As one of Clinton's former advisors recalls,

> Soon after Clinton took office, in 1993, it was apparent that his tenure was off to a rocky beginning. The early days of the Administration were marred by opposition within the military and the Democratic Party itself to Clinton's idea of gays and lesbians serving openly in the uniformed armed forces. The White House was unprepared to shepherd a major social-policy change through Congress. (Socarides 2013)

As remarkable as the road that California, or the American public, or Bill Clinton traveled between 1993 and 2013 was the transformation that occurred among American military officials and institutions between 1993 and 2011, when the rescinding of DADT was completed. The undoing of DADT has its own story arc. At a most important level, American attitudes toward the importance of the rule shifted over time.

Polls in 2009 from both Quinnipiac (April 2009) and Democracy Corps (November 2009) showed strong support for repealing DADT. In response to the survey item "Federal law currently prohibits openly gay men and women from serving in the military. Do you think this law should be repealed or not?" 55% answered yes, and only 35% no. Democracy Corps labeled this a "stable majority for change," that Americans favored the repeal of the federal rule. At another level, it took the election of Barack Obama to bring the first president from the Democratic Party since Clinton into office. And while Obama was much more of a follower than a leader on marriage equality and gay and lesbian issues, as we will see in Chapter 5, his eventual transformation had an effect on African American attitudes and votes.

> The perception was somehow that this would be this huge, ugly issue.... [There] hasn't been any notion of erosion and unit cohesion. In some ways what's been remarkable is how readily the public recognizes this is the right thing to do. (Nakamura 2012)

One axiom might be that when military leaders are prepared to support a change in a policy in a liberalizing direction—as Admiral Michael Mullen, the chair of the Joint Chiefs of Staff did with "Don't Ask, Don't Tell" in 2010 (Joint Chiefs of Staff 2010)—that change is indeed cemented. When one looks at the popular support for the reform of DADT over the last several years, it is apparent that the American people had long come to accept that recognition—rather than expulsion—of lesbian and gay troops was in keeping with American values.

When San Francisco supervisor Harvey Milk—one of the nation's first elected publicly gay politicians—was killed by a fellow supervisor in 1978, same-sex marriage was not even an issue that had been contemplated or suggested. San Francisco had been one of the first municipalities in the country to pass an anti-discrimination bill prohibiting discrimination in housing, employment, and accommodations along the lines of racial and religious anti-discrimination laws (Meeker et al. 1985). In 1975, when that ordinance was passed, there were few other municipalities in the United States that had passed similar laws. By 2013, there were over 174 counties and cities on the list, along with 21 states that prohibited discrimination either on the basis of sexual orientation or sexual identity (Human Rights Campaign 2013).

These changes were achieved over several decades by reformers and key organizations that worked tirelessly at changing American official response to gay rights through the many efforts at changing police practices, anti-sodomy legal reform, municipal and county anti-discrimination measures, and AIDS-era anti-discrimination measures before marriage and family issues became prominent (D'Emilio 2000; Hirshman 2012; Sullivan 2012b). As polls and surveys cited suggested, American public attitudes changed as a result of these organized efforts. By 2012, America had decidedly become less engrossed in seeing gay rights issues as a symbol of a core difference in Americans in social, religious, and political citizenship.

Clint

Clint Eastwood was a publicly unexpected, inspired, and unscripted speaker on the last night of the Republican National Convention in 2012. By occupying the second-to-last speaking slot before the acceptance

Figure 3.4. Actor Clint Eastwood addresses Obama's "empty chair" at the 2012 Republican National Convention.

speech of nominee Mitt Romney, the celebrated flinty-eyed actor and director was intended to give some cultural uplift to the then-flagging hopes of candidate Romney. What the Republican convention planner got—in a move orchestrated by Romney campaign director Stuart Stevens (a former television director who, by one account, vomited after the event; Balz 2013)—was an unscripted, seemingly stream-of-consciousness, 11-minute speech from a Hollywood icon so out of sync with his progressive colleagues that he was proudly supporting Herman Cain in the Republican primary contests. But it was not just an unscripted speech. In his now-famous diatribe, Eastwood used a set-up that was probably more familiar to actors trained in various Stella Adler acting techniques rather than to politicians used to employing predictable speech forms, particularly the kinds used for something as exalted as a presidential nomination acceptance speech. By addressing an empty chair that he had delivered onto the stage—which represented President Obama's "empty" leadership—Eastwood hoped to capture the sentiments and statements that many Republicans thought that their opponent Barack Obama should hear about the country they thought he was running into the ground in so many ways.

Partisans and critics had a field day ridiculing Eastwood for his rambling speech. The television cameras in the hall that night showed the seeming discomfort of many that such a moment of building drama for the Romney speech was being dissipated instead by the ad hoc ramblings of an octogenarian actor (even though it worked for Ronald Reagan, and Al Gore clearly thought that there was some cultural expansiveness possible by having his former Harvard roommate and Hollywood actor Tommy Lee Jones place his name in nomination at the 2000 Democratic Convention; *ABC News* 2000).

What went undiscussed after Eastwood's appearance was that the prominent cultural presence and former small-town California mayor had offered his decidedly libertarian thoughts on same-sex marriage less than a year earlier in an interview with *GQ* magazine before the opening of the film *J. Edgar* (2011), which he directed and which starred Leonardo DiCaprio (and which addressed, indirectly, the sexuality of America's long-serving FBI director J. Edgar Hoover).

> These people who are making a big deal out of gay marriage? I don't give a fuck about who wants to get married to anybody else! Why not?! We're making a big deal out of things we shouldn't be making a deal out of. . . . They go on and on with all this bullshit about "sanctity"—don't give me that sanctity crap! Just give everybody the chance to have the life they want. (Harris 2011)

Eastwood's comments in *GQ* were not exactly heresy in the Republican Party by 2012. Yes, Rick Santorum ran a decidedly social conservative campaign, and grassroots party activists in groups like American Values, the American Family Association, Focus on the Family, and the Family Research Council continued to describe the advent of same-sex marriage as abhorrent and an affront to traditional family values. American Values' Gary Bauer had said in 2006 that "your children and grandchildren will be taught that homosexuality is normal and same-sex unions equally valid to heterosexual marriages. So-called 'hate crimes' laws will make sure that anyone who objects is silenced." Yet there was a state of silence among Republican Party operatives in 2012 as same-sex marriage, and the president's support of it, moved steadily upward in Americans' approval index. Eastwood represented a growing acceptance of the inevitability of same-sex marriage among Republican operatives, some of whom felt strongly that this was an issue that could harmfully broadcast to the country, especially younger voters, how out of touch the party was.

To others, it may not have mattered much, but they saw the demographic changes and understood that a reliance upon culture war issues would be defeating for any Republican campaign that wishes to concentrate on its arguments on limited government and reduced taxation. But to many of the socially conservative band who had grown in importance and number during the Falwell years, culture war issues were still indeed a set of issues that spoke to large swaths of the American electorate—especially Republican primary voters—and that defined their ideas of what should be involved in policy debates. To them, the seemingly easy and rapid retreat from the culture war front was a sign that their voice was being diminished within the same party in which they had been important for decades. Their importance didn't always produce important results, though, as many from that movement expressed the feeling that they and their issues were given short shrift even during the Reagan administration, when the popular president seemed to focus more on the other two sides of his conservative triumvirate—economic pro-business conservatism, and foreign policy toughness/conservatism—and to pay only symbolic nods to social conservatism (Moen 1992).

There were those who, soon after the 2008 election, had commented on the diminishing utility of the gay rights/same-sex marriage focus as an organizing principle for the Republican Party. Some among those Republican strategists and analysts felt that demographic forces were pushing in the direction of support for marriage equality, since the youngest generation of voters were decidedly in support of it. With this demographic imperative, they felt it was unwise to yoke their party or cause to an issue that would slowly recede as a useful issue

Steve Schmidt, the McCain 2008 strategist, spoke out soon after that election about the need for Republicans to jettison this particular wedge issue. Schmidt would continue this line of reasoning in his 2012 appearances on MSNBC as a political analyst, and in 2013 he told Bill Maher that

> it's difficult to make the case to go work for a political party that wants to discriminate against their friend who happens to be gay. So, we have an enormous problem because of some of our issues in the Republican Party that are so out of step whether it is regard to women, with regard to gays, anti-immigrant rhetoric, it makes it difficult to attract the best and brightest. (*Real Time with Bill Maher* 2013)

Beyond the issue of reaching a younger portion of the electorate for whom this is such an clear sign of modernity—and potentially a surrogate for many other issues about the relevance of a political party—Schmidt addressed the hand-wringing issue of how the Democratic Party utilized the greatest skills and personnel of the Google generation while Republican operatives lamented their reliance on "blue hairs," the volunteer Republican women who had been their go-to staff for decades of party canvassing (supplemented in recent decades by social conservatives). This will discussed in more depth at the end of Chapter 6, especially as it is applied to the outreach differentials for the two campaigns and their respective ground games. In an era of deep data, narrowcasting, and finding persons based on their appetites, preferences, and habits, a deepening disadvantage would be troubling for a Republican party that believes it is again not attracting new generations.

The Republican Party sidestepped the impact of the 2013 announcement by Ohio Republican senator Rob Portman (on the short list for the Romney vice presidential consideration in 2012) that he supported same-sex marriage (or explained it away, as it had for Vice President

Dick Cheney) with the fact that Portman had a son who was gay. Meanwhile, Karl Rove allowed as to how a Republican nominee in 2016 might be in favor of same-sex marriage (Miller 2013). Only nine years before, during the 2004 presidential re-election campaign of George W. Bush, same-sex marriage had emerged as an important wedge issue, and the presence of defense of marriage referenda in key swing states like Ohio helped propel Bush to a close electoral victory (Stolberg 2013c).

Republicans might offer that they were in support of civil unions, once a plurality attitude, and a relatively safe middle ground that risk-averse politicians, even Democratic stalwarts such as President Bill Clinton, Senator and later President Barack Obama, and Senator and later Secretary of State Hillary Clinton supported up until 2013. Clearly this was an acceptable position for much of the straight American population without "overreaching" too much.

Obama would commit to supporting marriage equality during the 2012 campaign and go on to say in his 2013 inaugural address that "our journey is not complete until our gay brothers and sisters are treated like anyone else under the law—for if we are truly created equal, then surely the love we commit to one another must be equal as well" (Klein 2013). Hillary Clinton stated on March 17, 2013, that "L.G.B.T. Americans are our colleagues, our teachers, our soldiers, our friends, our loved ones, and they are full and equal citizens and deserve the rights of citizenship. . . . That includes marriage" (Robillard 2013).

Even California same-sex marriage repeal supporter David Blankenhorn, the founder of the Institute for American Values and the author of *The Future of Marriage* (2007), who had been a key expert witness in the Proposition 8 court case, announced in a *New York Times* op-ed piece in 2012 that he had changed his mind, and not only had he decided to withdraw his support for the anti same-sex marriage referendum and others like it, but, indeed, he also announced his support for same-sex marriage, writing,

> I don't believe that opposite-sex and same-sex relationships are the same, but I do believe, with growing numbers of Americans, that the time for denigrating or stigmatizing same-sex relationships is over. Whatever one's definition of marriage, legally recognizing gay and lesbian couples and their children is a victory for basic fairness. (Blankenhorn 2012)

And former Vice President Dick Cheney and his wife Lynne, leading American conservatives, were not social conservatives on the issue of marriage equality, appreciating the experience of their lesbian daughter, Mary.

Inevitability

According to a 2012 report, "For the first time ever, all 100 firms on *Fortune*'s Best Companies To Work For list this year have non-discrimination policies that include sexual orientation" (O'Toole 2012). Later, a poll from the Pew Research Center reported that even 59% of *opponents* to same-sex marriage think that legalization of same-sex marriage in the United States is inevitable (Pew Research Center 2013e). Even Rush Limbaugh agrees. But not all conservative movement leaders and organizations agree.

When President Obama had announced his support for same-sex marriage in 2012, it was met with a diversity of reactions. One social conservative reaction was,

> When President Obama publicly declared his support for same-sex marriage yesterday he was displaying his disdain and disrespect for anyone in this country who believes in Judeo-Christian values. Obama thinks that the same-sex marriage movement is so powerful and that we are so weak that his attack on normal marriage will actually help him win a second term. (Bauer 2012)

To some political analysts, Bauer and his colleagues were not joined in these assessments by what movement conservatives would call the "Republican establishment," which had chosen in 2012 to follow Steve Schmidt's 2009 message while hoping to keep included and motivated (at the polls in November 2012) the social conservatives who agreed with Bauer. Mark Halperin, the co-author of *Game Change* (Heilemann and Halperin 2010) comments,

> The greatest indication that public opinion on same-sex marriage has shifted over the past few years [is that] almost no prominent GOP elected officials raised the issue after the day of the endorsement; party leaders, almost to a person, changed the topic to the economy when asked about Obama's now evolved stance. . . . Rest assured, they will quietly commu-

nicate Obama's position to targeted voters via religious organizations and mail as the election nears. . . . And if Obama loses narrowly, some of his supporters are sure to look back and wonder if publicly backing gay marriage cost him his job. (Halperin 2012)

Social conservatives would have their way in the 2012 Republican Platform, which stated:

The institution of marriage is the foundation of civil society. Its success as an institution will determine our success as a nation. It has been proven by both experience and endless social science studies that traditional marriage is best for children. . . . We recognize and honor the courageous efforts of those who bear the many burdens of parenting alone, even as we believe that marriage, the union of one man and one woman must be upheld as the national standard, a goal to stand for, encourage, and promote through laws governing marriage. (Republican Party 2012)

Even after the 2012 election, the Republican National Committee passed a resolution in 2013, the "Resolution for Marriage and Children," that affirmed the social conservative stance (in anticipation of Supreme Court rulings that year):

Whereas, the institution of marriage is the solid foundation upon which our society is built and in which children thrive; it is based on the relationship that only a man and a woman can form; and

Whereas, support for marriage has been repeatedly affirmed nationally in the 2012 Republican National Platform, through the enactment of the Defense of Marriage Act in 1996, (signed into law by President Bill Clinton), and passed by the voters of 41 States including California via Proposition 8 in 2008; and

Whereas, no Act of human government can change the reality that marriage is a natural and most desirable union; especially when procreation is a goal; and

Whereas, the future of our country is children; it has been proven repeatedly that the most secure and nurturing environment in which to raise healthy well adjusted children is in a home where both mother and father are bound together in a loving marriage; and

Whereas, The U. S. Supreme Court is considering the constitutionality of laws adopted to protect marriage from the unfounded accusation that support for marriage is based only on irrational prejudice against homosexuals; therefore be it

Resolved, the Republican National Committee affirms its support for marriage as the union of one man and one woman, and as the optimum environment in which to raise healthy children for the future of America; and be it further

Resolved, the Republican National Committee implores the U. S. Supreme Court to uphold the sanctity of marriage in its rulings on California's Proposition 8 and the Federal Defense of Marriage Act. (Republican National Committee 2013b)

Supreme Court, 2013

For many decades, and certainly in earnest since the U.S. Supreme Court ruled in the 1954 school desegregation case of *Brown v. Board of Education*, the Supreme Court has been looked to as a source of legal reform in an America of often-contested legal and societal issues. While much has been written about the nature of judicial decision making, as compared to legislative enactment, and direct-democracy voting, the work of the Supreme Court has stood out as a source of criticism and organizing for conservatives—especially social conservatives—who feel that the court has been undemocratic in applying its decision to issues that the legislatures or the voting public has not yet embraced.

Supreme Court Justice Ruth Bader Ginsburg is not the first woman Supreme Court justice—that honor belongs to Sandra Day O'Connor, appointed by a conservative Republican president, Ronald Reagan, who had promised the move in his 1980 presidential campaign. But Bader Ginsburg is a different kind of scholar and jurist than O'Connor. Certainly she is a liberal advocate appointed by a Democratic president, Bill Clinton. She has made her reputation pursuing legal strategies for women's equality in employment, and her career has mirrored the transformation of American women's roles and rights during the latter part of the 20th century. As co-founder and head litigator for the Women's Rights Project of the American Civil Liberties Union, she had been instrumental in several lawsuits that attacked gender discrimination and argued for equal treatment. Along with legislative advances (and despite the failure of states to ratify the Equal Rights Amendment in the 1980s), Bader Ginsburg's work in this area, at this particular time in legal and societal evolution, was pathbreaking, a fact referred to by President Bill Clinton when he nominated her to the Supreme Court in 1993 (Clinton 1993).

But Bader Ginsburg's view on the Supreme Court's trailblazing action in 1973 legalizing abortion in *Roe v. Wade* was that the decision had been made prematurely and that the Court should have let the legislative process work its way through states that might have followed the first liberalizing states (New York, California, Hawaii, and others) into legal acceptance of abortion virtually on demand. But that was not the rapid path that state-sanctioned same-sex marriage and attitudinal changes in America were taking. One of the remarkable events with the issues considered in this book is that the June 2013 decisions made by the U.S. Supreme Court did not cause an immediate backlash echoing a social conservative view that the law had usurped in an undemocratic way, in part because the ruling against California's Proposition 8 (which amended the California state constitution to define marriage as the union between a man and a woman) was restricted to that state only, however large it was. Those social conservatives who half-hoped that the Supreme Court would offer them another "judicial tyranny" opportunity by authorizing *Roe*-like same-sex marriages in all 50 states (or in a limited number of chosen states) would not have that moment.

The Court ruled against the federal Defense of Marriage Act, passed in 1996. In considering the case of Edith Windsor—a legally married lesbian who was subject to increased federal taxes during the disposition of her late wife's will (they were married legally in New York State) and whose lawyers argued that the Constitution's Equal Protection Clause should invalidate the law (Levy 2013)—Justice Anthony Kennedy, authoring the majority opinion, wrote:

> DOMA instructs all federal officials, and indeed all persons with whom same-sex couples interact, including their own children, that their marriage is less worthy than the marriage of others. . . . DOMA is unconstitutional as a deprivation of the liberty of the person protected by the Fifth Amendment of the Constitution. (*United States v. Windsor* 2013)

In many ways, Justice Anthony Kennedy, who has now written the impressive triumvirate of majority opinions in key gay rights jurisprudence (*Romer v. Evans* in 1996, *Lawrence v. Texas* in 2003, and *United States v. Windsor* in 2013)—and been praised for them by gay rights activists, like the legal reformer Evan Wolfson of the group Freedom to Marry (Liptak 2013)—represented in a balancing way, the evolving views of Americans on these issues.

The rulings in June 2013 were widely anticipated, closely watched, and reported upon. Former Arkansas governor and 2008 Republican presidential nominee candidate Mike Huckabee, a minister and current television personality, tweeted "Jesus wept" and that "5 people in robes said they are bigger than the voters of CA and Congress combined. And bigger than God. May He forgive us all" (Huckabee 2013). The director of the Faith and Freedom Coalition (and formerly of the Christian Coalition) Ralph Reed called the decision "an Orwellian act of judicial fiat" (Faith and Freedom Coalition 2013). He added that the Proposition 8 ruling "endangers federalism as well as the most time-honored tradition in the history of Western civilization." Brian Brown, of the National Organization for Marriage stated: "There is a stench coming from this case that has now stained the Supreme Court. . . . They've allowed corrupt politicians and judges to betray the voters, rewarding them for their betrayal" (National Organization for Marriage 2013).

Conclusion

When Republican pollster Frank Luntz conducted a focus group immediately after the November 2012 elections, participants reported that they didn't want national or federal focus on abortion or social issues; "Republicans ultimately lose," he concluded (*CBS News* 2012). These findings would be of little surprise to America's Barack Obama. Nor would it be to France's Socialist president François Hollande and England's Conservative prime minister David Cameron, who both introduced and oversaw the legal reform for marriage equality that added their countries to the growing list of countries in the world that allow same-sex marriages.

But perhaps the sentiment about this sea change in American attitudes could be captured in another way. In 2013, as the end of the process signaling Britain's legal reform embracing marriage equality, Queen Elizabeth II offered her assent, as the British system mandates. For the queen, whose family had enjoyed much-celebrated royal weddings in 1981 and 2011, celebrated in the United States as well, her assent was a powerful symbol, however symbolic and expected, of how far marriage equality had come in that country.

Newly installed Catholic pope Francis made similar notice when he spoke to reporters after a trip to South America in 2013 (a continent with nations that have enacted marriage equality laws). The pope explained that he had no problem with gay priests. While not speaking in an official capacity or offering to overturn church teaching, the new pope told reporters, "Who am I to judge a gay person of goodwill who seeks the Lord? . . . You can't marginalize these people" (Meichtry 2013; Spadaro 2013).

Together with Admiral Michael Mullen, then the chair of the American Joint Chiefs of Staffs, who had articulated in 2010 that "devaluing them [gay and lesbian military] in that regard is just inconsistent with us as an institution" (Joint Chiefs of Staff 2010), these statements represent the sea change that Garin and others have spoken of (Haberman et al. 2012) and that D'Emilio (2000) and Hirshman (2012) have presented as a steady evolution toward societal normalization.

This convergence of opinions captures well the breadth and depth of global changes in marriage equality and gay rights generally. It is difficult to consider what more evocative triumvirate of symbolically powerful figures than the queen of England, the pope, and the American admiral who is the chair of the Joint Chiefs of Staff could bring to this issue.

Chapter 4 will now look at the issue of the growth of secularism—the "nones," the "unaffiliated," the "unchurched," the "spiritual but religious," and the nonbelievers and atheists. It will also reassert that to be religious in the United States is to be moderate, despite the consideration by the media and despite the 1980–2006 rise in evangelical political power. It includes discussion of the gay rights issues as one element of this change but ranges across a number of different ways in which the moderating of religion has made an impact in the "unwedging" of several of the prior core elements of the American culture war.

4

After Falwell

Shifts and Continuities in the Culture War and the Role of Religion in America

Coercing religious ministries and citizens to pay directly for actions that violate their teaching is an unprecedented incursion into freedom of conscience. . . . By its decision, the Obama administration has failed to show the same respect for the consciences of Catholics and others who object to treating pregnancy as a disease.
—New York Cardinal Timothy Dolan, chair of U.S. Conference of Catholic Bishops, 2012

Beginning in the late 1980s, early 1990s, we begin to see this rapid increase of people who say they have no religion—the "nones" because they have no religion. . . . So now they represent roughly 17 percent of the American population overall. But when you look at young people, it's an even higher percentage, up to a quarter, maybe even a third of all young people today say they have no religion.
—David E. Campbell, Pew, 2010

"Pope Says Church Is 'Obsessed' with Gays, Abortion, Birth Control."
—*New York Times*, September 20, 2013

The death of the reverend Jerry Falwell at age 73 in May 2007 came at a crossroads for social conservatives and culture wars they energized in the United States. Comments from those who were his allies softened his edges—saying he was biblically conservative but not mean. Dr. James Dobson remembered him as the awakening of the evangelical community, saying: " I don't know anyone who had a greater impact on the evangelical movement." To supporters, Falwell wasn't afraid of political correctness—for which, in their opinion, he got skewered by the media. To them, there was an effort to marginalize him because he had such political influence. The continuing influence of the groups that Falwell had started and supported was a major topic of the day's commentary. One libertarian newspaper described the movement that Falwell left as "past its peak," reiterating the classic libertarian position that "morality cannot be improved through the intervention of the state" (*Orange County Register* 2007). The *Los Angeles Times* (2007) wrote that the wall separating church and state in America was "porous long before Jerry Falwell started chipping away at it."

To the social conservative Gary Bauer, progressive notice of Falwell's passing was offensive:

> . . . the outright hatred that has been on display at leftwing web sites and media outlets. From the *Democratic Underground* to the *Daily Kos*, self-described leftists and so-called "progressives" have celebrated the news of Rev. Falwell's death. In San Francisco, a group danced on a "mock-up" of his grave. Outspoken atheist Christopher Hitchens told CNN's Anderson Cooper, "I think it's a pity there isn't a hell for him to go to." Radical homosexual rights groups spewed their hatred at the news, with many blaming Rev. Falwell for the AIDS epidemic, rather than the unsafe practices still prevalent in their community. For folks who pride themselves on "tolerance," they should be ashamed. (Bauer 2007)

With the death of Rev. Falwell, and the aging and deaths of some of the other leaders of the religious right in the United States, public attention was focused on an issue that social scientists and scholars of religion had been approaching—the decline of the size and influence of religious social conservatives in American law, politics, and culture. While there are some who question whether the "religious right" at its highest point could indeed claim as many members as some would have, the 2004 election—even after adjusting for poll faults—was taken as data showing that Karl Rove's notion of a conservative rule for a generation, based in no small part on religious votes, was within reach. Instead, with candidate Obama leading the way, the Democratic Party recalibrated the relationship between it and religion.

As social conservatives came to grips with the 2008 electoral defeats, there were those who argued for greater salience of culture war issues as a way of reviving their party (and maintaining the thrust of those wars). As one analyst explained: "Religious Right groups will use an Obama presidency to raise more funds and spur activism. They will say McCain lost because he failed to appease 'values voters' even though he put Sarah Palin, an evangelical, on the ticket" (Berkowitz 2008b). Soon after the election, one columnist for the *Washington Post* wrote of her desire to see the social conservative wing of her party reduced in importance so that other conservative wings could enlarge with a strategy to reclaim their share of governing:

> The lethal problem for Republicans is that while religion of a particular kind is central to their party today, it is also toxic to moderate, independent, suburban, young and, more inclusively, educated voters. . . . To win elections, Republicans will need to distance themselves from "social conservatism" and the religious right. (Parker 2008)

This assertion was answered quickly from several fronts, and with strategic and ideological comment. To one writer, "in fact, far from being the demise of the GOP, the coming generation of evangelicals, Catholics and fellow travelers can be the seeds for the conservative movement's intellectual rebirth" (Dreher 2008). To Dr. James Dobson, social conservative religious voices in the national debate "won't be silenced . . . the efforts and epithets of big media notwithstanding" (Dobson 2008). After promising during his campaign for president that he would overturn the Bush administration ban on federal funding for stem cell research, President Obama signed an executive order in March 2009 to permit it. At the same time, he referred the process for promulgating specific regulations to the National Institutes of Health. In signing the order, the president emphasized that he did so "as a person of faith" and insisted that it was "a false choice" to choose between science and religion on this issue (CNN 2009).

In so doing, President Obama returned to a topic that the newly elected Democratic Congress had placed at the top of its priorities for the 110th Congress and had passed, precipitating the veto of President Bush in 2007. And in moving forward, President Obama had chosen an issue where a large majority of American thought that the development of means to combat disease outweighed any pro-life considerations for any embryos used in the research procedures. The chairman of the U.S. Conference of Catholic Bishops' Committee on Pro-Life Activities referred to the action as "a sad victory of politics over science and ethics" (Archdiocese of Philadelphia 2009). However, a Pew poll in 2008 had reported that 59% of non-Hispanic Catholics supported stem cell research, as did 31% of white evangelicals, consistent with some of the data on moderation and progressive positions above.

Indeed, some religious leaders, reflecting the many denominations that have formally endorsed the need for such research, praised the decision as being consistent with their religious view of the importance of projecting exiting life. One Reform Judaism leader stated: "In giving government support to promising research utilizing stem cells, which can enhance the life and health of millions of Americans, President Obama has shown not just political courage, but a moral vision that resonates with deep religious reverence for life" (Saperstein 2009). These views combine with a demographic attitudinal shift that many have referenced as leading to the "eventual support for same-sex marriage, which Ruy Teixeira sees as a "'millennial generation' which signals [a] shift in [the] culture war" (as was discussed in Chapter 3):

> A strong majority (58 percent) of Millennials favor allowing gays to marry, compared to 35 percent who are opposed. Among older Americans, it is the reverse: 60 percent are opposed and only 31 percent in favor. Millennials' views on issues such as gay marriage are so liberal that their increasing weight in the adult population and the declining weight of older generations will, by itself, make a huge impact on taking these divisive culture issues off the agenda. (Teixeira 2009: 31–32)

This chapter analyzes the role of religion, and especially its conservative manifestations in contemporary American society. It buttresses the arguments elsewhere, especially the moderation of American religiosity and the diminution of the power of social conservatives to shape American politics and policy. This chapter supports the notion of an increasingly tolerant America. Along with Chapter 2, this chapter argues that the backlash of the 2008–2014 period was not being

Figure 4.1. An American roadside sign proclaims "Jesus saves."

driven by religious conservatism. Instead, the chapter argues that the moderating impulses within American religion have become dominant and that, with the maturation of its members, the evangelical movement has grown to more resemble the profile and positions of more mainstream religious denominations in America. This chapter discusses the continuing role of religion in American political discourse, shifts and evolution of religious denominations and positions in the 2008–2014 period, and their effects on the legal treatment of the key culture war issues. The 2008 election was an important moment in the re-adjustment of the politics and religion issue, and the 2009–2013 years of the first Obama administration (and the Obama re-election in 2012) were further tests of the extent to which religion would be a determinant in political sorting and the discussion and decision making of significant policy issues (like the 2010 Patient Protection and Affordable Care Act.)

Sin No More assessed the contours of the culture war in the 2000–2006 period, with significant analysis of the role of social conservatives and the religious right on issues especially within the purview of the legal system: gay rights, abortion, assisted suicide, and stem cell research (Dombrink and Hillyard 2007). In that work, Daniel Hillyard and I argued that more than simply rejecting social conservative positions, America had recently displayed an emerging of forces that had been increasing all along—our growing liberalization thesis. Our emphasis on "problematic normalization" as a key concept didn't deny that the dialectic of advance and backlash had formed the basis for much of the movement (and certainly the media focus; see Winston 2012). Nonetheless, we argued, many Americans are noncombatants in the culture wars (see Fiorina et al. 2005) and often stand outside the polarization. One ongoing interest of this current research is the assessment of the role of religion and the religious right in the contemporary culture war. In this observant country, the re-entry of religion into discussion of public policy in a pluralistic manner—rather than the rise of secularism—has produced a situation today that is different from what analysts, critics, and advocates might have foreseen in 2004, when a "God gap" was often mentioned as a feature of differences between the two major political parties, their constituents, and their appeals.

This chapter aims to introduce an attempt to inventory and analyze developments along the continuing themes of *Sin No More* in the American culture war since 2007, especially in the 2008 and 2012 presidential elections, and to do so especially as these shifts and reshaping and reframing emphasize the role of religion in American life. Of particular interest is the misreading of the 2004 election, as it applied to "value voters" and Americans' views on personal morality issues; the movement on these issues from 2008 to 2014; the meaning of the 2008 and 2012 elections for these culture war issues; and the role of religion in the display and change in these issues.

Religion, Overreach, and "Values Voters"

Figure 4.2 presents findings from the 2000, 2004, and 2008 elections and the correlation of religious membership with voting behavior. The figure shows how Barack Obama improved the performance of the Democratic Party in presidential voting in 2008, compared to John Kerry's performance in 2004. These voting patterns for Obama changed the perception of the party as being unfriendly toward religion. He lost some of this advantage in 2012 but still performed at a high enough level to earn reelection.

In 2008, Obama did markedly better than his immediate predecessor John Kerry in attracting votes among the religiously observant in America. While still trailing Republican nominee John McCain, Obama increased by 8 percentage points (from 35% to 43%) the Democratic share among those who attended worship services once a week or more than weekly (Luo 2008). (Some of this might be explained by his bringing into the mix observant black Protestants.) He overwhelmingly won Latino and other minority Catholics (mostly Latino) by capturing almost 80% of their vote. He also led among White Catholics who were less observant (over 50%), though he lost among more observant Catholics ("weekly attending" white Catholics—in 2012, Rick Santorum and Paul Ryan were exemplars of this group). Obama lost by less among weekly attending white mainline Protestants and most deeply among less-attending evangelicals and most among regularly attending white evangelicals. By focusing on this last group as the biggest story and neglecting their relative size among all Americans professing religion,

Presidential Vote by Religious Affiliation and Race						
	2000		2004		2008		Dem
	Gore %	Bush %	Kerry %	Bush %	Obama %	McCain %	Change 04-08
Total	**48**	**48**	**48**	**51**	**52**	**46**	**+4**
Protestant/Other Christian	42	56	40	59	45	54	+5
White Protestant/Other Christian	35	63	32	67	34	65	+2
Evangelical/Born-again	n/a	n/a	21	79	26	73	+5
Non-evangelical	n/a	n/a	44	56	44	54	0
Catholic	50	47	47	52	54	45	+7
White Catholic	45	52	43	56	47	52	+4
Jewish	79	19	74	25	78	21	+4
Other faiths	62	28	74	23	73	22	-1
Unafilliated	61	30	67	31	75	23	+8

Note: Throughout the report, "Protestant" refers to people who described themselves as "Protestant," "Mormon" or "other Christian" in exit polls.
Throughout the report, figures may not add to 100, and nested figures may not add to the subtotal indicated, due to rounding.
Source: 2006, 2004 and 2000 national exit polls. 2008 data from MSNBC.com.

Figure 4.2. Presidential candidate choice by religion, 2000–2008. Courtesy of the Pew Research Center.

many analyses lost track of the fact that American religions were indeed moderating and indeed also losing members (as Robert Putnam and David Campbell explained so well in *American Grace* in 2010). The rise of the "nones" coincided with Obama's mention of non-believers as a group in his 2009 inaugural speech. At the same time, that speech, with its religious imagery, was given between those of a modern white evangelical pastor (Rick Warren) and an African American minister and veteran of the civil rights movement (Hosea Williams).

Even before John Kerry's defeat in 2004, Democratic strategists were worried about their party's standing with those who profess religious beliefs. With the 2000 defeat in consideration, and the apparent success of President Bush in securing his party's standing on fiscal conservatives, foreign policy conservatives, and social conservatives, these strategists sought to address the "God gap" among their party's candidates. United after 2004 with a message that their party was not reflexively pro-choice and could offer a "big tent" for a range of positions on reproductive rights that could encompass a larger number of Americans (and especially religious Americans), the Democratic Party began an effort to redirect this issue. Even more so, the Democratic Party was in a position of denying that it was not "anti-religion," which would be a difficult position from which to build electoral majorities in an observant country.

As Sager (2010) and others have pointed out, the successes in 2008 were in large part due to a conscious strategy to identify and deploy progressive religious actors and constituencies and frames for policy discussion. One analysis in 2008 observed, describing the success to date of social conservatives:

> The idea was to argue that Democrats were fundamentally hostile to religious Christians, and thus put the onus on the opposition to show them appropriate respect and deference. So for several election cycles both parties bent over backwards to be respectful of evangelicals. This year, however, Democrats sought to do more than just show respect for people who identify strongly with religion—they wanted to match the Republicans in presenting their political ideas as grounded in religious values. (Canuelos 2008)

Former Clinton administration official William Galston considered the Obama campaign's outreach to religious voters as "night and day" different from the 2004 campaign (McKenzie 2008). The historian Randall Balmer observed:

> What happened between 2004 and 2008? The Democratic Party nominated a different candidate, of course, someone preternaturally gifted at communicating his message of hope and optimism, especially in the face of a discredited Republican administration. But there was another dynamic at work as well. While Dobson, Colson and their confreres continued to insist that the only salient moral issues were abortion and same-sex unions, this younger group of evangelicals saw things differently. They were prepared to see a moral valence in a much broader spectrum of issues: poverty, AIDS, the environment, the prosecution of an unjust war, human rights and torture. (Balmer 2009b)

To sociologist Christian Smith, "Evangelicalism is becoming somewhat less coherent as a movement or as an identity. . . . Younger people don't even want the label anymore. They don't believe the main goal of the church is to be political" (Banerjee 2008). In an op-ed article calling for compromise and liberalization as a way of advancing the same-sex marriage debate, conservatives David Blankenhorn and Jonathan Rauch (2009) emphasized that a recent poll had found that "58 percent of white evangelicals under age 30 favor some form of legal same-sex union." This percentage has only grown since then. When President-elect Obama chose the evangelical pastor Rick Warren to deliver a prayer at his 2009 inauguration, he signaled several issues regarding religion and politics. In choosing Warren, the best-selling author of *The Purpose-Driven Life* (2002), Obama chose a pastor who had welcomed him into an evangelical mega-church for a discussion on AIDS and Africa in 2006, before then-Senator Obama had announced his candidacy. He also signaled that he considered evangelical voters ripe for a shift to the Democratic Party, something that the prior years of the religious right had prevented.

A 2008 poll found that the strong support for Senator Obama among young Americans was largely reflected among white evangelical Protestants:

> Younger white evangelicals strongly oppose abortion rights but are less conservative and more supportive of same-sex marriage than older evangelicals. Young white evangelicals are strongly opposed to abortion rights, with two-thirds saying abortion should be illegal in all or most cases. Yet, less than a majority (49%) of younger evangelicals identify as conservative, compared to nearly two-thirds (65%) of older evangelicals. Among young evangelicals, a majority favor either same-sex marriage (24%) or civil unions (28%), compared to a majority (61%) of older evangelicals who favor no legal recognition of gay couples' relationships. (Faith in Public Life 2008)

Thus, President-elect Obama selected someone from a younger generation to offer a prayer at the inauguration—indeed, someone who paralleled his own generational representation of change. In so doing, he was probably also estimating that white Protestant evangelicals—who had done so much to further the social conservative agenda of the Republican Party in recent decades—would in time come to resemble in their political approaches American Catholics, a group marked by a sizeable moderate or centrist faction (Green 2004; Dionne 2008a).

Big Tents: Obama, Catholic Politicians, and the Vatican

Even with the loss of members to other denominations or to the unaffiliated or "none" category, Catholicism dwarfs other American religions. And despite efforts by bishops and conservative groups and their supporters to define out those who are not "real Catholics," research has shown a large moderate center for American Catholicism, even for personal morality issues on which the church leadership cares deeply and is socially conservative (reproductive rights, gay rights, aid in dying, and stem cell research—the "non-negotiables").

In 2008, this conflict in values between the official church and those in the pews played out on the issue of abortion, in instances in which portions of the American Catholic laity spoke against the single-issue politics, which would make then-Senator Obama's pro-choice position a disqualifying factor in their vote. Prominent among these was conservative law professor Douglas Kmiec, long an influential legal activist in pro-life circles, who wrote a notable 2008 op-ed article in the *Los Angeles Times* in which he argued that the totality of Senator Obama positions—many of them consistent with the social justice teaching of the Catholic Church—was more important to Kmiec than the single issue of reproductive rights (Kmiec 2008). Democrats also evidenced belief in bigger "tents" for a winning coalition (see Sager 2010). Kmiec's position fit in well with the movement of the Democratic Party toward a position that would welcome more who were centrist or moderate in their views toward reproductive rights. The use of the issue of late-term or "partial-birth" abortions to frame progressives as pro-abortion in situations and forms that the American public found objectionable (even if they didn't amount to many of the abortions carried out in the United States) had given social conservatives some traction in their efforts to undo *Roe v. Wade* (Lakoff 2004).

In 2012, this issue resonated through efforts by the Catholic bishops to carve out a sizeable exemption for religious institutions—including hospitals and schools—that wanted to have a "conscientious objection" waiver allowed for their institutions. This became a key issue in the 2012 election, with moments in which Cardinal Timothy Dolan insisted this, Georgetown law student Sandra Fluke disputed it, and Rush Limbaugh added the word "slut" as a key meme to the 2012 campaign (Chapter 6 discusses this at length).

Back in 2005, shortly after the Democratic defeat in the presidential election of 2004, one of the first elements to be recalibrated, rethought, and reframed was the issue of reproductive rights. Fearing that the Democratic Party was overresponsive to pro-choice groups (or pro-abortion groups, as social conservatives prefer to say), Democratic Party chief Howard Dean, Senator Hillary Clinton, and defeated presidential candidate and Senator John Kerry all spoke in concerted ways to the need for establishing a "bigger tent" in the Democratic Party, in respecting the diversity of opinion. The abortion plank of the 2008 Democratic Party Convention also reflected this. At the time of the same convention, then–House Speaker Nancy Pelosi would encounter opposition from the hierarchy of the Catholic Church, as she (and later, vice presidential nominee Joe Biden) explained how their pro-choice positions were both nuanced and not in total conflict with the official holdings of the Church (*NBC News* 2008; Phillips 2008).

As with young evangelicals, polls also found that the pull of Senator Obama and the Democratic Party among young voters was strong and also aligned along positions in this area:

> Younger Catholics more strongly support Obama, abortion rights, and more active government than older Catholics. While older Catholics (age 35 and older) are split between the candidates (46% for McCain and 44% for Obama), among younger Catholics Obama leads McCain by 15 points (55% to 40%). Six-in-ten younger Catholics say abortion should be legal in all or most cases, compared to half of older Catholics. Younger Catholics are more pro-government than any other religious group, with two-thirds preferring bigger government with more services, compared to 41% support among older Catholics. (Faith in Public Life 2008)

Exit polls from November 2008 showed a slight increase in support for Senator Obama among Catholics and a definite improvement in that regard from the 2004 campaign. In a close election, and among a sizeable constituency, and in battleground states, this movement was crucial.

In one sense, the explicit attempts to close the "God gap," and the nomination of a presidential candidate who was comfortable in discussing the importance of faith to his public policy, blunted attempts to portray the Democratic Party as anti-religious or largely secular in its orientation. Instead, the efforts from 2005 to 2008 can be seen as representing efforts to portray the full range of religiosity and political view in America and to challenge the hegemony on religion that the social conservatives had assumed.

After the 2008 election, the release of data from the American Religious Identification Survey showed an increase in those who did not consider themselves aligned with religion (Kosmin and Keysar 2009). The growth of secularism (including the "apatheists," as one observer termed the phenomenon; Petrenko 2009) should prove to be an important factor of any discussion of American religion and politics in the near future. Indeed, the religion professor Mark Silk, who helped design the survey, suggested that the growth in non-alignment may in part be reflective of some Americans' repugnance at the excesses of the culture wars waged in the name of religion (Stanek 2009).

Democratic activist and analyst Ruy Teixeira saw the combination of the two forces as driving a more progressive agenda, both in 2008 and in the future:

> This increased religious diversity, particularly the rise of secular Americans, is leading us toward a more tolerant, less culturally divisive politics. We are already seeing evidence of this shift. . . . 59 percent [of the respondents] agreed that "religious faith should focus more on promoting tolerance, social justice, and peace in society, and less on opposing abortion or gay rights." (Teixeira 2009: 31)

The Obama healthcare reform displayed cleavages within the body politics of the Catholic Church in the United States. Some were tied into long-standing division between the church hierarchy and the Catholics in the pews, which started taking shape after the papal encyclical on contraception, *Humanae Vitae*, in 1968 (Paul VI 1968). It became more noticeable with the orthodoxy imposed through the papacy of John Paul II (1978–2005), enforced in large part by the head of the Sacred Congregation for the Propagation of the Faith, Joseph Cardinal Ratzinger, later Pope Benedict XVI.

Change, 2008–2014

It would be difficult to imagine the progress on marriage equality presented in Chapter 3 if America remained at present a largely religiously observant and conservatively religious country. It does remain a religiously observant country, especially in comparison to our Western European counterparts, countries like England, where only 49% consider themselves as belonging to a religion (as opposed to 80% in the United States), and France, where less than 10% of those who declare a religious preference attend weekly services.

One of the key narratives out of the 1980–2014 period in America has been the growth of those who decline to affiliate themselves with a particular denomination or who view themselves as secular—or what the polls and analysts often refer to as the "nones." According to Robert Putnam and David Campbell (2010) and their insightful and exhaustive study of the meanings of religion and religious belonging in contemporary America, that number now approaches 20%. This is a steady growth from 1980, when Rev. Falwell first came to prominence.

Moreover, this development has clear demographic elements. Among those who are under 30—the often-called "millennial generation"—this number rises dramatically to 32% self-identifying as having no religious ties. This finding is replicated across a number of reputable studies and polling organizations. One study says that "one-quarter (25 percent) of Millennials identify as religiously unaffiliated" (Public Religion Research Institute 2012). This generational shift is profound. As Chapter 6 will demonstrate, this demographic shift away from organized religion has reduced the vitality of culture war wedge issues to stir the American voter. The "ascendant majority" that Obama relied upon to capture reelection in 2012 is a group that is in marked contrast to the socially conservative religiously influenced movement of the Reagan years and since, led by Rev. Falwell

Moderating Evangelicals

As noted in *Sin No More* (Dombrink and Hillyard 2007) and elsewhere, even the Falwell-styled American evangelical presence was losing some of its steam by 2004, when there were alternative brands of religious

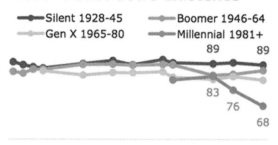

Figure 4.3. Belief in God by generation. Courtesy of the Pew Research Center.

focus among evangelical preachers and churches that did not emphasize the twin pillars of abortion and homosexuality, as Falwell had. A "kindler, gentler" evangelical Christianity—by which pollsters, analysts, political strategists, and scholars often mean "white evangelical Protestantism"—grew to focus on AIDS in Africa (despite the Falwell-era connection of AIDS, homosexuality, and sin) and environmentalism, emphasizing a biblically supported focus on stewardship of the earth and its creatures (see NPR 2008b). These young evangelicals might still be voting Republican in predictably high numbers (the 2012 exit polls put that level of support high, but only 22% of young voters are evangelicals). Many conservatives have argued that there were also millions of potential voters who stayed home and chose not to participate in the 2012 election because Republican presidential nominee Mitt Romney was not conservative enough or committed to their brand of social conservatism (or to whom his deep Mormonism was unattractive).

Among evangelicals, as among other groups, the millennial subpopulation is having an effect, with an expected result to keep following, as younger persons replace older persons in the voting population (and evangelical population).

Among evangelicals, the millennials are the most tolerant cohort, less likely to identify as conservative, more supportive of government solutions to social problems, and most in favor of that broader social agenda. At the same time, President Obama and his personal faith approach has offered a turning point in the contemporary American relationship between religion and politics, especially in the Democratic Party. The longstanding view of Americans (of both parties and independents) was that the Democratic Party was not simply the less friendly of the two major American political parties toward religion—it was, rather, perceived as being decidedly unfriendly to religion. To be effectively labeled as a secular party in a predominantly observant country and to be perceived as anti-religious would be to position oneself as uncompetitive. The careful dance that the Democratic Party has done over the past nine years has changed that perception. Obama's White House "personal pastor" and head of the Office of Religious Outreach, Joshua DuBois, "provided President Obama with a morning devotional weaving together scripture, song, prayer, and reflections to navigate the daily vagaries of life, doubt, and love for those called to lead in the 21st Century." The president commented that "every morning [Joshua] sends me via email a daily meditation—a snippet of Scripture for me to reflect on. And it has meant the world to me" (HarperCollins 2013). DuBois's 2013 book weaves together those daily messages along with reflections on the role of (and need for) religious reflection in contemporary society and leadership.

Adding to the turn of some evangelical organizations toward protection of the environment, even religious groups previously considered conservative moved to support two lines of action that leaned toward progressive policies. In this way, the evangelical and socially conservative Baptist groups were approximating the Catholic hierarchy, which had been prominent in supporting immigration reform and anti-poverty measures even as it adhered to a strong line against reproductive freedom and gay rights. In the first line, several evangelical groups argued for more progressive treatment under immigration reform. In this way, they tapped into the zeitgeist that was changing after the 2012 election, when even conservative stalwarts like Bill O'Reilly and Sean Hannity were speaking to the need for the Republican Party to be more inclusive (and especially to be perceived as such) on immigration. On the second issue, evangelical groups joined in a broader coalition of religious groups urging Congress to strike a deal before the sequester or fiscal cliff would result in the diminution or cutoff of benefits to the most vulnerable in society. This group, the "Circle of Protection" that issued a call for such legislative action in February 2013, included the president of the National Association of Evangelicals and the president of the National Baptist Convention.

2010–2014: The ACA and the Contraception Battle

Religion appeared in a major way in the first years of the Obama administration when the Catholic bishops objected to provisions in the Affordable Care Act that would have mandated that Catholic institutions, like other institutions, be required to provide for (pay for) women's reproductive coverage under their insurance plans. This benefit became a major issue in the period, as the bishops complained that the ACA took unusual presumption in delineating exactly which type of religious instructions could receive waivers from this requirement. To the bishops, the Obama exclusion of Catholic hospitals and Catholic universities unfairly provides waivers for some elements of their Church (parishes, essentially) while placing the hospitals and universities off-limits, considering them church-sponsored but not intrinsically religious institutions:

> For the first time in our history, the federal government will force religious institutions to fund and facilitate coverage of a drug or procedure contrary to their moral teaching, and purport to define which religious institutions are "religious enough" to merit an exemption. This is a matter of whether religious people and institutions may be forced by the government to provide such coverage even when it violates our consciences. . . . What is at stake is whether America will continue to have a free, creative, and robust civil society—or whether the state alone will determine who gets to contribute to the common good, and how they get to do it. (U.S. Conference of Catholic Bishops 2012)

Beyond this, the issue received significant public media coverage when a student at the Georgetown Law Center testified about how the Obama provision was a fair one for her and others in similar situations (Sandra Fluke's case, and the attention it received, receives greater coverage in Chapter 6, as an analysis of the issue as an important ingredient in the balance of the 2012 presidential election). As Maureen Dowd observed:

> So I wasn't surprised to see the Gallup poll Tuesday showing that 82 percent of U.S. Catholics say birth control is morally acceptable. Gallup tested the morality of 18 issues, and birth control came out on top as the most acceptable, beating divorce, which garnered 67 percent approval, and "buying and wearing clothing made of animal fur," which got a 60 percent thumbs-up. The poll appeared on the same day as headlines about Catholic Church leaders fighting President Obama's attempt to get insurance coverage for contraception for women who work or go to college at Catholic institutions. The church insists it's an argument about religious freedom. But, really, it's about birth control, and women's lower caste in the church. It's about conservative bishops targeting Democratic candidates who support contraception and abortion rights as a matter of public policy. (Dowd 2012d)

By endorsing the ACA, the Catholic Health Association (representing Catholic hospitals) and Network, a group of nuns focused on social justice issues, had in 2010 demonstrated that there were multiple voices that could speak authoritatively for American Catholics. In 2012, they would continue to represent an alternative position to the bishops. One newspaper report captured how that fissure provided an opportunity for the bill to pass through Congress:

> An unusual public split between U.S. Roman Catholic bishops, nuns and hospitals over abortion in the health care overhaul could undermine the church hierarchy's influence on the debate and give anti-abortion Democrats the political cover they need to vote for the bill. . . . The president of the U.S. Conference of Catholic Bishops, which opposes the Senate bill up for a House vote this weekend, warned that some forces are trying to use the rift to push the legislation through Congress. (Gorski 2010)

One Catholic bishop represented the most conservative wing of that position, although he was not alone in his critique (and his vitriol):

> Hitler and Stalin, at their better moments, would just barely tolerate some churches remaining open, but would not tolerate any competition with the state in education, social services and health care. . . . In clear violation of our First Amendment rights, Barack Obama—with his radical, pro-abortion and extreme secularist agenda—now seems intent on following a similar path. . . . This fall, every practicing Catholic must vote, and must vote their Catholic consciences, or by the following fall our Catholic schools, our Catholic hospitals, our Catholic Newman Centers, all our public ministries—only excepting our church buildings—could easily be shut down. (*Huffington Post* 2012b)

The Catholic Paradox

With their continued significant size among Americans with religious attachment, American Catholics can be rightfully considered a significant factor in American politics. And, if those Catholics—however defined, which we will see shortly is itself an issue at stake—were to largely follow the pronouncements and policies of their pope and American institutional church leaders (for example, the U.S. Conference of Catholic Bishops, or their various individual archbishops and bishops), this book and this chapter would unfold much differently. Even as the new pope Francis has impressed many as being open than his predecessors on personal morality issues, there have been few changes to the more rigid orthodoxy that predecessor popes Benedict XVI and John Paul II built. This line of thought emphasizes homosexuality as sin and emphasizes the importance of protecting human life, whether though opposition of reproductive rights/abortion, stem cell research and cloning, or end of life issues/assisted suicide (to the bishops credit, they have been consistently anti–death penalty, as befits an emphasis on honoring and protecting life, and strongly pro-immigrant, reflecting the church's mission and composition in America in the past and present). Throughout the last 50 years—a period during which many Catholics worldwide, especially in industrialized countries, have "fallen away"—American Catholics have displayed their independence from doctrinal teaching on the contraception and abortion issue for several decades, beginning with the reaction to the papal encyclical *Humanae Vitae* in 1968.

Even though the bishops were agitated by the Obamacare contraception issue, and even though Obama supporters (Like Catholic E. J. Dionne) thought that the Obama administration had misplayed the issue, there was also a long history of American Catholics choosing not to follow the pope's or bishops' lead on such personal morality issues:

> For months now the adjective Catholic has been affixed to the country's strange contraception debate, which began when many Catholic leaders took offense at a federal mandate that Catholic institutions provide insurance coverage for artificial birth control. But most American Catholics don't share their appointed leaders' qualms with the pill, condoms and such. . . . American Catholics have been merrily ignoring the church's official position on contraception for many years, often with the blessing of lower-level clerics. (Bruni 2012b)

Forty-four years after *Humanae Vitae*, the profile of American Catholics from the 2012 election was striking on the culture war issues. What is notable, and worth emphasizing here, as well in Chapters 5 and 7, is that these changes have taken place while the composition of American Catholicism has changed.

The Latinoization of the American Catholic Church

The shifts in American ethnic diversity that are characterizing the population in general are also having a tremendous effect on the Catholic Church, where the growth in Latino membership has changed some aspects of the church and amplified others (such as support for immigration reform). One 2013 report notes that

> while the proportion of the U.S. population that is Catholic—around a quarter—has remained fairly steady for several decades, there have been some striking demographic shifts. For example, the U.S. Catholic population has been heavily shaped by immigration and includes a rising share of Latinos. This is evident in the age structure of the U.S. Catholic popula-

tion, in which nearly half of Catholics under age 40 are Hispanic (47%), compared with about one-in-six (16%) Catholics 65 and older. (Pew Research Center 2013b)

As Putnam and Campbell conclude, "With immigration from heavily Catholic nations continuing apace, the Latinoization of the American Catholic Church will only be accelerated" (2010: 304). Several factors argue for this development: Latinos and Latino Catholics will be younger on average than non-Latino whites. They have both been shown to be similar to their non-Latino age cohort peers on reproductive rights issues. This means that they are dissimilar from their parents and grandparents and are *not* following elders in their views of religion and personal morality. There are also cohort-similar or secularization effects, with fewer Latino churchgoers (see Moses 2014). In addition, the salience of reproductive rights is seemingly lower among this population than among their non-Latino peers. They prioritize economic and pocketbook issues. Data show Latinos to be the biggest supporters of Obamacare and are among those most supportive of government's expansive role, similar to the characteristic of millennials generally. Finally, they are optimistic (see Baldassare 2002; Harmon 2012), which can be considered as having an effect on the consideration of public policy issues.

Religion in the 2012 Election: Of Nuns and "Nones"

Given the state of religion during and following the 2008 election, it was not to be expected that religion would be one of the fulcrum points around which the 2012 election would take place. There are two ways in which religiosity can be analyzed in the context of the 2012 election. One has to do with the explicit use of religious arguments and themes in the framing of issues, particularly personal majority issues. By 2012, many Americans had voiced an opinion that churches should keep out of politics. That poll also found that a record number of people (54%) said that churches and other houses of worship should "keep out of political matters" (Blow 2012b). The respondents also felt that religious conservatives held their significant sway through their influence within the Republican Party. "In fact, the poll found that most Americans (51 percent) believe that religious conservatives have too much control over the

Republican Party." Admittedly, that number could be mostly composed of Democratic partisans, who were anxious to see such an association between Republicans and religious/social conservatives' profile, to negatively affect the electoral chances of Republicans. But that number had to include a number of independents and undecided voters. By comparison, a plurality (49%) said they didn't believe the opposite, that secular liberals have too much control over the Democratic Party. In that way, the attempt from 2005 on worked to make Democratic politicians less perceived as a force against religion and to be seen as more friendly or neutral (Blow 2012b).

How the relatively small number of American Catholic nuns became an important consideration in the 2012 presidential campaign had a lot to do with the difference between the Catholic Church in the United States and other religious groups. The current ascendant religious groups, by all accounts, over the last 40 years have been those of evangelical Protestantism. But while Catholics have been less noteworthy—not seen as growing group with electoral and societal impact—their size and composition and have indeed been noteworthy. Strong conservative Catholic voices like the Catholic League's William Donohue have made it a primary mission to define out the legions of what they call "cultural Catholics"—those who were raised Catholic but are not key members of contemporary parishes, not contributors to the church, and not weekly church attendees. They also rail against the notion of "cafeteria Catholics," who pick and choose what aspects of the church doctrine they choose to comply with. This has been a long-standing critique from the church leadership.

The Catholic nuns had demonstrated their support for the ACA in 2010, breaking from the bishops as they supported Obama health reform, as did the Catholic Hospital Association. The nuns' actions generated debates among American Catholics, according to one report,

> between those who urge no cooperation with any government programs that support same-sex couples or abortion in any way . . . and others who favor policies that enhance social justice and provide benefits to the poor, even if this may mean some compromise on these issues. (Landsberg 2010)

The "Nuns on the Bus" tour was an unexpectedly provocative moment in the discussions of religion, social justice, and politics in 2012. The "Nuns on the Bus" campaign/road trip went to a national audience with their opposition to the Ryan budget plan (and its austerity and implications for the poor). The nuns articulated their objection to that Catholic congressman's austerity and budget-cutting plan while charging that such cuts would violate their own adherence to Catholic social justice teachings and concern for the poor. If "overreach" is one of the key concepts in the contests of the culture war, then the Catholic bishops in 2010–2012 were guilty of it, having taken a stand that was at odds with so much of their constituency.

The "Nones" and the Rise of Secular Millennials

Madalyn Murray O'Hair was an oddity in compliant 1960s America. She was recognized as a leading American atheist, having founded the group American Atheists. This group was responsible for one of the key U.S. Supreme Court decisions limiting religious expression in schools, one of a series of court rulings that still rankles American religious leaders, who worry that a resurgent secularism will tilt American law against their expression and practices. To some of them, the events in American society since *Roe. v. Wade*, other court decisions on gay rights, and the passage and approval of the Affordable Care Act followed this path. By 2012, O'Hair's legacy would make for a hot bookshelf in American bookstores, with prominent titles by Christopher Hitchens, Richard Dawkins, Sam Harris, and Bill Maher's 2008 documentary *Religulous* enjoying readership or viewership. And it was no wonder, as the size of the American "unaffiliated" (or "nones") audience edged toward 20%.

In 2012, President Obama's performance slipped among some of these religious groups, as it did among the population generally. But he was strong among the "nones," most of whom were repelled by the association of the Republican Party with conservative religious forces. Obama did less well among white Catholics (losing to Romney 56–43) but ended up winning Catholics overall, ostensibly because of his strong showing among Latino Catholics (74%). Obama stayed steady among non-evangelical Protestants (44%) but declined among white evangelical

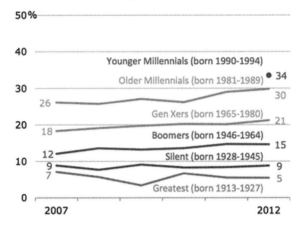

Source: Aggregated data from surveys conducted by the Pew Research Center for the People & the Press, 2007-2012.

PEW RESEARCH CENTER

Figure 4.4. Percent of age groups who are not religiously affiliated, by generation. Courtesy of the Pew Research Center.

Protestants. He went up slightly with Latino Catholics (Pew Religion and Public Life Project 2012b).

There was mostly stability among the denominations' share of the voters in 2012 (from 2008). Protestants remained the largest group, with 39% of the voting public. However, since the larger (23%) and growing evangelical Protestant group is joined by the smaller (16%) and declining mainline Protestant group, that category isn't unified. Catholics remained similar to their 2008 performance at 25%. But within the Catholic faithful, there were significant changes, as Latinos came to represent a larger share of the population (Pew Religion and Public Life Project 2012a, 2014). The idea that Latino Protestants, who are growing, report to be more religious than their Catholic peers, and tend to be more conservative theologically and socially does give support to those who feel that there is an opportunity for more socially conservative views and candidates to succeed among this growing population.

Conclusion

When social conservatives decry the reduction of religious freedom, they overlook the long tradition of Catholic and mainline Protestant religions and Jews in supporting liberal to moderate polices, from bingo, to end-of-life care in Catholic hospitals, to embracing of gays and lesbians in mainline Protestant churches. Certainly, this view of religion doesn't fit the evangelical Protestant groups that have grown in size and impact since Falwell and 1980. But they were never the whole story of religion in America, and they certainly now have a diminished profile. Witness a Southern Baptist national leader stating that it's time for groups like his to reduce emphasis on action in the political sphere: "This is the end of slouching toward Gomorrah. We were never promised that the culture would embrace us" (Riley 2013). Rev. Russell Moore added: "The Bible Belt is collapsing. It's bad for the country, but good for the church. . . . We are no longer the moral majority. We are a prophetic minority" (Moore 2014).

To many, it was this close association of religion and politics, and the politicization of religion (although we tend to talk more about this relationship in the context of the "religicization" of politics, as in Kevin Phillips's 2006 *American Theocracy*), that has caused this distaste among the American public, especially the young. To many younger Americans it was precisely this heavy-handedness that turned them off to religion. In addition to sullying younger Americans views of politics, it has also affected their view of religion. To many of the millennials, religion is overly conservative and overly political.

Maybe this would skew differently in a diversifying America, a country in which social conservative immigrants of color, coming to America with high levels of religiosity, impart to their children a sense of religion-based morality that makes them markedly different from their American-born peers. The next chapter analyzes the contention that a diversifying America will cause the liberalization of personal morality issues to slow, given the more traditional values and religion-influenced social conservatism of those populations set to increase in the near American future. If religiosity can't be the key ingredient to a successful conservative culture war as it has been in the recent past, maybe the influx of more socially conservative immigrants could be that factor.

5

"Vota Tus Valores"

The Culture War in a Diversifying America

Republicans should wake up and realize that Latinos are today's Reagan Democrats. They should pro-actively embrace
them based on shared conservative values to form a winning
conservative coalition in America.
—Alfonso Aguilar, American Principles Project, July 2013

Will the process of assimilation to the dominant Anglo culture lead Hispanics to abandon traditional family values?
We must interrupt this process of assimilation by making
support for marriage a key badge of Latino identity—a symbol of resistance to inappropriate assimilation.
—National Organization for Marriage, 2012 (internal strategy documents obtained by the Human Rights Campaign)

The new survey also finds rapidly growing support for same-
sex marriage among Latinos, mirroring growing support
among the general public. Half of Latinos now favor allowing gay and lesbian couples to marry legally, while one-third
are opposed. As recently as 2006, these figures were reversed. . . . White, non-Hispanic Catholics express about as
much support for same-sex marriage as Hispanic Catholics
do (53% and 54%, respectively).
—Pew Religion and Public Life Project, 2012a

On the same day in 2008 that Americans elected Barack Obama, in an historic election bringing America's first African American president into the White House, Californians voted to repeal that state's same-sex marriage law. The legal reform had resulted from a state supreme court's decision in May that had made California the second American state to reform their laws in this regard (alongside five countries at the time; Liptak 2008). California had been a predictably Democratic or blue state in presidential elections for several election cycles, since 1992—so much so that one analyst depicted it as: "California, a state so blue they could name a Crayon after it—Left Coast Azure"—that it was considered a leading progressive state for such reforms (Morrison 2005). At the same time, California was at the top of the list of America's states in celebrating an ethnically diverse population. With its location adjacent to Mexico (and formerly being Alta California as part of Mexico), and bordering the Pacific Ocean facing Asia, California is an immigrant-rich state. The state was transformed between 1970 and 2014 by both immigration and birth rates from a basis of 77% white to under 39% white (decades before the United States is projected to be a "majority minority" country).

But the same state that had given the nation the presidents Richard Nixon and Ronald Reagan was not predictably progressive on all issues. George H. W. Bush beat Michael Dukakis in 1988, for instance. California had passed an anti–affirmative action referendum in 1996. But the results of the 2008 election caused confusion in the analysis. While the state had overwhelmingly given Barack Obama its 55 electoral votes, its voters had voted for a repeal of the California supreme court's May 2008 decision allowing same-sex marriage.

Chapter 5 argues that the growing diversity of America does not present an opportunity for social conservatives to expand their influence. This chapter poses a provocative demographic question: What will be the effect of the growing ethnic diversity of the United States on legal consideration of the personal morality issues discussed in this book? Will a cohort replacement theory, which is so strong in other predictions of growing support and eventual same-sex marriage recognition, work in examples like the California context? Or will ethnic and racial diversity and religiosity make it less operable? Will a growing "Latinoization" of the American population continue in the direction of liberalization on these issues, or will cultural conservatism give rise to a slowdown in the granting of personal rights through the extension of personal autonomy? Will a generally religiously observant Latino population follow the precepts of their church leaders and embrace conservative pro-life measures on reproductive rights, same-sex marriage, and other social conservative issues? Will the secularization that defines America's millennials also describe the attitudes of young Latinos, many of whom were raised Catholic? (Pew Religion and Public Life Project 2014). Will the collision of different demographic impulses—youthful Latino voters trending one way, their elders another—produce a muted effect for the short term and a convergent liberalism in the long term?

Many of the analyses of the culture war in America presuppose a static America in which ongoing debates resurface and are resolved. Issues rise and decline, but some demographic factors are seen as key to their resolution. In the case of same-sex marriage, for example, the striking difference in support for this reform among younger American cohorts—as opposed to their most aged counterparts—indicates that in the not-too-distant future, all parts of America will formally embrace this change. The title for the chapter is taken from an outreach project for Spanish-speaking California voters for a Republican senatorial candidate in 2010. To "vote your values" is a reprise of the successful 2004 effort by President George W. Bush (however overblown the effect of this framing was) to rally "values voters" to his side in his reelection.

Conservative activists and political strategists were not satisfied in 2010 with letting the demographic changes produce perceived beneficial changes for them alone. Strategies were deployed in specific states—for example, California with Proposition 8 (which repealed the state supreme court granted right to same-sex marriage)—to alienate people of color from progressives on reproductive rights and same-sex marriage issues. However, this chapter demonstrates that this approach is not as promising as first thought, for several reasons. Foremost is the reliance upon religiosity and the beliefs that these diverse populations were both more religious and more conservative in their religiosity. This would theoretically have provided an opportunity for reluctance to embrace the progressive agenda on abortion and gay rights. This chapter analyzes findings that challenge that assumption.

Proposition 8

One of the first headlines after the Proposition 8 victory in November 2008 was "Liberal California Shuts Door on Same Sex Marriages" (*Rediff News* 2008). What most caught the attention of political analysts was that, at the same time that Californians voted overwhelmingly for Barack Obama as president (by a 61%-37% margin) in an historic election, it appeared there was a racial chasm in the opposition to Proposition 8. The first reporting on this, using the feature of the first exit polls, stated, "70% of African Americans Backed Prop. 8, Exit Poll Finds" (Grad 2008).

The origins of Proposition 8 were of an effort that came together quickly after the California state supreme court ruling in May 2008 permitted same-sex marriage in the nation's largest state. The funds for the eventual repeal campaign were primarily from several sources, including the Mormon Church (McKinley and Johnson 2008). The proponents spent $39 million, the majority of it from within California and $11 million from outside California. Those supporting the state supreme court decision (the opponents) spent $44 million, $13 million of it from out of state (*Los Angeles Times*, n.d.). One of the more used television advertisements of the 2008 Proposition 8 campaign, run by proponents of the repeal measure, featured San Francisco Mayor Gavin Newsom triumphantly exclaiming in 2008 that California is going to have same-sex marriage. The ad, with Newsom proclaiming: "This door's wide open now. It's gonna happen, whether you like it or not," was credited with shifting poll numbers.

That strategy emphasized the concept of "overreach" in statements, policy positions, and emotional tone like that of Newsom. The important agenda item for 2008 was the beginning of the deployment of an anti-equality strategy by social conservatives to take advantage of any racially influenced views of the preferability of same-sex marriage.

Critique of the Exit Polls

California Assembly Speaker Karen Bass, an African American woman, stated that she was "appalled at the hostility" that accompanied the interpretations from the exit poll (Rojas 2008). To her, such a result was "a generational issue." Political scientists Patrick Egan and Kenneth

Sherrill (2009) produced a socially scientific study of the support for Proposition 8 among communities of color. It offered a corrective to the immediate popular framing of the issue: that conflict existed between gays and the African American community over sexual orientation. The crux of that conflict was the issue of whether same-sex marriage and gay rights were as deserving of civil rights protection as were other civil rights concerns.

African American and Latino voters supported Proposition 8 to a greater degree, 58% and 59% respectively, than did whites and Asians. According to this survey, blacks' support for the ballot measure was much lower than reported by Election Day exit polls (Egan and Sherrill 2009).

Referencing the relationship between familiarity and tolerance, Egan and Sherrill identify the effect of gays and lesbians being less open at that time in African American communities: "Among those who do not know any gay people very well, 60% supported the amendment and 40% opposed it" (Egan and Sherrill 2009). Not surprisingly, Egan and Sherrill also found that Proposition 8 was supported by subgroups among the African American population that reflected the same areas of support in the population generally: "Across all models, men, older voters, the more religious, Republicans, and conservatives were all significantly more likely to support Proposition 8 than women, younger voters, the less religious, Democrats and liberals" (Egan and Sherrill 2009). When they eventually found a factor that was more important than the others, it was religiosity that stood out: "The analysis shows that African Americans and Latinos were stronger supporters of Proposition 8 than other groups (Model I), but not to a significant degree after controlling for religiosity (Models II and III)" (Egan and Sherrill 2009). To them, " black support for Proposition 8 can largely be explained by African Americans' higher levels of religiosity—a characteristic strongly associated with opposition to same-sex marriage" (Egan and Sherrill 2009).

Social Conservative Racial Wedge Strategies

The success of the Proposition 8 proponent campaign encouraged those who felt that the careful use of socially conservative messages in ethnically diverse locales was a good strategy. As one report explained:

The strategic goal of this project is to drive a wedge between gays and blacks—two key Democratic constituencies. Find, equip, energize and connect African American spokespeople for marriage; develop a media campaign around their objections to gay marriage as a civil right; provoke the gay marriage base into responding by denouncing these spokesmen and women as bigots. (Sparks 2012)

A strategy piece from the National Organization for Marriage, which pressed Proposition 8 in California in 2008, and which was disclosed in the discovery process of a lawsuit in Maine, announced and developed this kind of strategy: "We must interrupt this process of assimilation by making support for marriage a key badge of Latino identity—a symbol of resistance to inappropriate assimilation":

We aim to identify young Latino and Latina leaders, especially artists, actors, musicians, athletes, and other celebrities willing to stand for marriage, irrespective of international boundaries. . . . By searching for these leaders across national boundaries, we will assemble a community of next generation Latino leaders that Hispanics and other next generation elites in this country can aspire to be like. As "ethnic rebels" such spokespeople will have an appeal across racial lines, especially to young urbans in America. We will develop Spanish language radio and TV ads, as well as pamphlets, You Tube videos and church pamphlets and church handouts and popular songs. Our ultimate goal is to make opposition to gay marriage an identity market, a badge of youth rebellion to conformist assimilation to the bad side of "Anglo" culture. (National Organization for Marriage 2009: 20)

At a more establishment level, former Florida governor Jeb Bush, perennially on many lists of potential Republican presidential candidates, had been strongly urging Republican colleagues for a decade to get more involved with expanding the diversity of their party (as had his brother, former president George W. Bush):

Certainly the most important characteristics most conservatives and Hispanics share are religious and family values. Hispanics tend to be deeply religious, to practice conservative forms of Christianity, and to be politically influenced by their religion. But conservatism among religious Hispanics has not translated into Republican partisan affiliation. Democrats outnumber Republicans by 55 to 18% among Hispanic Catholics. Those findings reflect huge growth opportunities for Republicans. Obviously, a large part of Republican electoral successes since 1980 is attributable to mobilization of religious voters, particularly evangelicals. Republicans should make a similar effort to connect with Hispanics on religious faith and moral values. In particular, given the tremendous attachment among Hispanics to their families, policies that are pro-family are pro-Hispanic. That is an important message that Republicans need to communicate, and on which they can make common cause with Hispanics. (Bush and Bolick 2013: 219)

Later, social conservatives would be shown trying to make inroads into the generally progressive African American community and their reliable Democratic votes (Dewan 2010) by emphasizing abortion as a genocidal strategy, with prominent billboards near abortion clinics and in urban centers displaying messages like, "The most dangerous place for an African-American is in the womb," or "Black & Beautiful / toomanyaborted.com." One African American pastor quoted in the article said: "What's giving it momentum is blacks are finally figuring out what's going down. . . . The game changes when blacks get involved. And in the pro-life movement, a lot of the groups that have been ignored for years, they're now getting galvanized" (Dewan 2010).

From "Not a Civil Right" to "Not for Discrimination"

Writing a few years after the Proposition 8 vote, Adele Morrison analyzed the conflict between African Americans and the LGBT (lesbian, gay, bisexual, and transgendered) community in terms of rights claims and explained the ways in which this issue had evolved since then:

The 2008 election cancelled marriage rights for some in the most populous state in the country, while the 2012 voting extended marriage in more states. It is arguable that this change came because both Blacks and gays began to mend the split by realizing that an anti-same-sex marriage position is not a Black thing. (Morrison 2013)

Figure 5.1. Poster advertising *The New Black*, directed by Yoruba Richen.

Individuals and groups advocating marriage equality and LGBT rights have been successful in neighbor-to-neighbor campaigns that have brought opinion to focus on the question of whether those who have been discriminated against for race would be interested in preventing discrimination against others for sexual orientation. In the documentary *The New Black*, Yoruba Richen (2013) captures a similar phenomenon.

Morrison examined how these views "flipped." Views changed away from a stance of African Americans for a variety of ages, social standings, religious connections, and morality politics considering the validity of same-sex marriage. The new focus by marriage equality advocates was on why African Americans should want to support a movement (the anti-marriage equality movement) that denies benefits, memberships, and respect to a specified group of people, an experience with which they are very familiar. In this way, it could be argued, the focus changes from whether or not to embrace gays and lesbians to whether or not to embrace anti-equality activists.

Obama, 2012

This change in African American views followed an announcement by President Obama in May 2012 in which he stated that "at a certain point

I've just concluded that for me, personally, it is important for me to go ahead and affirm that I think same-sex couples should be able to get married" (Gast 2012). Obama, who had been chided for his slowness in coming to a fuller support of same-sex marriage, had initially opposed it as a candidate in 2008, then said that his views on it were "evolving." Speaking in a one-on-one interview with ABC's Robin Roberts, Obama cited the experience of his teenage daughters when he said, "It wouldn't dawn on them that somehow their friends' parents would be treated differently. It doesn't make sense to them and frankly, that's the kind of thing that prompts a change in perspective" (Gast 2012).

After 31 defeats at the ballot box, the first three victories for marriage equality that occurred at the ballot box came in November 2012 (Washington, Maine, and Maryland). In Maryland, where supporters were worried about the vote among African Americans, given the experience in California, one report spotlighted the shift in potential voters' attitudes:

The movement over the last two months can be explained almost entirely by a major shift in opinion about same-sex marriage among black voters. Previously 56 percent said they would vote against the new law with only

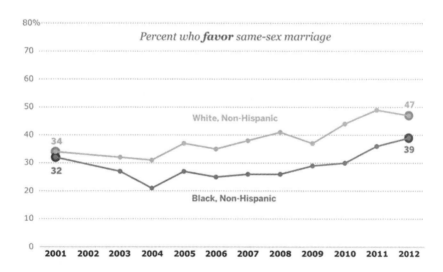

Pew Research Center's Forum on Religion & Public Life

Figure 5.2. Approval for gay marriage by race and by year. Courtesy of the Pew Research Center.

39 percent planning to uphold it. Those numbers have now almost completely flipped, with 55 percent of African Americans planning to vote for the law and only 36 percent now opposed. (Polasky 2012)

While African American pastors had opposed marriage equality when it was proposed in the Maryland House of Delegates, African American legislators voiced their support (Serwer 2012). The National Association for the Advancement of Colored People's National Voter Fund for Question 6 contributed funds for the measure's passage. Tamelyn Tucker-Worgs (2013) argues that the emergence of African American mega-churches, away from the traditional black churches closely connected to the civil rights movement, has advanced this new phenomenon. A large increase in African American support for marriage equality, though, came after the president's expression of support.

Latino Tolerance

Reports from the 2008 Proposition 8 campaign in California also pointed to the relatively close vote by Latinos on the ballot measure. While Latinos were not as supportive of the opposition as were whites, they were not nearly as supportive of the repeal as African Americans. The *Los Angeles Times* noted in a 2009 poll that followed soon after the vote that, "within the Latino population, there were additional divisions: Women, the young and people with a college education offered more backing for it [marriage] than men, older voters and those with less education" (*Los Angeles Times* 2009). To the Center for American Progress, and its analysis of racial and ethnic diversity on a range of issues in the United States, this finding made sense, two years later. And with even that short time for demographic and attitudinal shifts to take place, they felt the data was demonstrative:

> Consider the various approaches Republicans have taken to get their message out, particularly to Hispanics whom they believe (correctly) are a much better target for conversion than blacks. A longtime favorite has been the idea that Hispanics are socially conservative and can be induced to vote for the GOP if the party emphasizes "values" issues like abortion or gay marriage. This has not been effective so far, and there are no indi-

cations it will succeed in the future. Hispanics, it turns out, are actually much less likely than whites to vote on the basis of cultural issues. Hispanics overall also are not nearly as socially conservative as many believe. A Center for American Progress survey in 2009 showed that Hispanics actually had the highest average score of all racial groups on a 10-item progressive cultural index. Surveys have repeatedly shown that Hispanics are no more conservative on gay marriage than whites are. And younger Hispanics are typically more progressive than their older counterparts on social issues, so generational replacement will make tomorrow's Hispanic population less socially conservative than today's. (Teixeira 2010)

In 2013, the *New York Times* described a Public Religion Research Institute report on Latinos and social policies, with the finding that Latinos in the United States lean surprisingly liberally on social issues:

A new survey shows that Hispanics, the nation's largest minority group, have grown increasingly negative toward the Republican Party during the political battle over changing immigration law and lean surprisingly liberal on social issues like gay marriage—a combination of factors that presents a steep challenge for Republicans in trying to win back Hispanic voters. (Goodstein 2013)

A Pew research poll found similar findings:

The new survey also finds rapidly growing support for same-sex marriage among Latinos, mirroring growing support among the general public. Half of Latinos now favor allowing gay and lesbian couples to marry legally, while one-third are opposed. As recently as 2006, these figures were reversed (56% of Latinos opposed same-sex marriage, while 31% supported it). Latino evangelicals, however, remain strongly opposed to same-sex marriage (66% opposed vs. 25% in favor). (Pew Religion and Public Life Project 2012a)

These levels of support for marriage equality are similar to those in those South American countries that have legalized same-sex marriage in the last few years (Carrillo 2013). With Argentina, Uruguay, and Brazil providing such change, it appears that the hope of those social conser-

Half of Hispanics Now in Favor of Legal Marriage for Gays and Lesbians

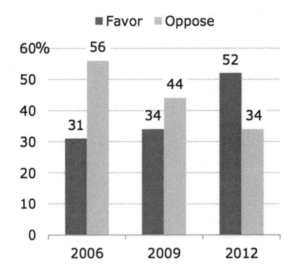

Source: Pew Hispanic Center, 2012 National Survey of Latinos. QN47b. Pew Hispanic Center 2006 National Survey of Latinos and 2009 National Survey of Latinos.

PEW RESEARCH CENTER

Figure 5.3. Support for same-sex marriage among Latinos, by year. Courtesy of the Pew Research Center.

vatives that Latinos in the United States would serve as a new bulwark against liberalizing social mores is not likely. The youthfulness of the Latino population, and the correlation of such liberal views with those cohorts, only exacerbates this situation.

Latino Catholics

If religiosity is a major factor in anyone's attitudes toward personal morality liberalization—especially important here as a theory about the attitudes and behavior of Latino immigrants, and also about African American voters, as in same-sex marriage and the passage of California's Proposition 8—then we would expect to find a disparity between

Figure 5.4. This political poster, designed by Latina artist Favianna Rodriguez, speaks to a trend of liberalism among young Latinos.

religious Latinos and unaffiliated Latinos, with the expectation that those religious-based beliefs would provide a roadblock to easy liberalization of reproductive rights and marriage equality issue. From the accounts examined here, this does not appear to be the case:

> A too-little-noticed 2010 poll by the Public Religion Research Institute found that a majority of Latino Catholics in California (57%) said they would vote to allow gay and lesbian couples to marry, compared to just 22% of Latino Protestants. This same Catholic-Protestant divide within the Latino community was evident across a wide range of public policy issues related to gay and lesbian rights. The Latino Catholic latitudinarianism on marriage tracks another almost-unreported finding, to wit: that the single most gay-friendly religious body in the U.S., bar none, is the lay Catholic community. Bishops, are you listening? (Laarman 2011)

Latinos in the United States had found many reasons to be increasingly positive toward progressive and Democratic Party positions. In 2012, President Obama added another with his announcement that he was using his prerogative to announce the halting of the deportations of as many as one million young immigrants who had come with their families to the United States. This move also generated debate among political analysts, and political operatives in the Republican Party, who had urged their leaders to adopt a more "Latino-friendly" set of policies, given the demographic changes that were taking place in the United States. To those who articulated that position, the fear that Latinos would go the way of African Americans—who voted for Democratic candidates by very wide margins—caused unease among Republican Party strategists. There were those who trumpeted the rise (and potential vice presidential possibility) of Senator Marco Rubio of Florida, a tea party favorite and Cuban American who was articulate on immigration issues. Not trying to attract more Latino voters would also cause the problem of having an increasingly white and aging party appear to be racially constructed—and bigoted—when it was increasingly populated by the decreasing share of the Anglo-American population.

As Latinos become a larger part of the American Catholic population, there is a reasonable probability that they will think and act more like the modern American Catholics who have shrugged off (or rejected)

Church policy and essentially gone their own way in large measure on issues like sex since Pope Paul VI's encyclical *Humanae Vitae* discussed contraception in 1968 (Paul VI 1968). Several factors argue for this development. Latinos, including Latino Catholics, will be younger on average than non-Latino whites and have been shown to be both similar to their non-Latino age cohort peers on reproductive rights issues and dissimilar from their parents and grandparents (meaning that they were *not* following Abuela [Grandmother] in her views of religion and personal morality). There are also cohort-similar or secularization effects, with fewer Latino churchgoers. The salience of reproductive rights is seemingly lower among this population then their non-Latinos peers. They prioritize economic and pocketbook issues. Data show Latinos to be the biggest supporters of Obamacare and among the most supportive of government's expansive role (which is true of the millennials generally).

Obama advisor David Plouffe articulates a point related to the salience of issues, and why social conservatives may be mistaken to believe that they can readily compete for the Latino vote, that Latino voters in America care more about pocketbook issues than immigration, although it can be easily argued that immigration carries great symbolic weight on many sides of the population and electorate:

> The Hispanic voters in Nevada, Colorado and New Mexico don't give a damn about Marco Rubio, the Tea Party Cuban-American from Florida. You know what? We won the Cuban vote! And it's because younger Cubans are behaving differently than their parents. It's probably my favorite stat of the whole campaign. So this notion that Marco Rubio is going to heal their problems—it's not even sophomoric; it's juvenile! And by the way: the bigger problem they've got with Latinos isn't immigration. It's their economic policies and health care. The group that supported the president's health care bill the most? Latinos. (Draper 2013a)

Putnam and Campbell also (2010) found a sharp contrast between white and Latino Catholics on the question of government aid to the poor: some 40% of white Catholics supported spending more, compared to 87% of Latino Catholics.

About 7 in 10 Latino Catholic registered voters identify as Democrats or lean toward the Democratic Party (71%), while only about 1 in 5 identify with or lean toward the Republican Party (21%). And fully 8 in 10 religiously unaffiliated Latinos identify with or lean toward the Democrats (81%), while only 1 in 10 are Republicans or lean Republican. Latino evangelical Protestants are more divided, with about half identifying as Democrats (52%) and 36% as Republicans (Pew Religion and Public Life Project 2012a).

America's Latino population is not alone in this evolution. As Hector Carrillo (2013) has pointed out, the shift to embrace marriage equality in Argentina, Uruguay, Mexico City, and potentially Chile belies any conception we have of Latinos as socially conservative and too caught up in elements of "machismo" to allow for any such societal and legal reform. In America, this observation also begs the salience issue.

Conclusion

This chapter has argued that the growing diversity of America does not present an opportunity for social conservatives to expand their influence, however much some of their leaders hypothesize. If social conservatives and the Republican Party thought that they had identified an inroad into African American and Latino voters through an appeal to their social conservative personal morality values, the results in 2012 could not have been encouraging.

There is still some possibility of inroads for social conservatives and Republicans among Latino evangelicals, which do represent a growing group among the Latino religious, who historically have been Catholic. At the same time, the growth in Latinos who are religiously unaffiliated—again a millennial characteristic—would potentially offset this growth. Even then, it is worth noting that Latino evangelical Protestants (a growing group—see Pew Religion and Public Life Project 2014) still voted for Obama at a comfortable margin of 50%-39%, suggesting that, even for them, the salience of these morality issues, compared to healthcare and economic issues, is not sufficient to compel their votes.

The belief that marriage and reproductive rights issues would be sufficient to pull Latinos away from the Democratic Party and progressive positions doesn't work out. Similarly, the belief that marriage and reproductive rights issues would be sufficient to pull African Americans away from the Democratic Party and progressive positions doesn't work out.

President Obama captured 93% of the African American vote and 73% of the Latino vote in 2012. Turnout was high, and the effect of the use of micro-targeting and the use of social media offset whatever suppression tactics were sought legislatively or actually deployed.

In all these groupings, the patterns are only made more pronounced by the attitudes of the millennials. In some cases, this amounts to a "double deficit" for social conservatives and the Republican Party, in the situation in which they are not able to make inroads into attracting the votes or views of young Latinos or young African Americans. When gender is added to this mix, there is the possibility of a "triple deficit."

The last three chapters have argued that three major factors (attitudes, religion, diversity) have undercut the potential power of the 2009–2010 backlash and the tea party message. However, the precarious campaign for the re-election of President Barack Obama in 2012 would be a measure of the strength of these arguments. It is plausible that this outcome, close as it was in some respects, could have been different. If so, then the analysis of this book—and particularly of those prior three chapters—would have to have been tempered by those alternate results. Chapter 6 provides an analysis of those culture war issues and the ways in which they were operational in the 2012 presidential campaign.

6

Campaign 2012

Of Plutocrats, Rape, and the "Ascendant Majority"

Barack Obama has failed America.
—Mitt Romney, 2011

What does it say about the college co-ed Susan [*sic*] Fluke, who goes before a congressional committee and says that she must be paid to have sex. What does that make her? It makes her a slut, right? It makes her a prostitute. She wants to be paid to have sex. She's having so much sex she can't afford the contraception. . . . Okay, so she's not a slut. She's "round heeled." I take it back.
—Rush Limbaugh, radio show, February 29, 2012

It seems to me, first of all, from what I understand from doctors, that's really rare. If it's a legitimate rape, the female body has ways to try to shut that whole thing down.
—Congressman Todd Akin (R-Missouri), Republican U.S. senatorial candidate, August 19, 2012

Writing after the re-election of Barack Obama in November 2012, political strategist and former Clinton White House official William Galston put into context the magnitude of president Obama's success:

> The fall of 2011, Barack Obama's prospects for reelection did not appear bright. . . . The president seemed unable to find a credible narrative to explain his plans; worse, he seemed to have lost the connection with the people that had fueled his remarkable victory in 2008. . . . What followed— between Labor Day of 2011 and Election Day in 2012—was one of the more noteworthy political comebacks in recent American history. . . . They de-

cided on a theme—fairness—and a strategy—using policies and events to mobilize key constituencies. And they waged a near-flawless tactical battle, including the decision to spend the summer—and much of their war-chest—characterizing Mitt Romney as a heartless plutocrat. (Galston 2013).

It was not too long ago—about 10 years ago, in 2004—that Karl Rove was crowing about the coming decades of Republican dominance, proclaiming that the 2004 reelection of President Bush had proven that America was a "center-right" country, a composition that a conservative base in the Republican Party could rely upon as it pursued policies and realignments in the coming decades. Within two years, the beginning of a challenge to Rove's prophecy was apparent, as the 2006 midterm elections brought the House of Representatives into Democratic control (admittedly second-term midterm elections usually don't increase the power of the party of the incumbent president).

Then 2008 signaled a thundering rebuke to Rove's claim. The election of America's first African American president (and an avowed "Chicago liberal," against the trend of recent Southern centrists from the Democratic Party) was greeted with glee from many progressive and Democratic circles. Interpretations of the 2008 election prompted some analysts to declare a turn in American politics and ideology. To them, the thrust of the Reagan Revolution was now subject to reversal. The decades of conservative realignment that had begun in 1980 with the election of the former California governor and that continued with his vice president George H. W. Bush in 1988 and the election of his ideological heir, George W. Bush, in 2000 and 2004, seemed to be in decline. One leading magazine trumpeted a cover story, "Conservatism Is Dead," featuring an essay that boldly proclaimed: "What conservatives have yet to do is confront the large but inescapable truth that movement conservatism is exhausted and quite possibly dead" (Tanenhaus 2009). These and other commentaries interpreted the election of Barack Obama, amid other changes, as a sign that the time of Reaganism had ended and that American conservatism had peaked.

The emergence and growth of the tea party in 2009, amid a time of soul searching for conservatives and the Republican Party, culminated in the 2010 midterm elections, at which time the tea-party-infused anger and rhetoric succeeded in bringing Republicans to a majority in the House of Representatives and put Barack Obama on the defensive with his 2012 reelection campaign ahead. Chapter 1 and especially Chapter 2 detail the many ways that the conservative movement groups and individuals and the national Republican Party came to focus on stopping Barack Obama and obstructing his administration and his party's agenda. This was the defining characteristic of their efforts in 2009–2012, as elected officials and their representatives tried to determine the best path back to retaking the Congress and the White House after the 2008 electoral defeats. To Senate Minority Leader Mitch McConnell (R-Kentucky), "The single most important thing we want to achieve is for President Obama to be a one-term president" (Garrett 2010).

To the conservative analyst and talk-show host Rush Limbaugh, the defeats of 2008 provided an opportunity for conservative elements in America—and especially in and around the Republican Party structure in Washington, D.C., in Congress, and in the states—to emphasize their deep conservatism—often including social conservatism as one of their elements—in the necessary revival of their party. The focus then turned to the most direct way to restrain Barack Obama and defeat his agenda. A House Republican attempt to derail and defeat the Patient Protection and Affordable Care Act came up short in 2010, but the anger and organizing after that resulted in the Republicans taking control of the House of Representatives in November 2010 by a wide margin.

What this chapter offers is severalfold: It highlights the planned and unplanned, inadvertent and unwise, use of culture war issues and symbols in the 2012 election. These are issues that had traditionally excited the social conservative religious base, stolen away "Reagan Democrats," and caused problems in national elections. While 2012 was meant to be an election about the economy, the times and tropes and discussions on some of these issues offered an opportunity for President Obama to win what was early on considered an unwinnable reelection.

Primary Season

With the sizeable changes in the Congress from the 2010 midterm elections and the apparent stalling of the American economic recovery, it appeared to many Republican strategists that the 2012 election year was ripe for a Republican resurgence, maybe even a return to the recent days of the George W. Bush administration, where their party controlled the presidency and both houses of Congress. There were times when the candidates clearly unloaded a wave of criticism on President Obama following the anger and memes of the tea party. In the early primary season, eventual Republican candidates referred to the president as the "The Great Complainer" (Friedman 2012).

The Republican campaign season began in earnest, seemingly starting increasingly earlier every four years. While it is easy to cut to the end and see who the eventual nominee is and then use the fully engaged political season as the real event, the primary season—in any party—often illuminates issues and strategies, with a residue of positions, usually extreme. Richard Nixon's much-referenced advice had been to run to the right in Republican primaries and run to the center in the general election.

The *New York Times*, viewed by conservatives as a typical bastion of liberal media, observed early in the Republican primary process that "primaries bring out the extremism in candidates, but this year seems much worse because the 'center' of the Republican Party has lurched so far to the right" (*New York Times* 2012a). The hope, to an opposing campaign strategist team, is that these extremist positions and pronouncements—whichever direction they lead, for either of the two main parties—could be used to demonstrate to moderate and centrist voters later that the specified party and the candidate himself, or herself, was out of step with a more centrist orientation of Americans. Republican pollster and analyst Frank Luntz predicted that the contested primary season (Romney being a putative, but hardly embraced, front-runner) would not be one that would advantage his party: "Republicans are not gonna like what's about to happen. . . . I think a war is about to break out within this primary field" (Sanders 2012). For example, as the primary schedule moved from first-in-the-nation Iowa caucuses (where social and religious conservatives are strong) to New Hampshire, a newspaper ad from former House Speaker Newt Gingrich called Mitt Romney a "timid Massachusetts moderate," while the ad portrayed Gingrich himself as a "bold Reagan conservative." To one *New York Times* analyst,

> this year, the very conservative Evangelical Christians in Iowa muddled the Republican presidential nominating contest, giving their support to an unelectable candidate, Rick Santorum, who fought to a draw with the

person Republicans seem most likely to settle for in the end, Mitt Romney. That means the G.O.P. will have to spend millions of more dollars, run more nasty ads and toss around more radical right-wing ideas before turning their attention to the general election. (Rosenthal 2012a)

To some analysts, the geometry of the contrast led to a series of one-offs with a rising candidate—or often all candidates—criticizing the front-runner (Collins 2012a). Social conservative movement leaders did try and coalesce around a candidate who was not Romney (Martin 2012a). Gingrich was himself an imperfect vessel for the conservative change he espoused and found lacking in Romney. His years as a K Street (Washington, D.C.) lobbyist had undercut the sincerity of his attacks on the ways in which Washington functioned, and his creative—some would say "harebrained"—ideas, like colonizing the moon, were risible and found a home in parodies on *Saturday Night Live* and the editorial cartoon pages.

Rick Santorum was different. Though he was later eclipsed by the emerging talent of those conservative senators and governors who were considered as potential running mates for Romney—such as Bobby Jindal, Marco Rubio, and Paul Ryan—he had made a conservative claim that Romney was compromised by the Massachusetts healthcare plan of 2006 and was perceived as not sufficiently conservative to excite the base—or to "light our hair on fire," as Sarah Palin had urged (McDonald 2012). What was ultimately a disconnect for him, even as he advanced far beyond what many had attributed to him at the beginning of the primary season, was that his flavor of conservatism was a decidedly social conservatism, rooted in the traditional bases of sex and life issues and more suited to the 2004 framing of issues than it was to the economy-centric focus of 2012. While Santorum espoused a belief that these issues had lasting power and demonstrated their salience in some victories and delegate successes, he was also vulnerable to criticisms that he had been a "statist" (one supporting large-scale government programs, such as George W. Bush's Medicare drug expansion) in the Bush years, as a senator and, later, as a lobbyist.

Still, to many, even to conservatives like David Brooks, the emphasis by Santorum on culture war issues that had riveted the Republican Party 20 and 30 years before were not apparent guides to a different electorate and society in 2012:

He seems to imagine America's problems can best be described as the result of a culture war between the God-fearing conservatives and the narcissistic liberals. Like most Americans, including most evangelicals under 40, I find this culture war language absurd. If conservative ideas were that much more virtuous than liberal ideas, then the conservative parts of the country would have fewer social pathologies than the liberal parts of the country. They don't. (Brooks 2012a)

While never remotely likely to emerge as a primary stop-Romney candidate—which almost everyone else did during the primary season—Texas representative Ron Paul nonetheless opened a door on a strain within Republicanism that wasn't being met by the establishment Romney or the social conservative Santorum. This libertarian strain would also reemerge as a potential road back to relevance after 2012. Paul, who had run for president before on the Libertarian ticket, was trying in 2012 to tap into the libertarian strain within the American Republican Party, a position that put him at odds with the prevailing pillars within the party:

To see Ron Paul on the Republican debate stage is to be reminded that the Party's libertarian streak is so thin as to be almost invisible. During the debates, when he warns against threatening Iran, or calls the war on drugs "a total failure," or observes that "rich white people don't get the death penalty very often," he seems like a man competing in an entirely separate contest, and perhaps he is. (Sanneh 2012a)

Ron Paul's criticism of Romney was in some ways little different from the broad-based critiques he had offered on the current American form of government and the lack of choices in the two parties. Paul's phenomenon was usually considered self-limited, and thus his capacity to expand beyond a base of acolytes and fervent followers—especially among the young, but also among those who resonated to his unique blend of anti-Obama, anti–drug war, and low-tax and less-government themes—was also limited. Romney gave as good as he took, with his well-funded operation airing ads in primary states. In one instance, when he critiqued conservative Newt Gingrich for being more of an "inside the Beltway" deal maker than Gingrich's conservative bombast would have preferred, one analyst observed:

The ads that Mr. Romney's allies ran against Mr. Gingrich in Iowa . . . proved eviscerating because they annihilated his confrontational persona. The video of the former speaker sharing that couch with Nancy Pelosi couldn't have been more disturbing to conservatives had it been the grainy tape from some convenience store, showing Mr. Gingrich with a hoodie and pistol. (Bai 2012)

Citizens United v. Federal Election Commission, protecting unlimited political action committee (Super-PAC) funding, counterintuitively worked in a progressive direction, allowing faltering Republican primary candidates to restock with funds and run negative ads in retaliation against each other, as Las Vegas billionaire Sheldon Adelson provided funds to the Gingrich Super-PAC, Winning Our Future.

These fissures, cleavages, and contradictions in part emerged and persisted because of the importance of the Reagan Democrats and blue-collar social conservatives who were not so convinced that that a candidate who emphasized the economic portion of the Reagan coalition would be there for them on issues that they considered most central—religion and the family.

The problems for Mitt Romney intensified during the 2012 Republican primaries when his nomination opponents began to criticize his tenure at Bain Capital and the nature of his relationship with workers and companies affected. While one might have anticipated this during a general campaign from Democratic opponents—and, as Galston indicates, it did form a central framing of Romney for the Obama forces—it was surprising to see the criticisms being leveled by his Republican counterparts. Admittedly, in such an often-bruising nomination contest, when negative charges and especially advertisements are plentiful, any line of attack might be used. But the way in which this particular one occurred reversed some of the expected and usual frames and policies. Governor Rick Perry of Texas, a bona fide conservative who was feeling the sting of Romney's attacks during debates and ads as he rose as conservative challenger to Romney's path to nomination, expressed this view:

Now I have no doubt that Mitt Romney was worried about pink slips— whether he was going to have enough of them to hand out because his company Bain Capital with all the jobs that they killed, I'm sure he was worried that he'd run out of pink slips. . . . There is something inherently wrong when getting rich off failure and sticking it to someone else is how you do your business and I happen to think that's indefensible. . . . Allowing these companies to come in and loot . . . people's jobs, loot their pensions, loot their ability to take care of their families and I will suggest they're just vultures. (Saenz 2012)

Newt Gingrich added: "There are some cases that look very suspicious where he and Bain Capital made a lot of money while other people went broke" (Easley 2012a).

With these exchanges, inherent contradictions are made visible—for example, a candidate courting both finance capitalists and blue-collar pro-lifers, or framing oneself as a populist to the party of more high school graduates—in other words, reshaping the culture war to one with culture more broadly. This is the price of courting the Reagan Democrats. At one point, conservative commentator Rush Limbaugh derided Gingrich for sounding like populist Obama administration official Elizabeth Warren (later a U.S. senator from Massachusetts) in her leading role impugning the excesses of Wall Street and the need for greater regulation of their activities. Even Rush Limbaugh was amazed at the turn of events:

The leading GOP candidates are on record arguing that Romney's practice of it—which he regularly cites as proof of his ability to create jobs, as a generally constructive force and even as synonymous with the American way—is not really capitalism at all, but a destructive, profit-driven perversion of it. Thanks to them, this is no longer a left-wing argument. (Sargent 2012)

To some analysts, all this framing had the unfortunate effect, for the anti-Obama crowd, of blurring the "Obama is a socialist" frame. William Galston analyzed this aspect of the attack on Romney and saw what would eventually be a successful use of it as a dividing or suppressing issue (as he would later write about the Obama campaign's successful exploitation of it as a Romney weakness):

Bain matters because it goes to the heart of the core case Romney is making: The economy is broken, Obama doesn't know how to fix it, and I do.

If his rivals can undermine his record as a job-creator and substitute the narrative of Romney as a "vulture capitalist" who makes money by looting firms and firing workers, his path to the presidency becomes a lot steeper. (Galston 2012a)

Of Mitt, "Anti-Mitts," and the "Enthusiasm Gap"

Maligned by opponents and movement activists in his party, Romney nonetheless represented a significant portion of the Republican coalition, those for whom a prudent fiscal manager would be a clear preference to another four years of the Obama administration. And Romney, while critiqued for being devoid of charisma and uninspiring as a speaker and candidate, made a point of always mentioning that he was determined to replace Barack Obama and make him as a one-term president. "Barack Obama has failed America," he said in 2011 (Balz 2013: 98). Romney generally made a personal or tactical decision to not malign Obama personally, probably a good choice given the public's split between Obama policies and ability to "re-steer" the economy and their consideration of him as a person. In this choice, he did, however, forfeit the opportunity to merge with the often angry vituperation that the tea parties and others had in their often nasty, often racist rejection of Obama from 2009 onward.

Several political analysts had described one of Romney's key vulnerabilities as that of an "enthusiasm gap." In electoral politics, this can be manifested in several ways. At one level, it can be a predictor of eventual turnout in voting on Election Day for the candidate and the entire party ticket. At another level, funding can dry up, or not rise to previously hoped for levels, as potential supporters either wait for another opportunity or fund different aspects of the electoral system—"down-ballot" representatives and senators, state legislators, important initiatives and ballot measures. At a third level, it can affect the party down-ballot, as those who depend upon turnout for their own electoral successes can also lose in a lackluster campaign and turnout effort. At still another level, it can diminish the number of people who are willing to walk precincts, stuff envelopes, cull voter data, and make phone calls or e-mails—the gritty "soldier work" of a campaign that can supplement the funding available for paid campaign staff and consultants. Finally, an enthusiasm gap can prompt a third-party effort, which can have the effect (see Ross Perot's effect on President George H. W. Bush's attempt for re-election in 1992) of allowing one's formal opponent to succeed electorally.

In this context, a schism is more pronounced than an enthusiasm gap (though not unrelated). In the case of 2012, it took on deeper meaning because it was directly a matter of social conservatives lamenting that they had yet been unable to propel a conservative, transformative candidate to the front of the nomination process. As Reagan-era strategist Richard Viguerie would write in 2014: "Conservatives are not going to get to the political Promised Land and be able to govern America according to conservative principles until flawed, big-government Republican leaders are replaced with constitutional conservatives." Nonetheless, the focus on removing Barack Obama from office was also a unifying theme in the primary contests. For a great deal of the primary season, the specter of "Obamacare" became a rallying force for Republican contestants. In the same way that it had fueled the tea party, the health law reform was often relied upon as an overextension of government and proof that the otherwise-mild Obama was indeed a socialist bent on driving government into corners of American commerce and personal life where it had not been previously. As Rick Santorum put it, "I believe Obamacare will rob America, the best way I can put it is, rob America of its soul" (Garofolo 2011).

After the election, "movement conservatives" like Rush Limbaugh would argue that many millions of conservative voters chose to stay home or not vote for Mitt Romney for president because they believed that he was too much a representative of the establishment. Enthusiasm gaps prompted parodies like this from *The Onion*: "Romneymania Sweeps America":

> As Romneymania has grown, the Republican candidate has crossed over from political figure to cultural phenomenon. Countless reverent portraits of Romney have appeared in storefront windows and on building facades throughout the country. (*The Onion* 2012a)

On a personal level, his mild demeanor, moderate record, and Mormon stolidness also fed into a sense that Romney was not capturing the anger of the tea party movement or the resentment of the anxious blue-collar voters whom Reagan and Falwell (and Nixon before them) had brought into the Republican Party, especially during an economic downturn.

Santorum, who was considered the candidate who most appealed to the social conservatives and their traditional culture-war emphasis on the pernicious policies changes and symbolism that the Obama Administration represented, often spoke to these issues in campaign appearances. One reporter captured this early on:

> He [Santorum] continued throwing out the cultural red meat for primary voters Sunday night, telling a rally at a Georgia church that Obama was intent on starting a cultural war. As the audience roared with applause, he called on the country to build a foundation that will "defend the church, defend the family, defend the nonprofit community, defend them from a government that wants to weaken them." (Tom Cohen 2012)

The ever-quotable Santorum—he on "man on dog sex" (Dombrink and Hillyard 2007)—had in 2008 warned that "Satan is attacking the great institutions of America, using those great vices of pride, vanity and sensuality as the root to attack all of the strong plants that has so deeply rooted in the American tradition" (Dowd 2012b). He also offered up this in the course of the 2012 campaign:

> Woodstock is the great American orgy. This is who the Democratic Party has become. They have become the party of Woodstock. They prey upon our most basic primal lusts, and that's sex. And the whole abortion culture, it's not about life. It's about sexual freedom. That's what it's about. Homosexuality. It's about sexual freedom. (Reeves 2012)

One analyst captured candidate Santorum's disdain for the president, a feature that had characterized some of the anti-Obama sentiment from 2008 onward:

> His portrayal of President Obama as an out-of-touch elitist who "thinks he's smarter than you" and "thinks he knows better than you" tickles the erogenous zones of right-wing Republicans . . . in a way that Romney, a genuine member of the élite to his bones, can't hope to mimic. (Cassidy 2012)

Political journalist John Heilemann, whose 2010 book *Game Change* (written with Mark Halperin) was seen as the definitive portrait of the 2008 Obama-McCain race (and which was made into an award-winning HBO movie, famed for its portrayal of Republican vice presidential candidate Sarah Palin) concluded that the changes by 2012 had led to a changed Republican Party (and some internal contradictions) :

> The transfiguration of the GOP isn't only about ideology, however. It is also about demography and temperament, as the party has grown whiter, less well schooled, more blue-collar, and more hair-curlingly populist. The result has been a party divided along the lines of culture and class: Establishment versus grassroots, secular versus religious, upscale versus downscale, highfalutin versus hoi polloi. (Heilemann 2012a)

Even the British press took notice, such as with a headline, "Election 2012: The Return of 'Culture Wars'" (Younge 2012).

However, the common notion among analysts and party strategists was that the united dislike of Obama and the Democrats, as expressed often from the sites of the Republican primary debates, would be enough to unite the party and generate a large turnout and victory in November 2012. But a failure to do so would be enough to untie the party.

The Bain Meme: Romney the Plutocrat

Mitt Romney escaped the Republican primary season with some negative impressions of him and fodder for the Democrats to begin using against him. One journalist writing at this time captured the effects on Romney's favorability, as early as February 2012:

> Even as he finds increasing success in the Republican primary, negative views of Romney have skyrocketed, particularly among independents, according to recent polls. An *ABC News/Washington Post* survey released last week, for example, found Romney viewed unfavorably by 49 percent of voters and favorably by just 31 percent. Among independents, just 23 percent viewed Romney favorably, compared to 51 percent who felt that way about President Obama. (Ball 2012a)

Figure 6.1. Mitt Romney and other Bain Capital executives pose in a 1984 photo.

There were emblematic moments during the campaign, some eva-
nescent and transitory, some retaining their power throughout, some
forgettable, others one wished to be forgotten. Like other presidents
and governors before him, Barack Obama and his campaign focused
on using the summer months before the national party conventions to
define his opponent in a negative light. For this, the Republican primary
season provided a great deal of material for the Obama attack ads. The
Obama campaign worked deliberately to create a Romney persona that
would be difficult for the Republican challenger to shrug off, especially
given the contours of the electoral calendar.

Several events (or inadvertent utterances) during the Romney campaign worked together to reinforce the notion that Romney was a "heartless plutocrat," in William Galston's term, (Galston 2013) or a practitioner
of "vulture capitalism" (competitor Rick Perry's term; see Sonmez 2012)
At one point, Romney, referring to his role as a finance capitalist involved
in the purchasing and restructuring of companies, stated, "I like to fire
people." When he later explained that he knew the impact of the rising
costs of fuel, since "my wife fills up two Cadillacs," or tried to connect

with NASCAR fans by claiming "I know NASCAR owners," he helped to reinforce the notion of his wealth. It was up to the Obama campaign to add the policy implications of being "heartless." Plans later surfaced for the Romneys to add a "car elevator" in proposed plans for their La Jolla, California, beach house. While it was understandable in the context of Ann Romney's multiple sclerosis, one journalist noted that "nobody who decides to build an indoor elevator for their car can get elected in America" (Hagan 2012). Still, it remained for America's first African American president, whose own birth certificate was often under attack from the "birther" element of conservatives, to make this image of Romney stick.

Late-night talk-show host Jimmy Fallon, one of many comedians who enjoyed the emerging characterizations from the campaign, offered: "A new survey found that only 31 percent of Americans would want to sit next to Mitt Romney on a flight. Romney was so upset, he was like, 'I don't understand. How would they get on my private jet?'" (Fallon 2012). Comedian Jay Leno also pounced on one Romney utterance ("My wife drives two Cadillacs") in a meme that would come to define Romney as rich and out of touch: "Gas prices are so high that Mitt Romney's wife can only afford to drive one Cadillac" (Leno 2012a). Fallon and Leno's jokes, months before the Republican National Convention, showed the extent to which the meme had sunk in during those months. As Rodell Mollineau, president of American Bridge 21st Century, explained, "They're smaller things, but I think after a while we've been able to add them up. It all funnels into that narrative that he is the guy that's not on the side of the middle class" (Ball 2012a). And it exemplified a point that political strategist William Galston made after the campaign:

> They [the Obama campaign] decided on a theme—fairness—and a strategy—using policies and events to mobilize key constituencies. And they waged a near-flawless tactical battle, including the decision to spend the summer—and much of their war-chest—characterizing Mitt Romney as a heartless plutocrat. (Galston 2013: 2)

Etch-a-Sketch

Though it turned out not necessarily to be a lasting meme of the campaign, a few news cycles captured the unfortunate expression of a Romney campaign official that his candidate was so flexible on policy that he was like an "Etch-a-Sketch" (a drawing toy that one erases by shaking)—if you didn't like the current position, you could shake, rearrange, and find a different policy position—"Everything changes. It's almost like an Etch A Sketch—you can kind of shake it up, and we start all over again" (Shear 2012a). This line of criticism, although it didn't eventually take hold in the general election (one could make the argument that movement conservatives considered it when deciding how strongly to work for Romney in the 2012 general election), played into conservatives' wariness of Romney's conservative core. Rick Santorum's campaign used a long-standing joke in one of its radio ads—"A liberal, a moderate and a conservative walk into a bar. The bartender says: 'Hi Mitt!'" (Santarelli 2012).

This invited attacks on Romney as a flip-flopper or, worse, a candidate without conservative rootedness, during the 2008 and 2012 campaigns. This is important, not in an inside-politics sense, but because it is so at odds with what the tea party (and Limbaugh) had been promoting for almost three years, the importance of a strong conservative pushback. One problem with this approach, former President Clinton cautioned the Obama campaign, was that voters, especially moderate or swing voters, liked flexibility and could see in the candidate hope that he or she would end up pursuing policies that aligned with their views:

> [President Bill] Clinton, echoing survey data presented by Obama's own pollster Joel Benenson, quietly argued that the empty-core approach failed to capitalize on what they see as Romney's greatest vulnerability: An embrace of a brand of tea party conservatism that turns off Hispanics, women and moderate independents. A more effective strategy, Clinton has told anyone who would listen, would be to focus almost exclusively on Romney's description of himself as a "severe conservative," to deny him any chance to tack back to the center. (Balz 2013)

Ascendant Majority

Beginning in 1968, and more represented in 1972, generational elements began to reshape the nature and salience of the ascendant majority for the Democratic Party. Years of civil rights activism surrounding the passage of the Civil Rights Act of 1964 (and Lyndon Johnson's fear that the act had "lost the South to the Democratic Party for a hundred years") paved the way for the influence of the women's movement and anti-war movements, and the counterculture, taken broadly. This shifted Democratic politics to the points where the onetime mainstay—the white working class—was reduced to one constituency among many. More pointedly, the group itself was accused—and often caricatured, a la Archie Bunker in Norman Lear's *All in the Family*, a popular television sitcom of the time—of being precisely the intolerant class. This group—for cultural, more than economic, issues—began to drift away from the Democratic Party. The election of 1976 was an aberration in many ways. As the immediate post-Watergate election, it featured a Southern governor as the Democratic candidate and, in Jimmy Carter, a candidate who spoke of his evangelical Christianity, a seeming cross-current to the trend identified in the prior two rounds (or specifically rising because of it).

The election year of 1980 represented a cyclic turn when the white working class was ripe for poaching, as the Republican Party and the Reagan campaign made inroads to the extent that the "Reagan Democrats" began to be discussed as a concept. Whether in places like Macomb County, Michigan, or other places that were strong in the traditional mores of the often religious group (who may have felt that they were looked down upon and marginalized by the growing Democratic coalitions—who themselves were often mocked because of their attention to equal speaking time and representation at Democratic gatherings, giving rise to the origins of the term "political correctness"), these Democrats combined with the intentional growth of Republican focus on, and the enlarged political participation of, evangelical Christians (see Winters 2012a), becoming a formidable group of voters for conservative policies and the Republican Party.

One analysis of 2012 turns first on the definition of "working class," especially whether it is primarily an economic difference, captured by job definitions—blue-collar or white-collar—or an emerging cultural and educational definition, especially preferred by pollsters, that emphasizes the attainment of a college degree—or more specifically, the lack of it—as a central defining characteristic. Looking back, one can see that the early plannings of the Obama campaign—supported by the polling and framing work of James Carville and Stan Greenberg and the analysis of their colleague Ruy Teixeira—had focused on a change in American society and the American electorate that would prove to be decisive in the November 2012 election.

Early on, Greenberg—who used the results of the 2008 election to dispute the notion of the vitality of the "Reagan Democrats" (Greenberg 2008)—and Carville promoted the idea that a change in American demographics had reduced the need for successful Democratic candidates in national elections to aim their arguments and policies at what they described as a thinning group of white blue-collar voters. They pointed out that these groups supported Nixon (and not McGovern) in 1972, along with Reagan (not Carter in 1980 or Mondale in 1984). Replacing them as the key components of a successful Democratic electoral coalition was a group often referred to as the "ascendant majority"—a combination of persons of color, youth, and single women.

If one views the 2012 election through this lens, then the ways in which issues related to them (such as contraception or immigration) loomed large. Through some planned events, as well as some unplanned ones, issues related to health care, to taxation, to contraception, and to immigration helped form the solidity and fervency of this population. The final turnout in November 2012 surprised (even stunned) some Republican operatives, who had assumed that the level on excitement shown for the transformative Obama election in 2008 would diminish, as economic opportunities had dwindled, the administration had taken some Republican-friendly policy directions (especially in foreign policy), and the newness of the Obama phenomenon had naturally faded. Although those like Teixeira who argued for the ultimate determinative quality of those demographic changes would be vindicated eventually, along the way they also had detractors from among their own colleagues. In "Seizing the New Progressive Common Ground" (Greenberg et al. 2011), instead of the white working class, Greenberg and Carville focused on a "new progressive coalition" made up of "young people, Hispanics, unmarried women, and affluent suburbanites."

Later analyses of the use of micro-targeting and facility with social media outreach (discussed in this chapter's final section) demonstrated how the Democratic campaign would be successful, even where skeptics thought that the youth segment—with its increased vulnerability to downward shifts in the American economy—would be particularly susceptible to a cooling off for the second election of Barack Obama. Demonstrating one way in which primary contests could cause overly strong policy proclamations that would seem extreme later in a campaign—and that further emphasized the problem the Republicans would have in attracting a key portion of the "ascendant majority"—Romney early on in 2012 praised some of Arizona's get-tough immigration policies as a model for federal policy at a time when Arizona exemplified a "one-state-going-extreme" immigration policy (Martin et al. 2012). Several analysts, like Teixeira, have argued that demographic changes in American society and the American electorate point to a lessening of the size and role of the "white working class." However defined—and the definition is important to construction of the argument—this group had been central to the Democratic coalition, especially since the time it was catalyzed in the campaigns and presidency of Franklin Roosevelt and in the growth of governmental support programs for those in need.

The implications of this choice (and bet) was that the Democrats could decide not to chase the white-working class voters, who had once been a key part of their winning coalition, on certain personal morality issues (abortion, gay rights, religion). Even in states like Ohio and Michigan, the fortuitous nomination of Mitt Romney allowed the Democrats to focus on economic populism issues in those Midwestern industrial states without worrying about blurring their message to those concerned about reproductive rights and the increasing conservatism of the Republican Party. For Democrats, these strategists predicted a road to success without going after working-class white voters generally (though they did in key states like Ohio).

Latinos were very positively disposed toward the Patient Protection and Affordable Care Act; they remain optimistic—even amid economic turmoil and insecurity (Baldassare 2002; Harmon 2012)—and supportive of the role of government in supporting those who are in need. While they joined many others in denoting the economy as a primary issue in 2012, they have a distinctive posture regarding these other issues. And it is for these reasons that they vote strongly Democratic. While immigration may not rise to the level of the economic issues, it also serves as an important litmus test and symbolic issue for the Democrats and may be also interpreted as a key to getting out the vote, increasing turnout among one element of the Democratic base. Conversely, the immigration issue displayed the ability to pin Republicans down and make them less able to expand their outreach to, and get support from, the Latino communities. It also made it difficult for them to not appear churlish, and it opened them to charges of racism at a time when America is growing more diverse.

Memes: The 47%

During the campaign season, Mitt Romney was filmed surreptitiously by a catering worker while he delivered a speech at a closed-door fundraiser in which he claimed that he needed assistance, since President Obama began the campaign with a great advantage: the support of the "47%" of the electorate who were dependent upon government largesse for their livelihood.

Romney's surreptitiously filmed comments, and the publicity and discussion they generated when made public, also resonated with a statement he had made earlier in the campaign in which he referred to his view of the lower-class in governance: "I'm not concerned about the very poor. We have a safety net there. If it needs repair, I'll fix it. I'm not concerned about the very rich, they're doing just fine. I'm concerned about the very heart of America, the 90%, 95% of Americans right now who are struggling and I'll continue to take that message across the nation" (Benen 2012). At several instances during the 2012 campaign, analysts wondered whether the "Occupy" movement, a loosely structured protest with encampments in some American cities against the excesses of capitalism, with their slogan "We are the 99%," were the counterpart to the tea party movement (Meyer 2013). Given the influence of the tea party on national events, it did not seem an apt comparison, but the concept of the top 1% of the American wealthy dictating policy at the expense of the many found resonance when Romney—often caricatured, as described earlier, as an out-of-touch and unfeeling representative of that 1%—used language dividing the country into those who were "makers" and those who were "takers" in such a stark manner.

Reproductive Rights: How "Slut" and Rape Turned a Potential Advantage into a Definite Disadvantage

One contributor to a *New York Times* forum had argued that the 2012 campaign would be devoid of such culture war issues, given the focus on the economy:

The great news for Romney is that, no matter how you slice the electorate into target groups, the economy and jobs are the top issues on voters'
minds. This is not an election that will be decided on social or cultural issues. Despite Democrats' efforts to turn fundamentally economic and fiscal issues into cultural issue wedges, the election will not hinge on issues
like free contraception or funding for Planned Parenthood. (Soltis 2012)

However, and in an unplanned manner that also showed the salience of
these issues for many in the Republican Party base, culture war issues
did rear their heads, as candidates hurried to activate some of the social
conservatives who formed a large part of the party's base.

The analyst Jeffrey Toobin, identifying what would later become a
unplanned campaign theme for the Republican Party, noted as early as
the early primary season that the fervent social conservatives who par-
ticipated zealously in the Iowa caucuses and in other early caucus and
primary states held strong pro-life views, which often led to a Republican
platform that became problematic for attempts to run toward the center in the general election and provided many opportunities for primary
candidates to prove their social conservative bona fides. Toobin wrote:

> Since Ronald Reagan, Republican Presidents (and Presidential nominees)
> have been committed to overturning *Roe v. Wade*, the Supreme Court's
> abortion-rights landmark from 1973. But as the debates last weekend in
> New Hampshire suggested, the G.O.P. appears to have taken a more ex-
> treme step in terms of rolling back the Constitutional right to privacy.
> (Toobin 2012a)

What Toobin had identified was the connection with the issue of re-
stricting contraception. The Catholic bishops helped create the focus on
contraception and women's reproductive rights in the modern era. Their
strong pushback to the Patient Protection and Affordable Care Act had
precipitated the action that helped make Sandra Fluke, a Georgetown
University law student who testified that she would lack to access to contraception at a Catholic university if elements of the Catholic Church's
suggested compromise with Obamacare took effect, a focus of Rush Limbaugh's attention. The seeds of this issue would grow during the campaign,
and the Sandra Fluke–Rush Limbaugh episode is an example of this:

Romney went beyond mere opposition to *Roe*. The New Hampshire debate provided Romney with the opportunity to state that he thought *Griswold v. Connecticut*, the 1965 case that first made explicit the right to privacy, in the context of contraception for married couples (and whose jurisprudence would form the basis for *Roe v. Wade* eight years later) was also wrong. Senator Santorum agreed that the Supreme Court in *Griswold* had ". . . created through a penumbra of rights a new right to privacy that was not in the Constitution." (Toobin 2012a)

One of the "sacred cows" of Democrats and progressives that social conservatives had fumed about since the *Roe v. Wade* ruling in 1973 was the issue of government support for reproductive services. Even though the Hyde Amendment had become law in 1976 and continued in 2012 to prohibit the expenditure of federal funds on abortion (except in dire circumstances), states were allowed to go their own way on this issue, and had for those decades. For example, in 2012, 17 states provided such use of Medicaid, while 32 states followed the federal example (and one more stringent than that), a situation representing the general pattern of red and blue states. In fact, progressive organizations and reproductive rights groups continued to be alarmed by the growing number of states that were actively implementing anti-choice laws in their states.

One of the leading elements in this effort was a focus on denial of state funding for the group Planned Parenthood under the argument that a portion of their funds were used for abortions. In the same way, "partial-birth abortion" had been a frame that social conservatives had used successfully to regain some of the ground in the "pro-life versus pro-choice" battle (and it had helped drive the pro-life position in a 2009 Gallup poll to a position above pro-choice sentiments among Americans; see Saad 2009). The tying together of abortion and government payment for such services had long been a losing combination, as the Hyde Amendment proved. It combined the power of fiscal stringency with that of social conservative and religious moral objections and had polled low throughout the post-*Roe* era (Craig and O'Brien 1993). In 2011, Indiana became the first state to prohibit state funding (a decision that a federal judge would stay and that the Supreme Court would decline to hear) for the organization Planned Parenthood. It appeared that the framing of those particular issues broke in a beneficial way for Republican campaign strategies, particularly in those swing states in which socially conservative voters—the historical Reagan Democrats, now evolved into their own potent force—might tilt a general election.

The campaign also took a turn toward culture war issues in an unexpected way, or in a miscalculated way, in which the Democrats were more than happy to welcome the Republican attacks, knowing that they did not represent the many voters in America—particularly women, especially young women:

> For the first time in our history, the federal government will force religious institutions to fund and facilitate coverage of a drug or procedure contrary to their moral teaching, and purport to define which religious institutions are "religious enough" to merit an exemption. This is a matter of whether religious people and institutions may be forced by the government to provide such coverage even when it violates our consciences. . . . What is at stake is whether America will continue to have a free, creative, and robust civil society—or whether the state alone will determine who gets to contribute to the common good, and how they get to do it. (U.S. Conference of Catholic Bishops 2012)

Soon after, the House Oversight and Government Reform Committee (all male, for those who might have misread the symbolic importance of the moment) held a hearing at which a Georgetown University law student, Sandra Fluke, was not allowed to testify about the deleterious effects of having contraception coverage denied for students at a Catholic school, a provision that the U.S. Catholic bishops were trying to get included back into the Obama administration's policies on the waiver process for religious institutions. What happened next became an unexpected part of the theatre that is often a political campaign. On his February 29, 2012, and March 1, 2012, radio shows, Rush Limbaugh referred to Ms. Fluke as a "slut" and offered that women who want free contraception should have to make an online sex tape:

> What does it say about the college co-ed Susan [sic] Fluke, who goes before a congressional committee and says that she must be paid to have sex? What does that make her? It makes her a slut, right? It makes her a prostitute. She wants to be paid to have sex. She's having so much sex she can't afford the contraception. She wants you and me and the taxpayers to

Figure 6.2. Sandra Fluke speaks with Democrats on women's need for contraception coverage at religious institutions.

pay her to have sex. Okay, so she's not a slut. She's "round heeled." I take it back. (*ABC News* 2012; YouTube 2012)

Limbaugh naturally created a controversy. The abortion-rights organization NARAL referred to him as "revolting Rush."

After the criticism, Limbaugh added: "If we are going to pay for your contraceptives and thus pay for you to have sex, we want something. We want you to post the videos online so we can all watch" (Whitcomb 2012). President Obama spoke with Ms. Fluke by phone, offering his encouragement. As Ms. Fluke reported in an interview with MSNBC's Andrea Mitchell,

He encouraged me and supported me and thanked me for speaking out about the concerns of American women . . . And what was really personal for me was he said to tell my parents they should be proud. And that meant a lot because Rush Limbaugh had questioned whether or not my family would be proud of me. I appreciated that very much. (MSNBC 2012a)

In time, former Republican presidential candidate John McCain expressed his belief that the focus on contraception had gone on too long:

I think we have to fix that. I think that there is a perception out there, because of the way that this whole contraception issue played out. We need to get off of that issue, in my view. I think we ought to respect the right of women to make choices in their lives, and make that clear, and get back on to what the American people really care about: jobs and the economy. (Kapur 2012)

Another moderate Republican, retiring Republican senator Kay Bailey Hutchison (R-Texas), expressed a similar view, but with more policy focus, in an interview:

HUTCHISON: We cannot afford to lose the Medicaid funding for low-income women to have health care services. We cannot. We can't keep turning back federal funds that every state gets and then try to find money in our budget, which is already being cut in key areas like education. I do think that the governor needs to sit down with the federal government and work it out so that we can have our share—our fair share not more—of money for Medicaid to help low-income women have their health care services.

MSNBC's CHUCK TODD: So it sounds like you think he should not be excluding Planned Parenthood?

HUTCHISON: I think Planned Parenthood does mammograms, they do so much of the health care—the preventive health care and if they're doing that, we need to provide those services, absolutely. (MSNBC 2012b)

Hutchison would later be followed by Republican governors (including some unlikely candidates in Arizona's Jan Brewer and Florida's Rick Scott) who saw the need for federal funding of their expanded Medicaid program, whatever their rhetoric had been previously (and after the 2012 election, some governor critics would relent to let Obamacare-related funding flow into their state).

A leitmotif for the 2012 campaign, and issues of gender and age, had been created. One analyst observed:

In Ms. Fluke and the scorn she has drawn from conservative commentators, Democrats may have found a symbol for what they have called a Republican war on women that could spell more difficulty for a Republican Party already showing signs of trouble with female voters. (Weisman 2012)

Figure 6.3. Former U.S. representative Todd Akin.

When the Republican Missouri Senatorial candidate Todd Akin told an interviewer in August 2012: "It seems to me, first of all, from what I understand from doctors, that's really rare. If it's a legitimate rape, the female body has ways to try to shut that whole thing down" (Eligon and Schwirtz 2012), it was met with alarm by Republican strategists who were looking closely at Missouri for potential control of the Senate. Missouri was one of the states that Obama had not won in 2008, wasn't expected to win in 2012, and in which a Democratic senator—in this case, first-term Senator Claire McCaskill—was vulnerable. The Democratic Party pounced, and women's rights and reproductive rights groups made Akin's comments a focus of what they perceived as part of the "Republican war on women," connecting it with a range of economic and health policies.

Akin's bizarre statement propelled him into the spotlight in an unplanned manner. The Republican Senatorial Committee and the leading outside 527 funding groups announced that they would no longer financially support his candidacy and exhorted him to step aside by the September 25 ballot deadline and let another candidate replace him. Akin declined and became a significant part of the 2012 Fall campaign. (Similarly, the idea that Akin chaired a House science committee raised issues of science and modernity, even beyond reproductive rights, at a time when climate change and evolution were topics of contention.)

While this seemed marginal, critics pointed out that Rep. Paul Ryan, the vice presidential candidate, and other members of the growingly conservative Republican house majority felt similar in their opposition to abortion, even in access of rape or incest. For so many years, social conservatives had emphasized the importance of value issues, providing them as wedge issues for general elections in which many differences divided the two parties—but, at least until 2011, debt and deficit issues were of secondary or tertiary importance. Dan Balz talks about how the Obama campaign also put their emphasis on values, by emphasizing economic fairness as a core societal value, and on that they thought differentiated them from their Republican opponents (Balz 2013).

The problem in 2012 was that, while abortion can be mined as an ambivalent issue in contemporary American society, contraception really could not. Rape certainly and emphatically could not either. The earlier strategy on late-term abortion (see *Sin No More*, Dombrink and Hillyard 2007) had given social conservatives an opening in the reproductive wars. But the 2012 framing by anti–Planned Parenthood politicians and activists, the opposition to contraceptives' inclusion in the Patient Protection and Affordable Care Act by politicians and religious leaders, the seeming glee with which Rush Limbaugh and others attacked reproductive rights advocates, all combined to portray Republicans as wrongdoers in what was called by Democrats and women's groups as the "War on Women." As Republican strategist Ed Gillespie observed (months before Todd Akin and Richard Mourdock—discussed later—would offer their thoughts), emphasizing the tenuous nature with which the reproductive rights issue is displayed in an often ambivalent American societal and political life, that

> life is a winning issue for conservatives. But it's always been an issue where tone matters and imagery matters. How you talk about it matters. We win on life. . . . Whichever side is deemed as extreme on the issue is losing. If you're seen as extreme or trying to impose your views on others you run into trouble on either the pro-life side or pro-choice side. (Harris and Martin 2012)

To the Democrats, these actions, sentiments, and statements added up to a "Republican war on women," and they reacted with a series of critiques and policy comparisons that they hoped would expose the extreme nature of Republican policies on reproductive rights (among other gender issues, with the issue of equal pay being given great prominence as well).

It was important that the issue was not as narrow as abortion—on which the American public is consistently ambivalent and arguably centrist—or even one as narrow as late-term abortion (or "partial-birth abortion," in the preferred parlance of the pro-life movement). It was, instead, a rather wide-ranging and often heated discussion of the availability of *contraception* for American women, an issue of great salience for them. It also had the effect of making the Republican Party look very out of step with modern American women and their lives and choices (later, when Mitt Romney mentioned in the second presidential debate that, as Massachusetts governor trying to diversify the governmental workforce, he had asked an aide to get him "binders full of women," a series of tweets and Tumblr pictures followed, further enforcing the sense of Romney and the Republican Party as out-of-date).

Bishop Daniel Jenky of Peoria represented the most conservative wing of that position in a Sunday homily, although he was not alone in his critique:

> Hitler and Stalin, at their better moments, would just barely tolerate some churches remaining open, but would not tolerate any competition with the state in education, social services and health care. . . . In clear violation of our First Amendment rights, Barack Obama—with his radical, pro-abortion and extreme secularist agenda—now seems intent on following a similar path. This fall, every practicing Catholic must vote, and must vote their Catholic consciences, or by the following fall our Catholic schools, our Catholic hospitals, our Catholic Newman Centers, all our public ministries—only excepting our church buildings—could easily be shut down. (*Huffington Post* 2012b)

At a time when the top concerns of Americans, as reported in a March 5, 2012, NBC/*Wall Street Journal* poll were, in descending order, job creation and economic growth (68%, top two choices), the deficit and government spending (40%), health care (27%), energy and the cost of gas (23%), national security and terrorism (16%), the war and Afghanistan (10%), and immigration (9%), a focus on birth control seemed ill placed (Public Opinion Strategies 2012). After Rush Limbaugh apologized to Ms. Fluke, he was nonetheless defended by some of his allies and supporters. Sarah Palin declared:

> I think the definition of hypocrisy is for Rush Limbaugh to have been called out, forced to apologize and retract what it is that he said in exercising his First Amendment rights. . . . And never is . . . the same applied to the leftist radicals who say such horrible things about the handicapped, about women, about the defenseless. So I think that's the definition of hypocrisy. (CNN 2012)

One large problem for the Republican Party was that they had, at least implicitly, allowed Limbaugh to occupy a place of privilege in the discussion of political issues in the country. With his searing approach, Limbaugh had often called out Democrats and liberals and been willing to go a click too far in his cauterizing, in a display that might have brought chuckles, with some eye rolling. However, in the bright light of examination, many of Limbaugh's moments could not be excused as entertainment:

> The cop-out for Republicans is to dismiss Limbaugh as a showman, and not a consequential political messenger. . . . But the general public probably doesn't see such a sharp distinction. Limbaugh's show is almost entirely about politics, and the themes he stresses invariably echo and influence the themes that Republican politicians across the country emphasize. (Kornacki 2012a)

While Rush Limbaugh's statements often caused problems for Republican attempts to provide broader and more moderate messages on issues as needed, there were also attempts by notable conservatives to try and provide a parallel spokesperson for the Democratic Party, as when Fox television figure Sean Hannity stated that the satirist Bill Maher, host of HBO's weekly show, *Real Time with Bill Maher*, was the "defacto head of the Democratic Party" (Sheppard 2012).

Looking back at Akin's rape comment and the significance and size of pronouncements from the much-listened-to Limbaugh, it might be easy to lose track of some of the other unfortunate utterances coming from various Republican players, such as this from Santorum fundraiser Foster Friess: "On this contraceptive thing, my gosh it's such [sic] inexpensive. You know, back in my days, they used Bayer aspirin for contraception. The gals put it between their knees, and it wasn't that costly" (Haberman 2012). The raising of the contraception issue was presumably not scripted as a strategic advance in itself, but it emerged as a by-product of some of the discussions on the implementation of the Patient Protection and Affordable Care Act. As one analyst wrote:

> The real attraction of the birth-control issue was that it could be used to bash Obamacare. It's not proving to be a very effective weapon, however. When birth control is uncoupled from the religious-freedom argument— and when conservatives start talking in ugly ad-hominem language, like Limbaugh's, or clueless anachronistic language, like Santorum's—women, in particular, do not respond well. (Talbot 2012)

Even as there were these attempts to modify the strident positions expressed by Limbaugh and others and to contain the damage done by the prominence of the Catholic bishops, there was doubt among observers that the attack, once unleashed, would be softened. As one historian and author wrote: "The establishment GOP is trying to claw its way back to the center after its monthlong bender over birth control, breast cancer, and slutty law students. The question is, will the sexual fundamentalists in the base and Rick Santorum let them?" (Cohen 2012c).

South Carolina Republican governor Nikki Haley explained why she thought this was a spurious issue to worry about in the heat of a presidential campaign: "Women don't care about contraception," she said (Devlin 2012). But Toobin explains why the emergence of the tea party doesn't necessarily remove this as a topic of discussion but instead plays into a focus on issues on which the American electorate was not as conservative anymore:

> When the Tea Party first appeared as a national political force, in 2009, it was often described as libertarian—focused mostly on lowering taxes and

repealing health-care reform. Social issues, it appeared, were distinctly secondary concerns. This view now appears precisely wrong. Following their victories in the 2010 midterm elections, the Tea Partiers and their allies have proven to be preoccupied with, even obsessed by, social issues—most especially abortion. (Toobin 2012b)

Progressive groups (and women's groups and reproductive rights groups) used the ongoing issues of what they termed the "Republican War on Women" to rally support (and fundraising). For example, one group captured it in portraying the Republicans as out of touch with modern women: "You and I know that it's 2012 and not 1952. Republicans don't. They've decided now's the time to declare an all-out war on women" (Tanden 2012).

Even though the bishops were agitated by the Obamacare contraception issue, and though even Obama supporters (like the Catholic progressive political analyst and writer E. J. Dionne, Jr.) thought that the Obama administration had misplayed the issue, there was also a long history (as discussed in Chapter 4) of American Catholics' independence from the bishops. As *New York Times* columnist Frank Bruni explains:

> Most American Catholics don't share their appointed leaders' qualms with the pill, condoms and such. . . . American Catholics have been merrily ignoring the church's official position on contraception for many years, often with the blessing of lower-level clerics. (Bruni 2012b)

Columnist Maureen Dowd, referring to a poll of American Catholics, supported this notion:

> So I wasn't surprised to see the Gallup poll Tuesday showing that 82 percent of U.S. Catholics say birth control is morally acceptable. Gallup tested the morality of 18 issues, and birth control came out on top as the most acceptable, beating divorce, which garnered 67 percent approval, and "buying and wearing clothing made of animal fur," which got a 60 percent thumbs-up. (Dowd 2012d)

Another poll trumpeted that the percentage of Carbolic women who had even used birth control was at 98% (Guttmacher Institute 2012), disabusing some of the notion that the celibate male bishops' pronouncements on the subject—and that of the church, dating back to 1968's papal encyclical *Humanae Vitae*—was in touch with the modernization and worldview of the female American Catholic (Paul VI 1968) Some political analysts downplayed the capacity of such a culture war issue to have any effect upon the 2012 election, especially regarding the salience of same-sex marriage and other culture war issues as drivers in the 2012 election (among undecided voters). To one: "The only thing likely to move these undecided voters is the economy and whether they decide things are getting better or getting worse and/but whose fault it is. Everything else is just noise" (Cilliza 2012c). But Obama strategists appreciated the significance of some of Romney's positions, as well as some he moved closer to during the primary season (and many that would become enshrined in the 2012 platform at the Republican National Convention). As one Obama strategist told a reporter: "But we're also gonna say, 'We know where he stands; he's way off to the right on abortion, contraception, immigration, and gay rights.'" (Heilemann 2012b).

However, several issues—some planned, some clearly unplanned (Todd Akin), some consistent but unwise in full explanation (Richard Mourdock, discussed later in this chapter), and some beyond the control of political forces but clearly thought by movement conservatives to be rich with possibility of conservative gathering (Rush Limbaugh on Sandra Fluke)—would combine to raise issues of reproductive freedom into the 2012 campaign in a way that, combined with the ascendant majority hypothesis of Teixeira and others, would become a source of strength, rather than weakness or defensiveness, for the Obama campaign

Obamacare and the Supreme Court

In the middle of the campaign season, a U.S. Supreme Court decision on the Patient Protection and Affordable Care Act loomed as an important element in the campaign, especially to the extent that it was a critical issue of focus and galvanizing for the tea party and conservatives and, indeed, as an agreed-upon dictum for the Republican Party. The complicating factor was always that, since he had initiated a similar reform as governor of Massachusetts, Mitt Romney was ill positioned to give a full-throated attack on the concept and plan (not that he didn't try).

Snipes from primary challengers—such as former Minnesota governor Tim Pawlenty, who referred to the Affordable Care Act as "Obamney-care" (but later endorsed Romney, anyway)—didn't help (Balz 2013).

In anticipation of the June 2012 U.S. Supreme Court decision on the constitutionality of the Patient Protection and Affordable Care Act, pundits and political analysts and strategists were preparing to emerge from the ruling with whatever strategic momentum they could design. For the president's advisors, a loss on the constitutionality of the individual mandate—the key provision that underpinned the means of financing the broad coverage that the act provided for—would have a negative effect. But the Court said that the mandate could be construed as a tax: "Because the Constitution permits such a tax, it is not our role to forbid it, or to pass upon its wisdom or fairness":

> The Framers created a Federal Government of limited powers, and assigned to this Court the duty of enforcing those limits. The Court does so today. But the Court does not express any opinion on the wisdom of the Affordable Care Act. Under the Constitution, that judgment is reserved to the people. (*National Federation of Independent Business et al. v. Sebelius* 2012)

Pundits mentioned it as a "huge political win" for Obama. At the same time, FOX News quickly focused on the opt-out provisions. Senator Rubio's comment was that, while the ACA was ruled constitutional, it didn't mean that it was good politics, good law, or good for the economy. Rubio expressed hope that the November 2012 elections would bring a Republican majority to both houses of the Congress—and to the Presidency—which would result in the repeal of the law. To conservatives, was Chief Justice Roberts a sellout? One t-shirt available featured his face and one word; "Coward." To some, he was too concerned about the legacy of the court, perhaps mindful of its lowered rating recently as an institution. To one, "John Roberts' opinion seems to clearly suggest he wants to keep the Supreme Court out of political fights and was willing to destroy his reputation with conservatives to do it" (Erickson 2012).

Romney was poorly positioned to capitalize on the sentiment, since he had supported the individual mandate as governor of Massachusetts, which had passed the prototype legislation that the federal effort had been based upon—the individual mandate, a key piece of the plan. It had, after all, been a policy idea created by the American Enterprise Institute, a conservative think tank. Romney's response, in front of a banner reading, "Help us against the liberal agenda. . . . And it's killing jobs across the country," was pointed: "What the Court did not do on its last day in session, I will do on my first if elected President of the United States" (LoGiurato 2012). Sarah Palin used the brevity of a tweet to express her displeasure: "Obama lied to the American people. Again. He said it wasn't a tax. Obama lies; freedom dies." (Palin 2012).

Debates

The three debates were, as in prior elections, "must-see TV." They were watched by over 65 million viewers. In the first debate, Romney seemingly surprised Obama—and most of the political analysts—by following Nixon's strategy and portraying his most moderate positions of the general campaign to date. It paid off with higher favorability and competitiveness ratings after the debate, including increased support among women. This move, which at one time seemed necessary, was inevitable, but it had not presented itself during the post-convention summer or during September, perhaps portending a different type of base-activating (and polarized) appeal to voters in the general election. Indeed, Romney's pivot to moderating his views was precisely the move that seemingly flummoxed Obama and produced his detachment and underperformance in the first debate.

Comedian Jay Leno chided Obama for his lackluster performance: "Unemployment is 7.8 percent, the lowest it's been since Obama took office. The Obama campaign said they can't wait to take these statistics and not use them in the next debate" (Leno 2012b). To critics, Obama lost much of his luster in that first debate, undoing (they hoped) some of the exalted consideration that was present in Grant Park in Chicago on Election Night 2008:

> Perhaps Barack Obama can likewise reassert himself in Tuesday evening's town hall in Long Island. But his problem is this: In Denver he didn't just lose a debate—he lost the carefully cultivated illusion of a larger-than-life figure who was Lincoln and FDR and Moses all wrapped in one. (McGurn 2012)

Then Joe Biden gave the full-throated and aggrieved defense of the administration in the vice presidential debate. Comedian Bill Maher tweeted, "Hello 911? There's an old man beating a child on my tv'" (Green 2012). Most analysts agreed Biden had shown up for the fight and gave a clear defense of the Obama administration's choices and accomplishment through his performance (although Ryan also performed well).

The second 2012 presidential debate played to conservatives' view of the role of the mainstream media (or "lamestream," as Rush Limbaugh views it) in supporting the arguments and candidacy of President Obama and the Obama administration. Conservatives and partisans claimed that the moderator in the second presidential debate, CNN's Candy Crowley, was favorable toward Obama (and unfavorable toward Romney) in her questions and demeanor, allowing Obama to slip out of the public unease that the first debate had landed him in. One *FoxNews* reporter wrote: "CNN's Crowley first plays umpire, then joins Team Obama" (Gainor 2012). While providing post-debate analysis, former George H. W. Bush advisor John Sununu said to CNN anchor Soledad O'Brien: "It's always good to come on the groupie channel" (Real Clear Politics 2012b). Rush Limbaugh said the next day on his radio program: "In the real world, she would've committed career suicide last night. . . . She committed an act of journalistic . . . malpractice last night" (Limbaugh 2012c). Following the debate, the Obama-supporting Super-PAC Priorities USA Action re-released its most effective ad from the summer, "Stage," in key swing states. The spot featured an employee at a Bain-controlled company discussing how he had to build a stage for a company announcement, only to find out that the announcement was that the workers had been fired.

Having seen the increase for Romney among women voters after the first debate, some of Obama's focus in the second debate was specifically aimed at loosening that tie. The culture war issues present in the Republican primaries reappeared, with Obama saying of Romney that "he's gone to a more extreme place on social policy than Bush (who didn't support the defunding of Planned Parenthood)." Obama continued:

> A major difference in this campaign is that Governor Romney feels comfortable having politicians in Washington decide the health care decisions for women. . . . These are not just women's issues. These are family issues.

These are economic issues. . . . I've got two daughters, and I want to make sure that they have the same opportunities that anyone's sons have.

There are some things where Governor Romney is different from George Bush. . . . You know, George Bush didn't propose turning Medicare into a voucher. George Bush embraced comprehensive immigration reform. He didn't call for self-deportation. George Bush never suggested that we eliminate funding for Planned Parenthood. So there are differences between Governor Romney and George Bush, but they're not on economic policy. In some ways he's gone to a more extreme place when it comes to social policy. I think that's a mistake. (Commission on Presidential Debates 2012)

To reproductive rights leader Cecile Richards (2014), it was crucial that President Obama referred to reproductive choice several times during the second debate and that many subsequent ads were aired in that time period. These ads were used to further draw sharp distinctions and rally the base. The national Democratic Party was no longer strategically worrying about the Reagan Democrats who had been so central to the culture war for 30 years.

The Final Weeks: A Different Kind of "October Surprise"

Much has been made of the beneficial effect to President Obama in both providing crucial federal government assistance and in cutting through partisan argument when he was welcomed by Republican New Jersey governor Chris Christie to that state to spotlight federal emergency assistance in the aftermath of that year's destructive storm Hurricane Sandy in October 2012. This was in marked contrast to Christie's 2012 Republican National Convention keynote speech, in which he exhorted his party, saying: "It's time to end this era of absentee leadership in the Oval Office and send real leaders to the White House" (NPR 2012). In allowing the president to appear and appeal to potential voters as a problem solver, and in showing that such efforts transcended the partisan bickering that typified the late stages of most presidential campaigns, Christie provided the president with a chance to bolster his favorability ratings at a time when candidates are usually under attack. Christie himself was vilified by Republican partisans. Romney would later express dismay that the storm had landed when it did.

Going against the tradition that a classic "October surprise" is late-season campaign strategic move by a campaign to further its position, Republicans instead also had to deal with a self-inflicted surprise days before the election when Indiana state treasurer and Republican senate candidate Richard Mourdock—a tea party supporter who defeated six-term centrist Republican Richard Lugar in that state's primary—explained in a televised senate debate that he was not in favor of abortion in case of rape, with the reasoning that

> the only exception I have to have an abortion is in the case of the life of the mother. I struggled with it myself for a long time, but I came to realize life is that gift from God. I think that even when life begins in that horrible situation of rape, that it is something that God intended to happen. (McAuliff 2012)

Some Republican senatorial candidates tried to distance themselves from Mourdock. Massachusetts's incumbent senator Scott Brown was first, followed soon by Connecticut's candidate Linda McMahon, who said in a statement: "Richard Mourdock's comments were highly inappropriate and offensive. They do not reflect my beliefs as a woman or a pro-choice candidate." (Both were unsuccessful candidates in November 2012.) Even anti-abortion candidates sought distance from the intemperate Mourdock. A spokesman for Arizona congressman and Republican senatorial candidate Jeff Flake stated: "Jeff Flake's pro-life position has always included exceptions for rape, incest, and to protect the life of the mother, so he does not agree with some of the comments made by other candidates on this issue." Political scientist Larry Sabato observed: "A lot of the Democrats have aired one or more ads about contraception, abortion, Todd Akin, you name it, it's been in there. . . . In those campaigns, the ones that have used this cluster of issues, I would think it reinforces their message" (McAuliff and Siddiqui 2012).

Indiana Democratic Congressman and Democratic senatorial candidate Joe Donnelly, who successfully opposed Mourdock (and stated his own pro-life leanings), commented: " I think for someone running for the United States Senate, it is hurtful to women to survivors of rape and their families to have said this. . . . When you say, in regards to rape, that pregnancy from rape is God's intention that it will happen, I just think that is hurtful and insulting to women, to rape survivors, and to the families" (McAuliff and Siddiqui 2012). President Obama obliged the unfolding of the issue and criticized Indiana candidate Mourdock by reiterating a point about his own stance on women's issues, including reproductive rights issues:

> I don't know how these guys come up with these ideas. Let me make a very simple proposition. Rape is rape. It is a crime. And so these various distinctions about rape don't make too much sense to me—don't make any sense to me. . . . This is exactly why you don't want a bunch of politicians, mostly male, making decisions about women's health care decisions. Women are capable of making these decisions in consultation with their partners, with their doctors. And for politicians to want to intrude in this stuff, oftentimes without any information, is a huge problem. And this is obviously part of what's stake at this election. (Feller 2012)

A campaign that had hoped to focus on the state of the national economy and to portray its nominee as a tested businessman and executive instead found itself increasingly vulnerable for its role in what the Democrats defined as a "War on Women."

Conclusion: The "Ground Game"

In the last seven years, one of the transformations in communications technology has had a decided effect on the American consumer. The "smart phone" reached a saturation point of use by 50% of American households/adults/individuals faster than other notable 20th-century technological advances—faster than color television, telephones, washing machines, and microwave ovens. The cell phone, including the smart phone, and social-networking services like Facebook were instrumental in the surprising ability of the Obama campaign to target voters, especially resulting in their strong showing among youthful voters in 2012, which was unexpected, given the state of the economy as well as common wisdom about the lassitude of young voters when they were displaying an ordinary political vote, rather than an historic one, as they did in 2008.

One revelatory statistic indicated that the Obama campaign had a 1:50 ratio of campaign field staff to contacts with voters in the very contested swing states, like Nevada and Colorado. As one volunteer in Nevada describes the function of "the contacts, both by phone call and face-to-face, [was] to urge the need to vote, to continue contact, to check on the voter's plan for election day or early voting or absentee voting" (Anderson 2012). There is also the challenge of producing a nominee who has exemplified enough conservative mettle in the exposition of his or her policies and positions through a series of challenging, sometimes tedious, usually protracted, and cutting interchanges—which in today's 24/7 media environment includes Twitter, Facebook, Instagram, Reddit, and Tumblr, as well as the ubiquity of amateur and often surreptitious audio and video chronicles of record—for example, the important video of Mitt Romney's melancholy complaint at a 2012 fundraising event that fully 47% of Americans were predisposed to vote for his opponent because of their reliance upon government support and programs. Unfortunately, in that video he also tarnished people he didn't necessarily want to publicly malign—soldiers, the elderly—as well as the many who felt that, instead of being considered parasites on society, they were worthy recipients of aid granted by government to those in need.

With each passing election, data gatherers and strategists are better able to "crunch" and "massage" data and "slice and dice" voters in their many attributes and sub-categories. This activity has long been deployed but has recently become much more attenuated and possible through the use of technology and the wide array of information available about individuals and their proclivities (the National Security Agency issue aside). The highly sophisticated Obama re-election campaign drew upon experts in the data-mining area and applied advances in assembly and communication technologies to their campaign (Alter 2013), something that Republican officials would admit they should have done in their 2013 "post-mortem" (Republican National Committee 2013a). To one volunteer involved in the process,

> the Obama campaign also had a geeky edge to add to that raw passion in the form of superior data and technology. Calls to "clean your data" still ring in my ears: nothing was more important that accurately reporting numbers, so that the in-house IT [information technology] teams could analyse, refresh and recreate our targets and numbers nightly. (Anderson 2012)

At the same time, the Obama campaign orchestrated these use of these skills locally: "[Campaign manager Jim] Messina stressed the hyper-local nature of the reelection campaign's voter contacts, saying 'We ran county commission campaigns in each of these places.'" (Donovan Black 2012). Blending the local focus, the data mining, and the use of social networking together, Messina employed a strategy that fit the changing communications world of America in 2012. As one account described it:

> Messina's bet was the first stage of a two-part strategy. . . . The summer airwave blitz would soften up the opponent in the eyes of voters, but victory would be carried home by Obama's volunteer army on the ground. "We believe that, in this age of saturation television, eventually people are going to throw their TV as far as they can out their window, and look to their neighbors and family to have a discussion about how they've going to vote," Messina said. "And we're going to be integral to that moment— that is our entire moment." (Lizza 2012b)

One volunteer described her experience in the swing state of Nevada:

> The real key to victory, however, was this: we didn't just knock on each door once. We knocked on the doors of known Obama supporters again, and again, and again, until we knew that they knew where and when to vote. And then, we just kept on knocking until they had voted. We provided them with a ride to the polls if they couldn't get there and we redirected them if they turned up at the wrong place. . . . The Democrats registered just under 100,000 new Nevadan voters in the year preceding the election, and there was an 81% turnout to the polls. We eventually won by the biggest margin of all swing states. (Anderson 2012)

On November 6, 2012, Obama won 51% of the popular vote to Romney's 48%. Obama won 332 electoral votes, more than the 270 needed for victory. Obama won almost all of the swing states that the two campaigns had targeted, losing only Indiana and North Carolina from his 2008 list.

Optimistic Romney forces had seen movements and momentum in the large crowds at the end of the campaign and optimistically thought that the predictions of their model maker would come true and pro-vide a close victory on Election Night. It was not to be. That night signaled the transition to a new era in which chastised movement con-servatives and Republican regulars who had thought that the times and signs were right to defeat Barack Obama had to reflect and analyze the ways in which they were connecting—or not connecting—with a changing America.

Whither the Culture War?

The "Unwedging" of Old Frames

The culture war is over and conservatives lost.
—Matt K. Lewis, January 3, 2013

Focus group participants told us that they don't want national or federal focus on abortion or social issues. Republicans ultimately lose.
—Republican pollster/consultant Frank Luntz, November 13, 2012

The battle for our values and religious liberty will only become more intense.
—Gary Bauer, *American Values*, November 7, 2012

On November 6, 2012, Barack Obama concluded his reelection campaign with a somewhat more comfortable margin than many had been predicting even a week earlier, gathering 51% of the popular vote and a sizeable margin with 332 electoral votes. Mitt Romney's vote-modeling team had constructed an altogether different outcome. That optimistic model was built around misconceptions on turnout for Obama in several states, especially among young, minority, and low-income voters.

There would be much lamenting among Republicans and conservatives after the 2012 election results were in. Republican strategist Karl Rove became upset with the news readers on *FoxNews* when that predictably pro-Republican network attempted to call the election for President Obama along with the other major television networks and media outlets at 11:12 p.m. Eastern Standard Time on Election Day. Rove blurted: "I think this is premature [to declare President Obama the winner of Ohio]. We have to be very cautious about intruding into this process" (Weinger 2012). Romney was slow in coming down from his suite to offer his concession speech, which was ultimately very gracious. Reports surfaced that he didn't prepare a concession speech. Paul Ryan particularly looked crestfallen.

As with John McCain in 2008, the handwringing and second guessing after the Romney defeat in November 2012 was widespread, embittered, and immediate. Newt Gingrich reminded analysts that he had criticized Romney throughout the primary season for not being conservative enough, for being a flip-flopper, and for being unappealing to the Republican base in the general election. When the analyses of turnout were completed, they indeed showed that many of those voters who resembled the winning Bush coalition in 2004 had stayed away from voting—"sat on their hands" in the parlance—and contributed to Romney's defeat in crucial swing states like Florida, Virginia, Nevada, and Ohio.

After the immediate response, there were waves of assessment and response. Newt Gingrich added that the "economic fundamentals" favored the Republicans but that "politics beats fundamentals." Former Florida governor Jeb Bush called Romney's campaign "a tragic lost opportunity made more so because it was largely self-inflicted." He described his unease at watching the GOP primary debates, especially Romney's "missteps" on immigration, which "hung like an anvil around his candidacy" (Bush and Bolick 2013). Mitt Romney later commented on the great job that Obama did with the "ground game" and the inability of Romney and the Republicans to reach minorities. To him, it helped enormously that the Obama health policy (i.e., "giving things to the 47%") had great salience for this population:

> MITT ROMNEY: We did very well with the majority population, but not with minority populations. And that was a—that was a failing. That was a real mistake.
>
> WALLACE: Why do you think that was?
>
> MITT ROMNEY: Well, I think the Obamacare attractiveness and feature was something we underestimated in a—particularly among lower incomes. And we just didn't do as—as good a job at connecting with that audience as we should have. (*FoxNews* 2013b)

Romney and Ryan and their strategists made arguments about how well Romney did among the "majority population" (read "whites"). Ryan stated: "I don't think we lost it on those budget issues, especially on Medicare, we clearly didn't lose it on those issues. I think the surprise was some of the turnout, some of the turnout especially in urban areas, which gave President Obama the big margin to win this race" (Shear 2012b).

What do we make of the 2012 results? Was it a "realigning election"? Do we go forward as a country demonstrably changed by the last six years of liberalization and backlash? In the long run, as historians look back at the "Obama years," what might they say about the nature of American society based on these contests?

In the same way that Chapter 1 began with the implications of the election of Barack Obama as American president on November 4, 2008, this concluding chapter begins with his re-election four years later, on November 6, 2012. It presents data on the impact of the millennial generation and the rise of the progressive "ascendant majority" (and issues such as contraception), the suggestion of strategic plans and "rebranding" of the Republican Party and the internecine struggles that has produced, an analysis of the role of polarization in the body politic, and the conclusion, which analyzes these elements and predicts the complications of populism (including "libertarian populism"), the reduced salience/role of social conservatives, and the end, finally, of the potency and relevance of "Reagan Democrats" (Greenberg 2008).

The "Ascendant Majority"

As the Republican Party began to analyze the ways in which it had underperformed at the presidential level in 2012, various strategists and analysts considered a number of factors that caused a seemingly winnable contest against a president in a difficult economic time to be lost. Several of those analysts pointed to the superior outreach and get-out-the-vote actions of the Obama campaign. As the Republican National Committee's self-reflection ("autopsy") report of March 2013 stated: "Our message was weak; our ground game was insufficient; we weren't inclusive; we were behind in both data and digital; our primary and debate process needed improvement. . . . So, there's no one solution: There's a long list of them." (Republican National Committee 2013a).

Many analysts concluded that the combination of young and minority voters that President Obama and the Democrats secured in 2012 were ultimately responsible for the victory in November. To Democratic strategists James Carville and Stan Greenberg,

> the Rising American electorate [RAE] not only delivered huge margins to the President, but also turned out for the President as well. According to estimates in the National Exit survey, voters in the RAE make up nearly half (48 percent) of the 2012 electorate. The number of unmarried Americans, male and female, accounted for the largest change in the composition in the electorate—jumping 6 points to 40 percent in 2012. (Democracy Corps 2012)

With the strong belief of young and minority voters in government not interfering in their personal lives—for example, their very strong support of same-sex marriage, which presumably won't recede in the near future—this has been a societal-level shift. Fully 74% of millennials support same-sex marriage (Pew Research Center 2013d). This phenomenon runs across religious orientation (to greater and lesser degrees), across racial and class lines, and across party affiliation. It also parallels their overwhelming support for the legal reform of marijuana laws. According to a Pew research report, in addition to same-sex marriage and contraception, the younger cohort is also noticeably supportive of a strong government role: "A majority said the government should do more to fix problems" (Pew Research Social and Democratic Trends 2012). One *New York Times* analysis in 2013 described this ascendant majority as "young, liberal and open to big government" (Stolberg 2013a).

The Role of Old-Time "Wedge Issues": Reproductive Rights

When Gallup, Pew, and other polling organizations reported in 2009 and 2010 that Americans' self-description as "pro-choice" had fallen to its lowest level since *Roe*—and, most important, that the self-description had crossed the line to where more than 50% of American

% of each generation who say …

Abortion should be legal in all or most cases

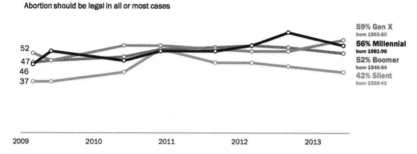

Figure 7.1. Approval for abortion, by generation and year. Courtesy of the Pew Research Center.

described themselves as "pro-life"—it was not surprising then that social conservative Gary Bauer and others found that data to be supportive of a reading of an American society that was trending toward pro-life positions.

Following the success of the use of the concept of "partial-birth abortion" to undercut support for choice positions among the American public (Dombrink and Hillyard 2007), a flurry of activity in mostly red states has taken place over the last several years to pass laws that restrict reproductive rights. Currently, there is a move by several states (and the federal Congress) to enact bans on abortions after 20 weeks using the concept of "fetal pain." This has given hope to social conservatives, who also see the decline in youth self-identifying as pro-choice. Social conservatives like evangelical leader and Baptist theologian Albert Mohler have expressed their support for this concept:

> The pro-life movement must also reflect on the 40th anniversary of *Roe v. Wade*, and there is cause for much humble thankfulness. There has been a great and measurable shift in public opinion on abortion. The extremism of the abortion rights movement has not been appreciated by the American people, who do not see abortion as just any other medical procedure. Younger Americans are more likely than their parents to be pro-life in a general sense. The generation that knows ultrasound pictures on the refrigerator is not going to accept the fact that their unborn sibling is a non-person. (Mohler 2013)

The paradox for social conservatives and those who hope to use these results to challenge *Roe v. Wade* or expand *Planned Parenthood v. Casey* is that Americans continue to respond that they favor keeping *Roe v. Wade* in place. In a 2013 poll, fully 70% of respondents to an NBC/*Wall Street Journal* poll said that they would favor keeping *Roe* (Murray 2013). This level of support has generally been consistent since the ruling in *Roe* in 1973.

Unfortunately for the Republicans in 2012 (and going forward), the issues of reproductive rights veered away from an area where they might have held an advantage—late-term abortions and even funding for Planned Parenthood (Lepore 2011), issues where they hoped to frame the discussion to their advantage and the Democrats' detriment. Instead, the issue frame became focused on rape and contraception—one that is abhorrent, and the other that has been a settled issue for some time. In 2012, 89% of respondents to a Gallup poll reported that contraception was morally acceptable, while only 8% opposed that statement (Newport 2012). Importantly, fully 82% of Catholics responded similarly:

> The Catholic Bishops made the forced mandatory coverage of contraception in the employee health plans of many Catholic hospitals and colleges under the Affordable Care Act an important campaign issue in 2012. They encouraged those who felt that this issue could provide a "wedge" in the same way as gay rights and abortion had done for prior campaigns. However, the focus on contraception was not as beneficial. 40% of American adult women are single, and Obama won these by 36%. Romney carried married women by 11%—this is where contraception and reproductive politics seemed to have its greatest effect. (Newport 2012)

Same-Sex Marriage

As the amicus briefs were being prepared for the 2013 U.S. Supreme Court argument in two marriage equality cases, former George W. Bush administration official and campaign strategist Ken Mehlman (having recently publically announced his gay sexual orientation) assembled a group of Republican officeholders, strategists, and others to submit an amicus brief in the Court's consideration of both the federal Defense

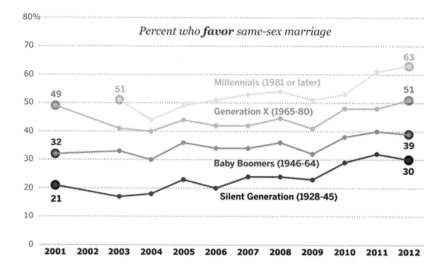

Percent who *favor* same-sex marriage

Millennials (1981 or later)

Generation X (1965-80)

Baby Boomers (1946-64)

Silent Generation (1928-45)

Pew Research Center's Forum on Religion & Public Life

Figure 7.2. Approval for same-sex marriage, by generation and year.

of Marriage Act and the challenge to the constitutionality of California's Proposition 8, the 2008 referendum item that repealed the state's court-decided right to same-sex marriage. Signatories also included several Republican strategists, like former McCain (2008) strategist Steve Schmidt. Schmidt had argued after the 2008 campaign that the Republican Party should avoid stressing the issue that had previously been a centerpiece of social conservative campaigning in the Republican Party (and once an important part of the successful tripartite Reagan-era coalition). Included in the 2013 amicus briefs were other Republican strategists like Alex Castellanos. To some, like David Frum,

> as a conservative concerned with stabilizing families to rely less on government aid, I have been convinced: I've been worrying about the wrong thing. Stopping same-sex marriages does nothing to support families battered by economic adversity. Instead, it excludes and punishes people who seek only to live as conservatives would urge them to live. Treating same-sex partnerships differently from husband-wife marriages only serves to divide and antagonize those who ought to be working together. (Frum 2013)

Pointedly, the 2012 election had not played upon social conservatives' displeasure with the rapid expansion of marriage equality in the country. Much of the strategy had been to avoid the discussion, even as President Obama eventually spoke in its favor, and various Democratic candidates, operatives, and interests groups trumpeted their support for the legal reform. Even as social conservatives like Gary Bauer warned of incursions on religious freedom in the country, these strategists had decided that, especially demographically, offering a strong opposition to a rapidly changing societal social support of marriage equality would be dysfunctional to the party's stability and potential growth. When former Republican governor and 2012 presidential primary candidate Jon Huntsman argued in an article in the *American Conservative* (2013) that marriage equality was a "conservative issue," he was expressing an opinion that was gaining greater currency among former opponents of marriage equality, including those like him who had favored civil unions. Finally, in 2012, when given the choice between only two choices, for the first time a majority of Americans supported same-sex marriage. Similarly, leading conservative litigator and legal scholar Theodore Olson, a founder of the Federalist Society, and former solicitor general in the George W. Bush administration, joined up with fellow litigator David Boies (against whom he had argued in a U.S. Supreme Court case on antitrust and the Microsoft Corporation) to challenge in federal court the validity of California's Proposition 8. That proposition, which was passed by voters there in November 2008, invalidated the May 2008 California state supreme court decision allowing same-sex marriages in the state, but it was eventually set aside by the U.S. Supreme Court (Becker 2014).

Even Rush Limbaugh, thinking prospectively, saw inevitability: "I don't care what this court does with this particular ruling, Proposition 8. I think the inertia is clearly moving in the direction that there is going to be gay marriage at some point nationwide" (Limbaugh 2013).

Growing Diversity

Soon after the 2012 election results were clear, some were astonished at the rapidity at which some conservative analysts (*FoxNews* pundits prominent among them, but also including legislators and Republican

Party strategists) concluded that the changing demographics of the country (the "ascendant majority"), coupled with their party's woeful progress in attracting those voters, convinced them that proposed immigration reform would now be a good and necessary thing for the country. It seems that the electoral growth (and perceived attractiveness) of the growing Latino population has generated a shift in proposed immigration policy among Republicans and conservative elites, including the U.S. Chamber of Commerce and the editorial page of the *Wall Street Journal*. But this was not without some division and analysis as to whether that—or attracting and turning out more conservatives as in 2004—was the path back to electoral competitiveness at the federal level. (And it has not yet been dealt with by the current Congress).

Within a few days after the 2012 presidential election, conservative *FoxNews* analyst Sean Hannity expressed an ameliorative view toward immigration reform:

It's simple to me to fix it [immigration]. . . . I think you control the border first. You create a pathway for those people that are here—you don't say you've got to go home. And that is a position that I've evolved on. Because, you know what, it's got to be resolved. (Byers 2012)

Former President George W. Bush, who had tried to effectuate immigration reform in his second term, argued that immigration reform was needed to boost the economy. Republican Senator Lindsay Graham warned that Republicans are "in a demographic death spiral" and will fail in their effort to win the presidency if the party blocks an immigration overhaul.

To political analyst Thomas Edsall, the demographic issues were dire:

Right now, the Republican Party is caught in a vise: it is dependent on support from a diminishing but still powerful constituency of socially, culturally and morally conservative whites from across the economic spectrum, many of whom oppose gay rights and immigration reform. But the party must also deal with two ascendant constituencies: culturally tolerant—indeed, permissive—young and suburban voters of all races, along with Hispanic voters who place a priority on immigration reform that gives undocumented aliens a path to citizenship. (Edsall 2013d)

Mitt Romney's chief strategist agreed:

> The greatest appeal that the Obama campaign had for Hispanic voters turned out to be Obamacare. And they ran a tremendous amount of their advertising appealing to Hispanic voters . . . because an extraordinary percentage of Hispanic voters are uninsured. And that was smart politics. They did it well. The [Republican] party was also known as the party that was against Obamacare, and that hurt us. . . . I hope and pray we can get through this stage and . . . come to some sort of [immigration] consensus . . . and go forward. (*ABC News* 2013)

Obama strategist David Plouffe, successful in 2008 as Obama's campaign manager and afterward an advisor to the president, made the point in an interview that the Obama 2012 campaign's success with Latinos ran deep:

> The Hispanic voters in Nevada, Colorado and New Mexico don't give a damn about Marco Rubio, the Tea Party Cuban-American from Florida. You know what? We won the Cuban vote! And it's because younger Cubans are behaving differently than their parents. It's probably my favorite stat of the whole campaign. So this notion that Marco Rubio is going to heal their problems—it's not even sophomoric; it's juvenile! And by the way: the bigger problem they've got with Latinos isn't immigration. It's their economic policies and health care. The group that supported the president's health care bill the most? Latinos. (Draper 2013a)

Beyond the growing number of Latinos, and their very poor ability to attract African American voters, the Republicans also demonstrated problems with Asian Americans, with Romney only winning 26% of the vote. To one observer:

> these days, the GOP strikes Asian-Americans, along with many other Americans, as hostile to science and modernity. . . . in a sense, Asian-Americans are not just another ethnic group waiting for a politician to march in a parade, eat some exotic food, and then announce a community grant or shill for votes. Rather, they are also a subset of high-tech America, and one thing is clear: high-tech America is not in love with the Republican Party. (Green 2013)

These developments have generated a significant debate within Republican strategy circles and have informed the basis of how that party would respond to the "ascendant majority" demographic issue.

In another notable demographic shift, America is rapidly becoming a "nation of singles." In a break from the past, today (and in the future) sociologists explain that the typical American will spend more of his or her life unmarried rather than married, and that time mostly living alone (Klinenberg 2012). Healthcare and reproductive freedom are important to this heterogeneous group. In his comprehensive and incisive work on the 2012 election, *Washington Post* political report Dan Balz examined the potential impact of the "ascendant majority." In 2012, he noted, only 20% of American households contained a nuclear family of a man, a woman/wife, and children. In 1952, it was 80%. To him, social conservatives decry the decline of the family, but "large portions of the progressive community are indifferent or hostile to the idea of the nuclear family, while many on the right argue that it's key to a Republican revival." (Balz 2013).

Rebrand? The Republican Post-mortem

Louisiana governor Bobby Jindal, often mentioned as a rising star in the Republican Party (and one who could bring ethnic diversity to a political party often criticized for its whiteness) was one of the first to be strong in his analysis of the party's direction." At the GOP's January 2013 retreat, he said: "We must stop being the stupid party . . . I'm serious. It's time for a new Republican Party that talks like adults" (Rosenthal 2013). Jindal re-emphasized this in an interview:

> The fact that we lost a winnable election has caused Republicans to take this very, very seriously. . . . I don't think it's just a marketing change. I don't think it's just cosmetic changes. It is going to require some serious changes, not in principles, but in the way we talk and act. (Vanderhei and Allen 2013)

Former Florida governor Jeb Bush, a son and brother of two former presidents and someone often mentioned as a potential presidential candidate himself, had another take: "We need to learn from past mistakes. . . . All too often we're associated with being 'anti' everything. . . .

Way too many people believe Republicans are anti-immigrant, anti-woman, anti-science, anti-gay, anti-worker" (Martha Moore 2013). One Republican donor summarized his frustration, saying that the GOP has had too many candidates who are "nut cases . . . I don't think anybody anywhere with any sense is going to want to elect a candidate who says, 'If your daughter gets raped, it's God's will'" (Vogel et al. 2013). To Republican pollster and strategist Frank Luntz, culture war issues were the root cause: "Focus group participants told us that they don't want national or federal focus on abortion or social issues. Republicans ultimately lose" (Luntz 2013).

The post-mortem done by the Republican National Committee, labeled the "Growth and Opportunity Project," was blunt in its articulation of the party's short fallings in November 2012.

The official report was cautionary yet optimistic:

> The GOP today is a tale of two parties. One of them, the gubernatorial wing, is growing and successful. The other, the federal wing, is increasingly marginalizing itself, and unless changes are made, it will be increasingly difficult for Republicans to win another presidential election in the near future. . . . The Republican Party needs to stop talking to itself. We have become expert in how to provide ideological reinforcement to like-minded people, but devastatingly we have lost the ability to be persuasive with, or welcoming to, those who do not agree with us on every issue. (Republican National Committee 2013a: 6–7)

To progressives who may have taken delight in the November 2012 outcome, and thus the post-mortem, there was a strong sense of schadenfreude:

> President Obama's campaign staff boasted throughout the 2012 race that the GOP's dismissal of minority concerns, intolerance towards gays, celebration of wealth, and fetishism of Ronald Reagan would doom them in November. Today the RNC released their official response: "You were right." (Sarlin 2013)

What, then is the takeaway message of conservatives after the 2012 election? No one wants to be considered obsolete or irrelevant, and social conservatives have rejected the notion that their framing and efforts led to the party's demise in what was thought to be a very winnable presidential race. Some observers, analyzing the election data from a nonpartisan position, considered the Republican image and "branding" issues of import:

> While there are no catchy phrases for the Republicans of 2013, their image problems are readily apparent in national polls. The GOP has come to be seen as the more extreme party, the side unwilling to compromise or negotiate seriously to tackle the economic turmoil that challenges the nation. (Kohut 2013)

But then David Frum writes, chastising the culture war politics and polarization:

> I have also been swayed by an intensifying awareness of the harm culture-war politics has done to my party. Culture-war politics have isolated the GOP from the America of the present and future, fastening it to politics of nostalgia for a (mis)remembered past. Culture-war politics have substituted for relevant cultural policies aimed at encouraging the raising of children within married families. Worst of all, culture-war politics has taught the GOP to talk to America as if the nation were split into hostile halves, as if more separates Americans than unites them. (Frum 2013)

But leading social conservative Gary Bauer countered:

> Anyone who thinks we need a "values truce," or who suggests we should toss aside life, liberty and marriage in order to deal with the "important" stuff, is missing the crisis that is plaguing America's urban centers and spreading rapidly—the breakdown of the family. Nearly half of all children today are born to unwed mothers.
>
> There is a moral dimension to marriage, and to suggest otherwise is simply absurd. But I would ask my libertarian friends this question: If the country can't get marriage right, why would such a country ever get the moral dimension of imposing debt on the next generation? If we can't comprehend the sanctity of life, why should we understand the virtue of balanced budgets? (Bauer 2013a)

The "Growth and Opportunity Project" (Republican National Committee 2013a) spent a good deal of space on discussing the importance of diversity and demography and the simultaneous importance of immigration as a topic of legislative policy reform that would aid in this endeavor:

> If Hispanic Americans perceive that a GOP nominee or candidate does not want them in the United States (i.e. self-deportation), they will not pay attention to our next sentence. It does not matter what we say about education, jobs or the economy; if Hispanics think we do not want them here, they will close their ears to our policies. In the last election, Governor Romney received just 27 percent of the Hispanic vote. . . . Among the steps Republicans take in the Hispanic community and beyond, we must embrace and champion comprehensive immigration reform. If we do not, our Party's appeal will continue to shrink to its core constituencies only. We also believe that comprehensive immigration reform is consistent with Republican economic policies that promote job growth and opportunity for all. (Republican National Committee 2013a: 10)

Reflecting on the turnout and decidedly Democratic and Obama advantage in Latino votes in November 2012, and the realization of the growth in the Latino population in the United States in the near future, influential Republicans began to argue for shifts in the party's approach to immigration reform, lest they get so far behind in a demographic sense that they would not be competitive in national races in the near future. This view was expressed by Jeb Bush and Clint Bolick in a 2013 book. It was embraced by Senator John McCain and was seconded by two architects of the George W. Bush immigration reform measure of his second term, Karl Rove and Bush himself. Whether immigration emerges as such a vehicle is unclear, for a variety of reasons. In some ways, it has developed as a polarizing issue in ways that are equivalent to the moral resentment of other aspects of the culture war, such as abortion. Immigration is an issue in which one must distinguish between racism and bigoted comments and some of the class-based fears and competitions as a source of the resentment. To those for whom a steady flow of illegal Mexican immigrants has brought job competition to their specific trades and unskilled, low- skilled, and medium-skilled manual labor jobs, illegal immigration has posed a real threat to their livelihood. Republican strategist and political analyst Steve Schmidt succinctly commented that the rise in ethnic diversity among the American population should trigger a strategic response from Republican policy-makers, concluding that "this is a simple math equation" (Draper 2013b). To former George W. Bush campaign official Ken Mehlman, "A political party that ignores demography or ignores broader cultural trends does so at its own peril" (Bruni 2012d).

One major analysis by Sean Trende argued that the Republican Party could re-emerge with dominance by reclaiming those who had failed to turnout in 2012, rather than focus on an outreach to Latinos and other persons of color. Trende considered questionable any theory that such Latinos would vote Republican, since they had been proving to be reliable Democratic voters in recent elections. In his four-part series, Trende started his analysis of race in the 2012 election with "The Case of the Missing White Voters, Revisited" (Trende 2013a; the other parts to the series are Trende 2013b, 2013c, and 2013d). One of his arguments has generated discussion: his assertion that the "ascendant majority" analysis isn't necessarily the correct reading of the 2012 election. To him, "the 2012 elections actually weren't about a demographic explosion with non-white voters. . . . Instead, they were about a large group of white voters not showing up" (Trende 2013a). Ronald Brownstein presents this sentiment, as he himself presents data on why the Democratic Party is relying less on working-class white voters:

> But through 2013, the sense of demographic urgency inside the GOP has palpably dissipated. Instead, an array of conservative analysts has advanced a competing theory for Romney's defeat: He failed to generate a big enough margin among whites. (Brownstein 2013d)

This internecine struggle, between an establishment side of the Republican Party and a movement conservative side (often with roots in the 2010 tea party surge), then became visible, especially circling around House Speaker John Boehner for his supposed apostasy in brokering a debt-ceiling deal. The conservative Internet activist Matt Drudge wrote, "It's now Authoritarian vs. Libertarian. Since Democrats vs. Republicans has been obliterated, no real difference between parties" and "Why would anyone vote Republican? Please give reason. Raised taxes; marching us off to war again; approved more NSA snooping. WHO ARE THEY?!" (Drudge 2013).

Movement conservative and blogger Erick Erickson (*RedState*) expressed the unwillingness of some to reduce their conservative impulses and fold into a big Republican tent:

> We inch ever closer to a third party as Republican Leaders commit suicide by lie. The leadership willing to fight the base to pass a terrible immigration reform bill won't lift a finger to fight against Obamacare. . . . The best chance we, as conservative activists have, is to deliver the third party from within by picking off Republican establishment leaders in primaries. (Erickson 2013)

In 2015, it is too early to say decisively which of several competing narratives will emerge triumphant. The idea of the victorious Obama was seen by many in 2008 and 2009 as an embrace of change and a sign that the culture war would wane (a good thing to those who foretold its demise). The backlash against the Obama administration, phrased in the angry "town hall" meetings of 2009, coalescing in the tea party opposition of 2009 and 2010, and culminating in the midterm election reversals of November 2010, offered a competing narrative—a rejection of the Obama change and a chance to "take our country back." The shooting of Democratic congresswoman Gabrielle Giffords in Arizona in January 2011 (and the killing of six other persons), at a time when the second narrative would seem to be ascendant, called that interpretation into question (Balz and Cohen 2011; Zoellner 2011). However indirectly connected to the political divisiveness, the violence unleashed on a moderate Democratic congresswoman and the killing of a federal judge and a nine-year old girl, among others, caused a pause in American discourse, as the often conflicting values of civility and partisanship became discordant.

Analyses of the early 2012 election season warned that it was focusing so much on the economy that the issues that had underpinned the culture were eclipsed. Indeed, several analysts and advisors had suggested to Republican Party strategists that they should downplay the issue of same-sex marriage as a useful issue for organizing and encouraging voter turnout in recent elections. Instead, it was suggested, the demographic trends would harm the "Republican brand" with younger voters. This schema seemed sturdily constructed with a "non–culture warrior" as the leading Republican primary candidate (in the person of former Massachusetts governor Mitt Romney). The economy—polling as it did so high on Americans' list of important issues—seemed likely to dominate discussions. Despite detours into the issues of contraception coverage under the Affordable Care Act, the rights of religious institutions, and both sides' claiming that the other side was waging a "War on Women," the culture war issues seemed destined to be an undernote in the 2012 election (Alexander 2012). But they weren't, as Chapter 6 demonstrated.

As the tea party—which was so successful in the midterm elections of 2010—veered into the more candidate-oriented nomination process of 2011–2012, it became vulnerable to the wishes and reserved power of the Republican establishment. By the end of the nominating process, with the nomination of the former Massachusetts governor all but assured, the party that had positioned itself as the voice of the anti-government, anti-Obama tea party movement found itself promoting a candidate who had caused divisions in the nominating process because he had espoused pro-choice sentiments in Massachusetts and had enacted a form of health coverage plan that was the template for the much-maligned "Obamacare."

The Limits of Social Conservatism

Chapters 3, 4, and 5 each took one strand of analysis looking at why the change contemplated by tea party adherents, and particularly their sizeable social conservative element, won't be forthcoming. Chapter 6 examined that weakness in the context of the 2012 presidential election. What all these chapters refer back to are the data (as demonstrated in various polls and studies) that show that tea party members and adherents were *more* likely than their other Republican Party member counterparts to oppose abortion and otherwise take social conservative positions.

Chapter 3 presented the rapid sea change in America and among Americans toward gay rights generally and marriage equality specifically. This is important because of the historical importance of gay rights as one of the pillars of social conservative opposition to modernity in the United States (the others being reproductive rights and the role of religion). From the period starting from 2004, when it was a significant national "wedge" issue drawing socially conservative voters, marriage equality has declined dramatically as both an issue of support among conservatives generally (especially millennials) and in the Republican Party, which has chosen not to pursue the issue as a way of attracting voters. There may not be many Republican politicians supporting marriage equality currently, but there is also little desire to fan the flames by raising it as a key issue. (In fact, Karl Rove even envisioned the possibility of a GOP presidential nominee in 2016 who supported marriage equality.) The pivot here instead has been toward embracing federalism as a way of also supporting states that have passed DOMA laws and restrictive abortion laws or the defunding of Planned Parenthood. The shift of the salience of the same-sex marriage issue after 2004 was seen as early as polling in 2006 (Pew Research Center 2006) and can best be characterized by the rapidity of the ascent of its tenets.

Here is the conundrum—is the opposition to reproductive rights the way back for socially conservative culture warriors in the era of a changing American demographic landscape? In supporting *Roe v. Wade* in the compromise decision in *Planned Parenthood v. Casey* in 1992 (which was attacked by both progressives and conservatives and hailed by few), Justice O'Connor pointed out that a generation of women had grown up with *Roe* and the expectation that they will have control over their reproductive destiny—and thus their lives. This is even more true now more than 20 years after *Casey* (and more than 40 after *Roe*). In June 2013, Maggie Gallagher, of a socially conservative organization, the National Organization for Marriage, called the U.S. Supreme Court progressive decisions in *United States v. Windsor* and California's Proposition 8 (*Hollingsworth v. Perry*) "our generation's *Roe*" (*National Review* 2013). One point of this book is that this wishful statement has been proven wrong by the movement of several states toward marriage equality as well as by American attitudes generally in a fairly rapid pattern. It has caused the Republican Party to approach this issue rarely and gingerly. Even conservative icons like Rush Limbaugh have declared that same-sex marriage is inevitable and shouldn't form a basis for conservative regeneration, re-emergence, and "redominance" (Limbaugh 2013). And Gallagher herself noted that anti–marriage equality spokespersons didn't rate coverage on even *FoxNews* (Becker 2014).

Chapter 4 explained why appeals to conservative religiosity will fall short and why religion will not be the source of a regeneration of support for social conservative policies in the near future in America. When conservatives decry the reduction of religious freedom, they overlook the long tradition of Catholic and mainline Protestant denominations (and Jews) in supporting liberal to moderate polices, from bingo, to aid-in-dying in Catholic hospitals, to the embracing of gays and lesbians in mainline churches. There are only about 56,000 Catholic women religious in the United States, and they are a markedly older group (Gibson 2012; Leadership Conference of Women Religious 2013). Still, the 2012 work of the organization Network and its leader, Sr. Simone Campbell, and the popularity of the "Nuns on the Bus" tour, showed that their progressive views still had resonance (Campbell 2014; Miller 2014). This was especially true for the many Catholics who may have been taught by such nuns or who consider them an equal counterpart to the bishops and the Vatican when it comes to articulating "Catholic values."

Certainly, this view of religion doesn't fit the evangelical Protestant groups that have grown in size and impact since Falwell and 1980. But they were never the whole story of religion in America, and they certainly now have a reduced profile. Witness Russell Moore, the new president of the Southern Baptist Convention's Ethics and Religious Liberty Commission (a platform for social conservative policy for his predecessor, Richard Land), who stated in 2013 that he would prioritize a return to inner spirituality and place less of an emphasis on the political sphere (without calling for a retreat; see Russell Moore 2013). This is far different from the increased connection that Falwell and others preached (Riley 2013). To many, it was this close association of religion and politics and the politicization of religion that is most troublesome—though we tend to talk more about the "religicization" of politics and the "theocracy" that Kevin Phillips and others critiqued. (Phillips 2006). To many younger Americans today, it is precisely this heavy-handedness that has turned them off to religion. In addition to sullying younger Americans views of politics, it has also affected their view of religion. To many of the millennials, religion is overly conservative and overly political.

Chapter 5 explained why any reliance on America's changing demographics to revive this social conservatism is misguided. Specifically, any hope that the rising Latino population will be as socially conservative as their elders—and will care about those issues more than they care about health care, education, and the economy—seem far-fetched. Chapter 6 examined these issues in the context of the 2012 presidential election. Taken together, these three chapters explain why the predictions of the effect and rootedness of the tea party backlash, presented in Chapter 2, or the continuing influence of social conservatives, is not likely to shape the near future of American politics and public policy.

Conclusion: The Withering of the Culture War

The 2008 predictions of realignment and hopes for post-partisanship after the Obama election seem far distant now. Whether the near future will hold vestiges of past conflicts, sometimes dressed as other efforts (deficit reduction) or taking a secondary role to economic concerns (such as a "truce" in the culture wars), is unclear (Ferguson 2010). It is unlikely that the election of 2012 offered a solution to this or whether electoral politics themselves are the measure of where Americans have moved on these issues and on the salience they attribute to them. However represented, the American culture war seems to have been redefined for a new era. With the new Democratic majority of minorities, millennials, young progressive upscale and college-educated whites—especially women—by 2012, Beinart's (2009) enthusiastic prediction of the perceived end of the culture war as previously constituted could be proved right.

Some progressives expect backlash, again. Frank Rich worries that "no matter how many times the conservative bogeyman came back from the dead along the way, liberals were shocked at every resurrection . . . we were always gobsmacked" (Rich 2012d). Polarization and hyper-partisanship are the "new normal." There were still bumper stickers in 2014 that read: "Honk for Impeachment" and "Worst President Ever." It is hard to envision a national presidential candidate arguing in 2016 that America craves—and needs—a return to bipartisanship, to undo the gridlock that characterizes Washington these days and that has led to historically low numbers for Americans' estimation of Congress. According to Gallup, only 10% of Americans now have a "great deal" or "quite a lot" of confidence in Congress. (The president and the Supreme Court do somewhat better—36% for the presidency; Blow 2013).

Figure 7.3. An anti-Obamacare protest.

Republicans can point to their success in the states, where they control 23 states with both governor seats and legislatures, as signs that they are a dominant force. Maybe the forces that the *Citizens United* decision unleashed, demonstrably unsuccessful in 2012, will coalesce and matter in subsequent elections: groups like Americans for Prosperity (the Koch brothers), American Crossroads (Karl Rove), and now the Conservative Victory Project (Karl Rove). Maybe a racial or gender or age or personality change at the top—perhaps Sen. Marco Rubio, promising diversity, or Sen. Rand Paul, with a libertarian bent—can turn things back in their favor. At the federal level, Republicans continued to hold the House of Representatives and took the Senate in 2014, relying upon winning currently Democratic held Senate seats in states that voted against President Obama in 2012 and in which he is unpopular.

Conservatism will probably continue to maintain its status, maybe even more so as the results of the 2012 presidential election allows conservatives in the Republican Party to win arguments and run candidates who agree with a more decidedly conservative direction. The effects of moderate Republicans being "primaried" (because they are considered to be "Republicans in Name Only"—RINOs) suggests that this could continue to shape the profile of Congress and the debates that ensue. But then the "establishment" resurgence in 2014 party primaries suggests that any depiction of the nature and size and influence of conservatives is complex—have the ideas and personae of the tea party fizzled and foundered, or have their ideas been absorbed into mainstream conservative republican dogma by now?

Although some think this rift is overstated (Holland 2013), one result of the creation of the Reagan Democrats for the Republican Party has been to privilege those social conservatives. This can be unproblematic until the social conservatives come into conflict with the big business–economic conservatives whom Reagan also relied upon. In 2007 Mike Huckabee referred to the pro-growth anti-tax group Club for Growth as the "Club for Greed" (Rubin 2007). In 2012, Newt Gingrich and Rick Perry both criticized Republican primary front-runner Mitt Romney as being a "vulture capitalist." Observing this, Rush Limbaugh, referring to candidates Perry and Gingrich and their criticism of Romney's financial history, realized that there is an inherent conflict, given the absorption of so many blue-collar social conservatives into the Republican Party from Reagan forward. This problematic populism naturally engenders discontent:

> So now we've got all this talk about corporate raiders, vulture capitalists plundering companies and greed. All this talk about sucking the blood out of companies and leaving corpses? Limiting how much somebody can make in profits? This is the language of leftists like Michael Moore and Oliver Stone. They popularized this. This is the way Fidel Castro thinks, or says he thinks. (Limbaugh 2012a)

But it seems likely in the near future that *social* conservatives will be reduced in their importance—along with the salience of their favored issues. They have enjoyed a favored position they have maintained since the reverend Jerry Falwell first organized the "Moral Majority" and contributed to a Ronald Reagan victory in 1980. Is abortion a winning issue for social conservatives? Or is there some evidence that the gender gap and the 2012 results were more than the errant statements by some fringe candidates? As the last few decades have demonstrated, women's reproductive rights may continue to be a wedge that is used to help divide voters—with the 20-week abortion ban and restrictive abortion laws in many states attempting to undo the holdings of *Roe*. But any efforts will have to come to grips with how the discussion on contraception as part of the Affordable Care Act compromises unfolded. There is a belief by many women that any party that continues to run candidates who speak so freely and insensitively about rape, as two Republican senatorial candidates did in 2012, are far out of touch with women's rights in the modern era. The 12-percentage-point gender deficit among females for Mitt Romney in the 2012 election illustrates this (Easley 2012b). It is questionable whether a renewed emphasis by social conservatives on second-term abortion or fetal pain will end up reversing this situation.

Still, what are we to make of the claims of social conservatives that there is a downward change in the pro-choice self-labeling? This takes some parsing out. It may reflect the fact that, for both sides, there is more rallying around the poles—supporting access to reproductive choice, for example. What about reproductive rights and the influence of technology? The birth-control pill revolutionized sex. The morning-after pill, used by almost one-quarter of women 18–24, has expanded that, and the various fights over RU-486 (Greenhouse 2013) may well do the same. It is this creeping normalization that ardent pro-life activists fear and hope to stop through the courts (as well as in the states where they wield influence). There was real decline in pro-choice self-identification after 2008, although the positive responses supporting *Roe* complicate that interpretation. And some of that can be placed at the youngest voters, who may not be as "conscienticized" on reproductive issues as their 1970s predecessors (Erdreich 2013).

Meanwhile, there remain many who are perplexed as to why such seemingly lower-level issues are the crux of controversy while global economic situations, poverty and its relief, and international conflicts and wars compete for attention (Skolnick 2005). The distaste (disgust, disappointment, alarm) that many people have over the inability of the federal government to solve problems that the general population place a high priority on—energy and the cost of gas, jobs, and the dictates of a changing economy in a world of globalization in which young people have different (lowered) expectations of what their future holds in store for them—is evident (Skolnick 2005). One locus for continuation of the culture war seems to be at the state, rather than federal or national, level. It is possible that we will see a greater division or "balkanization" into redder red states and bluer blue states as the newly created laws on abortion restriction, and existing laws against same-sex marriage, indicate.

Even with the growth of the "unaffiliated" status, especially among younger cohorts, religion should continue to be an influential topic in the American near future. America is a religious country, especially by industrial country standards. But with a rising number of religiously "unaffiliated" citizens (or "nones," as the term often used) in the country, and a much larger number of them among the millennial generation of young Americans, the capacity of explicitly religious appeals to gather in undecided or "cross-pressured" voters appears to be diminishing. And it is unclear how many politically attuned people will agree with Gary Bauer's sentiment and make it a core issue for them going forward: "It seems as though America is on the verge of criminalizing the Book of Genesis. And with Obamacare's assault on conscience, the danger to religious liberty cannot be overstated" (Bauer 2013b). With a downturn in the culture war, is America back to life pre-Falwell? Will the post-Falwell era now resemble the pre-Falwell era, in smoldering resentment, exacerbated not only by the success of the libertine left, but also defined by anxiety over the economic rise of China and the economic decline of America, more pronounced in certain sectors and regions?

The new conservative backlash post-2012 appears to be rooted is a visceral dislike of government programs, from the Affordable Care Act ("Obamacare") to entitlement programs. The intense dislike of Obamacare, from the "You lie!" moments of the Congress in 2009, to the willingness of some conservative representatives to support a shutdown of the federal government in order to eviscerate the ACA, continues to hold sway over a large portion of conservative Republicans politicians, even if it is not supported by the American public. (And when 10 Republican governors expressed their desire to have a federally funded expansion of the Medicaid program that is part of the ACA, it was apparent that such an obstructionist strategy might have limits from various directions.)

The 2012 election, as carried out by the Obama team, and as suggested by Ruy Teixeira and other strategists, showed that an "ascendant majority" of youth (especially single women), including liberals and people of color, means that the Democratic Party no longer is trying to figure out ways to bring the "Reagan Democrats" back into the fold. Post- Falwell, given this new electoral base, the Obama administration and the Democrats don't need to worry as much about "right-leaning whites"—socially conservative, mostly white, working-class voters. Brownstein presented the snapshot of this remarkable change: non-college educated whites were 62% of the voters in 1984; in 2012, they were only 36% (Brownstein 2013d). Stan Greenberg had argued that the 2008 election had proved the demise of the Reagan Democrats (Greenberg 2008). Results from 2012 proved him prescient.

One way to interpret the events and results of 2012 is to suggest that we are facing the end of the "Reagan Democrats." It is not the end of conservatism, although the contours it takes will necessarily be different. Will there be "Paul Ryan Democrats," persons for whom budgetary strictures, entitlement reform, and austerity measures are central and motivating? Will there be "Rand Paul Democrats," who are libertarian in their leaning, wanting to reduce foreign military adventures and keep government out of the regulation of business and regulation of personal morality? Will there be "Marco Rubio Democrats," Latinos who are pro-business and wishing for a limited government but also mindful of diversity and interested in immigration reform?

The Republican Party could win the presidency again soon, maybe even in 2016—lessons are learned, funds and resources are refocused, and events do intervene. The 2014 electoral results can be read in that way, but even they were not a referendum on social conservative issues.

Whether one of these possibilities or others emerge, it seems apparent that the culture war "wedge issues" that have been successful for over 30 years in politics appear to be losing their edge. This "unwedging" is what characterizes America in 2015, especially amid the effect of the rising importance of the millennial generation. It seems improbable that these wedge issues will again regain their potency.

BIBLIOGRAPHY

Abcarian, Robin. 2012. "Birth Control Uproar: The 60's All over Again." *Los Angeles Times*. March 25, A10 at col. 1.

ABC News. 2000. "Tommy Lee Jones' Speech Text." www.abcnews.go.com. August 16.

ABC News. 2012. "Rush Limbaugh/Sandra Fluke controversy." *YouTube*. www.youtube. com/watch?v=Jfb9f7yFYgw.

ABC News. 2013. "Roundtable II: This Week in Politics." *This Week*. www.abcnews. go.com. February 17.

ABC News/Washington Post Poll. 2010. "Anger, Anti-incumbency; It's Frustration, 2010-Style." *ABC News*. www.abcnews.go.com. June 8.

Abramowitz, Alan I. 2010. *The Disappearing Center: Engaged Citizens, Polarization and American Democracy*. New Haven, Conn.: Yale University Press.

Abramowitz, Alan I. 2012a. *The Polarized Public: Why American Government Is So Dysfunctional*. Upper Saddle River, N.J.: Prentice-Hall.

Abramowitz, Alan I. 2012b. "Grand Old Tea Party: Partisan Polarization and the Rise of the Tea Party Movement." In Lawrence Rosenthal and Christine Trost, eds., *Steep: The Precipitous Rise of the Tea Party*. Berkeley: University of California Press.

Acemoglu, Daron. 2012. "The World Our Grandchildren Will Inherit: The Rights Revolution and Beyond." Working Paper no. 17994. Washington, D.C.: National Bureau of Economic Research. April.

Adler, Ben. 2010. "Palin Pushes Back against 'Lamestream' Media over Video." *Newsweek*. www.newsweek.com/blogs/the-gaggle. August 10.

Aguilar, Alfonso. 2013. "My Fellow Republicans, Wake Up—Latinos Are Today's Reagan Democrats." American Principles Project. www.americanprinciplesproject.com. July 18.

Aguilar, Rose. 2008. *Red Highways: A Liberal's Journey into the Heartland*. Sausalito, Calif.: PoliPointPress.

Alexander, Bryan. 2013. "Oscars in 'Good Hands' with Ellen DeGeneres." *USA Today*. www.usatoday.com. August 4.

Alexander, Rachel. 2012. "The Democrats' War on Women." *Townhall.com*. www. townhallcom. May 2.

Allen, Mike. 2011. Playbook. *Politico*. www.politico.com. February 13.

Alter, Jonathan. 2010. *The Promise: President Obama, Year One*. New York: Simon & Schuster.

Alter, Jonathan. 2011. *The Promise: President Obama, Year One*. Revised paperback ed. New York: Simon & Schuster.

Alter, Jonathan. 2013. *The Center Holds: Obama and His Enemies*. New York: Simon & Schuster.

Americans for Prosperity. 2010. www.americansfor prosperity.com.

Anderson, Maisie. 2012. "How Obama's 2012 Election Ground Game Won Nevada." *Guardian*. www.theguardian.com. November 21.

Antle, W. James, III. 2012a. "Getting It Right Next Time." *American Spectator*. www. spectator.org. April 11.

Antle, W. James, III. 2012b. "Supreme Beings." *American Spectator*. www.spectator.org. July 2.

Aravosis, John. 2007. "'Barack, the Magic Negro'—a New Song Played on the Rush Limbaugh Show." *Americablog*. www.americablog.com. April 30.

Archdiocese of Philadelphia. 2009. "Executive Order on Embryonic Stem Cells a Sad Victory of Politics over Science and Ethics, Says Cardinal Rigali." www.archphila. org. March 9.

ARIS (American Religious Identification Surveys). 2008. "ARIS 2008 Summary Report." Hartford, Conn.: Trinity College. http://commons.trincoll.edu/aris/ publications/2008–2/aris-2008-summary-report. March.

Armbinder, Matt. 2012a. "How Democrats Will Explain an Obama Loss." *The Week*. www.theweek.com. November 2.

Armbinder, Matt. 2012b. "How Republcians Will Explain a Romney Loss." *The Week*. www.theweek.com. November 2.

Bacon, Perry, Jr. 2010. "Republican Fundraising Document Portrays Democrats as Evil." *Washington Post*. www.washingtonpost.com. March 4.

Bai, Matt. 2012. "The Caucus: Why Bain Attacks Could Stick to Romney." *New York Times*. www.thecaucus.blogs.nytimes.com. January 9.

Bailey, Fenton, and Randy Barbato, dirs. 2011. *The Strange History of Don't Ask, Don't Tell*. Documentary. New York: HBO Films.

Baldassare, Mark. 2002. *A California State of Mind: The Conflicted Voter in a Changing World*. Berkeley: University of California Press.

Ball, Molly. 2012a. "Have Democrats Succeeded in Pre-destroying Romney?" *Atlantic*. www.theatlantic.com. February 2.

Ball, Molly. 2012b. "Praise for Obama on Immigration from the Religious." *Atlantic*. www.theatlantic.com. June 15.

Balmer, Randall. 2009a. "By the Way: A Radically Conservative 'Faith-Based Initiative.'" *Religion Dispatches*. www.religiondispatches.org. February 7.

Balmer, Randall. 2009b. "By the Way: James Dobson Departs the Scene," *Religion Dispatches*. www.religiondispatches.org. March 3.

Balz, Dan. 2010. "Voters' Anger at Washington May Overpower Any Fixes." *Washington Post*. www.washingtonpost.com. May 19.

Balz, Dan. 2012a. "Mitt Romney and the Enthusiasm Gap." *Washington Post*. www. washingtonpost.com. February 8.

Balz, Dan. 2012b. "A Most Poisonous Campaign." *Washington Post*. www.washingtonpost.com. August 15.

Balz, Dan. 2013. *Collision 2012: Obama vs. Romney and the Future of Elections in America*. New York: Viking/A James H. Silberman Book.

Balz, Dan, and Jon Cohen. 2010. "Voters' Support for Members of Congress Is at an All-Time Low, Poll Finds." *Washington Post*. www.washingtonpost.com. June 8.

Balz, Dan, and Jon Cohen. 2011. "Poll Shows High Marks for Obama on Tucson, Low Regard for Political Dialogue." *Washington Post*. www.washingtonpost.com. January 18.

Balz, Dan, and Jon Cohen. 2012. "Obama Holds Edge over Romney in General Election Matchup, Poll Finds." *Washington Post*. www.washingtonpost.com. February 5.

Balz, Dan, and Haynes Johnson. 2009. *The Battle for America 2008: The Story of an Extraordinary Election*. New York: Viking.

Banerjee, Neela. 2008. "Taking Their Faith, But Not Their Politics, to the People." *New York Times*. www.nytimes.com. June 1.

Barabak, Mark. 2010. "Passion Alone Can't Sustain the 'Tea Party.'" *Los Angeles Times*. June 25, A1 at col. 6.

Barr, Andy. 2009. "Mike Huckabee: Big Tent Will 'Kill' GOP," *Politico*. www.politico.com. December 9.

Barr, Andy. 2011. "Poll: Majority Favors Gay Marriage." *Politico*. www.politico.com. March 18.

Barrett, Wes. 2011. "Palin on Obama's Call to Win the Future: WTF?" *FoxNews*. www.foxnews.com. January 27.

Barro, Josh. 2013. "The Ticker: Republicans' No-Fingerprints Strategy on Gay Marriage." *Bloomberg*. www.bloomberg.com. January 30.

Bassett, Laura. 2012. "Obama Administration Announces New Decision on Birth Control, to Chagrin of Religious Groups." *Huffington Post*. www.huffingtonpost.com. January 20.

Bauder, David. 2009. "Young Get News from Comedy Central." *CBS News*. www.cbsnews.com. February 11.

Bauer, Gary. 2006. "Congress Returns This Week." *American Values*. www.ouramericanvalues.org. April 24.

Bauer, Gary. 2007. "Have They No Shame?" *American Values*. www.ouramericanvalues.org. May 18.

Bauer, Gary. 2008. "Just Say NO!" *American Values*. www.ouramericanvalues.org. November 8.

Bauer, Gary. 2009a. "Great Shame?" *American Values*. www.ouramericanvalues.org. February 23.

Bauer, Gary. 2009b. "Long Live the Culture Wars." *Politico*. www.politico.com. September 10.

Bauer, Gary. 2010a. "Who Are the Tea Party Patriots?" *American Values*. www.ouramericanvalues.org. February 25.

Bauer, Gary. 2010b. "Obamacare = Abortion." *American Values*. www.ouramericanvalues.org. March 12.

Bauer, Gary. 2011a. "Divisive Rhetoric Is Not the Problem." *American Values*. www.ouramericanvalues.org. January 31.

Bauer, Gary. 2011b. "Call Your Congressmen Now." *American Values*. www.ourameri-canvalues.org. March 23.

Bauer, Gary. 2011c. "The New Red Menace." *American Values*. www.ouramericanvalues. org. April 1.

Bauer, Gary. 2011d. "Help Us Defend Our Values." *American Values*. www.ourameri-canvalues.org. September 27.

Bauer, Gary. 2012. *American Values*. www.ouramericanvalues.org. May 10.

Bauer, Gary. 2013a. "Will America Survive This Fight?" *American Values*. www.oura-mericanvalues.org. March 26.

Bauer, Gary. 2013b. "Taking a Bullet for Biblical Marriage." *American Values*. www. ouramericanvalues.org. August 15.

Beaujon, Andrew. 2012. "Karl Rove Challenges Fox's Election-Night Data Operation in 'Odd Civil War.'" *Poynter*. www.poynter.org. November 7.

Becker, Jo. 2014. *Forcing the Spring: Inside the Fight for Marriage Equality*. New York: Penguin Press.

Bedard, Paul. 2013. "Limbaugh, Hannity, Levin Eyed as 2016 GOP Debate Moderators." *Washington Examiner*. http:washingtonexaminer.com. August 15.

Beinart, Peter. 2009. "The End of the Culture Wars." *Daily Beast*. www.thedailybeast. com. January 26.

Beinart, Peter. 2010. "Palin Is the New McGovern." *Daily Beast*. www.thedailybeast. com. September 20.

Bell, Jeffrey. 2010. "A Big Tent on the Right." *Weekly Standard* 16, no. 1 (September 20). www.weeklystandard.com.

Bell, Jeffrey. 2012. *The Case for Polarized Politics: Why America Needs Social Conserva-tism*. Jackson, Tenn.: Encounter Books.

Ben Barka, Mokhtar. 2010. "Rôle et place des « guerres culturelles » dans le discours politique des évangéliques nord-américains." Presented at the conference "Culture Wars in the United States: The Politics of Religious Conservatism in Obama's Time." Simultaneous translation. Center for United States Studies, University of Quebec at Montreal. October 14.

Benen, Steve. 2010. "Political Animal." *Washington Monthly*. April 15.

Benen, Steve. 2012. "Romney Rejects Concern for the 'Very Poor.'" *The Rachel Maddow Show*. http://maddowblog.msnbc.com, February 1.

Bennett, William. 2010. "The Corner: Saturday Night Beck." *National Review*. www. nro.com. January 21.

Berkowitz, Bill. 2008a. "Even after an Obama Victory Reports of the Death of the Reli-gious Right Are Greatly Exaggerated." *Religion Dispatches*. http://religiondispatches. com. November 5.

Berkowitz, Bill. 2008b. "No Retreat, No Surrender: The Future for the Religious Right." *The Smirking Chimp*. www.smirkingchimp.com. December 9.

Berlet, Chip. 2009. "Toxic to Democracy: Conspiracy Theories, Demonization, and Scapegoating." Report. Somerville, MA: Political Research Associates.

Bernstein, Jonathan. 2011. "Sarah Palin's Missed Presidential Moment." *New Republic.* www.tnr.com. January 10.

Bishin, Benjamin G., and Charles Anthony Smith. 2011. "Gay Rights and Legislative Wrongs: Representation of Gays and Lesbians." Unpublished paper. Irvine: University of California, Irvine.

Black, Donovan. 2012. "It's the Ground Game, Stupid . . ." *Politico.* www.politico.com. November 10.

Black, William K. 2012. "Romney Dooms His Candidacy by Doing the Full Murray." *Huffington Post.* www.huffingtonpost.com. September 18.

Blake, Aaron. 2012a. "Has the Tea Party Become a GOP Liability?" *Washington Post.* www.washingtonpost.com. April 5.

Blake, Aaron. 2012b. "The Fix: President Obama: Pot-Stirrer." *Washington Post.* www.washingtonpost.com. June 15.

Blake, Aaron. 2012c. "Romney Moves to Embrace 'Romneycare.'" *Washington Post.* www.washingtonpost.com. August 8.

Blankenhorn, David. 2007. *The Future of Marriage.* New York: Encounter Books.

Blankenhorn, David. 2012. "How My View on Gay Marriage Changed." *New York Times.* www.nytimes.com. June 22.

Blankenhorn, David, and Jonathan Rauch. 2009. "A Reconciliation on Gay Marriage." *New York Times.* www.nytimes.com. February 22.

Blow, Charles. 2012a. "Newt's Southern Strategy." *New York Times.* www.nytimes.com. January 20.

Blow, Charles. 2012b. "Down with Religion?" *New York Times.* http://campaignstops. blogs.nytimes.com. May 30.

Blow, Charles. 2013. "The Era of Disbelief." *New York Times.* www.nytimes.com. September 4.

Blue, Miranda. 2013. "Phyllis Schlafly's Totally Coherent Defense of North Carolina's Voter Suppression Law." *Right Wing Watch.* www.rightwingwatch.org. August 20.

Boaz, David, and David Kirby. 2012. *The Libertarian Vote: Swing Voters, Tea Parties, and the Fiscally Conservative, Socially Liberal Center.* Washington, D.C.: Cato Institute.

Boehnerteaparty. 2011. "Pro-life Demands to Mr. Boehner and House GOP." www. boehnerteaparty.com. n.d.

Boren, David, Christine Todd Whitman, and William Cohen. 2012. "Challenging the Two Parties." *Politico,* www.politico.com. March 16.

Bottum, Joseph. 2013. "The Things We Share: A Catholic's Case for Same-Sex Marriage." *Commonweal.* www.commonwealmagazine.org. August 23.

Boule, Jamelle. 2012. "Who Is to Blame for Polarization?" *American Prospect.* http:// prospect.org. January 30.

Bowler, Shaun, and Todd Donovan. 2000. *Demanding Choices: Opinion, Voting, and Direct Democracy.* Ann Arbor: University of Michigan Press.

Brazile, Donna. 2010. "GOP Fosters Anger on Phony Issues." CNN. www.cnn.com. June 8.

Brock, William, Jack Danforth, Trent Lott, and Don Nickles. 2012. "Opinions: A Republican Litmus Test Harms Our Party." *Washington Post.* www.washingtonpost. com. March 22.

Bromwich, David. 2010. "The Rebel Germ." *New York Review of Books.* November 25.

Broockman, David E., and Christopher Skovron. 2013. "What Politicians Believe about Their Constituents: Asymmetric Misperceptions and Prospects for Constituency Control." Working paper. Department of Political Science, University of California, Berkeley.

Brooks, Albert. 2011. *2030: The Real Story of What Happens to America.* New York: St. Martin's Press.

Brooks, David. 2010. "Midwest at Dusk." *New York Times.* www.nytimes.com. November 4.

Brooks, David. 2012a. "A New Social Agenda." *New York Times.* www.nytimes.com. January 5.

Brooks, David. 2012b. "Where Are the Liberals?" *New York Times.* www.nytimes.com. January 10.

Brooks, David. 2012c. "Dullest Campaign Ever." *New York Times.* www.nytimes.com. July 31.

Brooks, David. 2012d. "Thurston Howell Romney." *New York Times.* www.nytimes.com. September 18.

Brooks, Joanna. 2012a. "Will Romney's VP Pick Win Catholic Voters?" *Religion Dispatches.* www.religiondispatches.com. August 11.

Brooks, Joanna. 2012b. "'Mitt Romney Style'—a Virtually Religion Free 2012 Contest?" *Religion Dispatches.* www.religiondispatches.com. October 29.

Brown, Carrie Budoff, and Jake Sherman. 2013. "New Immigration Attack: It's Too Pricey." *Politico.* www.politico.com. April 9.

Brown, Sherrod. 2010. "How to Fight Tea Party's Faux Populism." *USA Today.* October 9.

Brownstein, Ronald. 2010. "Mistrust: Election's Wild Card." *Los Angeles Times.* June 25, A21 at col. 1.

Brownstein, Ronald. 2012a. "The Gray and the Brown: The Generational Mismatch." *National Journal.* http://decoded.nationaljournal.com. April 16.

Brownstein, Ronald. 2012b. "Obama Sinks to Historic Lows among Blue-Collar Men." *National Journal.* http://decoded.nationaljournal.com. July 11.

Brownstein, Ronald. 2013a. "Why Obama Is Giving Up on Right-Leaning Whites." *National Journal.* January 31.

Brownstein, Ronald. 2013b. "Courting the Twenty-Somethings." *National Journal.* February 14.

Brownstein, Ronald. 2013c. "Why the Culture Wars Now Favor Democrats." *National Journal.* April 4.

Brownstein, Ronald. 2013d. "Republicans Can't Win with White Voters Alone." *Atlantic.* www.theatlantic.com. September 7.

Bruni, Frank. 2011. "Pizzas and Pessimism." *New York Times.* www.nytimes.com. October 30.

Bruni, Frank. 2012a. "A Campaign Pruned of Bushes." *New York Times Sunday Review*. www.nytimes.com. January 8, 3 at col. 1.

Bruni, Frank. 2012b. "Many Kinds of Catholic." *New York Times*. www.nytimes.com. March 19.

Bruni, Frank. 2012c. "The Emotional Tug of Obama." *New York Times*. www.nytimes. com. May 26.

Bruni, Frank. 2012d. "The GOP's Gay Trajectory." *New York Times*. www.nytimes.com. June 9.

Bruni, Frank. 2012e. "An Election Half Empty." *New York Times*. www.nytimes.com. June 12.

Bruni, Frank. 2012f. "Risky Ryan." *New York Times*. www.nytimes.com. August 8.

Bruns, Alex. 2012. "The Rundown: Mitt Romney and Evangelical Voters: An Arranged Marriage." *PBS Newshour*. PBS. www.pbs.com. July 11.

Buchanan, Patrick J. 1992. Address to the Republican National Convention, Houston, Texas. *American Rhetoric*. www.americanrhetoric.com. August 17.

Buckley, William F., Jr. 1955. "Our Mission Statement." *National Review* 1, no. 1 (November 19): 5. www.nationalreview.com/articles/223549/our-mission-statement/ william-f-buckley-jr.

Burke, Daniel. 2009. "Big Churches Posting Small Membership Losses." *Pew Forum on Religion and Public Life*. www.pewforum.org. March 2.

Burns, Alexander. 2011. "Right Grapples with Social 'Truce.'" *Politico*. www.politico. com. March 2.

Burns, Alexander. 2012. "Obama's Demographic Gamble." *Politico*. www.politico.com. November 3.

Burns, Alexander. 2013. "GOP Elite Embraces Portman Gay Marriage Switch." *Politico*. www.politico.com. March 15.

Bush, Jeb, and Clint Bolick. 2013. *Immigration Wars: Forging an American Solution*. New York: Threshhold edition/Simon & Schuster.

Butler, Anthea. 2012. *The Gospel according to Sarah: How Sarah Palin's Tea Party Angels Are Galvanizing the Religious Right*. New York: New Press.

Byers, Dylan. 2012. "Hannity: I've 'Evolved' on Immigration and Support a 'Pathway to Citizenship.'" *Politico*. www.politico.com. November 8.

Calmes, Jackie. 2013. "For 'Party of Business,' Allegiances Are Shifting." *New York Times*. www.nytimes.com. January 15.

Campbell, David E., and Robert D. Putnam. 2011. "Crashing the Tea Party." *New York Times*. www.nytimes.com. August 16.

Campbell, Simone. 2014. *A Nun on the Bus: How All of Us Can Create Hope, Change, and Community*. New York: HarperOne.

Canuelos, Peter S. 2008. "Mix of Politics, Religion Appears a Recipe for Disaster." *Boston Globe*. June 3.

Capehart, Jonathan. 2013. "The GOP Better Listen to Colin Powell." *Washington Post*. www.washingtonpost.com. January 14.

Carlson, Margaret. 2012. "How Democrats Lost Their Way on Abortion." *Bloomberg*. September 5.

Carmon, Irin. 2012. "Rove's Plan Won't Work: Don't Count on Latino Social Conservatism." *Salon*. www.salon.com. November 23.

Carrillo, Hector. 2013. "How Latin Culture Got More Gay." *New York Times*. www.nytimes.com. May 15.

Carroll, James. 2013. "Who Am I to Judge?" *New Yorker*. www.newyorker.com. December 17.

Carter, Joe. 2010. "There Is No Tea Party Movement." *First Things*. www.firstthings.com. November 3.

Carville, James, and Stan Greenberg. 2012. *It's the Middle Class, Stupid!* New York: Blue Rider Press/Penguin.

Cassata, Donna. 2011. "Tea Partiers Demanding Budget Cuts Say Military in the Mix, Setting Up Hard Choices for Reps." Associated Press. January 23.

Cassidy, John. 2012. "The Meaning of Rick: Santorum Could Be for Real," *New Yorker*. www.newyorker.com/online/blogs. February 8.

Catanese, David, and Manu Raju. 2012. "GOP's Problems Exposed in Struggle for Senate." *Politico*. www.politico.com. October 18.

CBS News. 2011. "Poll: High Marks for Obama's State of the Union Speech." CBS News Polling Unit. www.cbsnews.com. January 25.

CBS News. 2012. "Luntz: GOP Has to Learn Language of the American People." November 14.

Centers for Disease Control. 2009. *"Nearly 44 Million in United States without Health Insurance in 2008." Atlanta*: Centers for Disease Control *Newsroom*. July 1.

Chait, Jonathan. 2010. "Conservative Hatred vs. Liberal Hatred." *New Republic*. www.tnr.com. July 28.

Chait, Jonathan. 2011a. "The Pathology of Repeal." *New Republic*. www.tnr.com. February 2.

Chait, Jonathan. 2011b. "Obama 'Very Vulnerable'?" *New Republic*. www.tnr.com. February 12.

Chait, Jonathan. 2012. "The Real Romney Captured on Tape Turns Out to Be a Sneering Plutocrat." *New Republic*. www.tnr.com. September 17.

Chellew-Hodge, Candace. 2012. "Surprises in Survey of Hispanics on Homosexuality." *Religion Dispatches*. www.religiondispatches.com. April 16.

Christian Broadcasting Network. 2001. *The 700 Club with Pat Robertson*. September 13.

Cillizza, Chris. 2012a. "The Fix: In GOP Circles, Some Wonder Whether the Party Needs to Lose Big to Eventually Win." *Washington Post*. www.washingtonpost.com. March 4.

Cillizza, Chris. 2012b. "The Fix: Is the Tea Party Still Relevant?" *Washington Post*. www.washingtonpost.com. April 22.

Cillizza, Chris. 2012c. "The Fix: Gay Marriage? Bullying? Voters Don't Care." *Washington Post*. www.washingtonpost.com. May 23.

Cillizza, Chris. 2012d. "The Fix: Did Republicans Lose The Health Care Battle but Win the Health Care War?" *Washington Post*. www.washingtonpost.com. June 29.

Cirilli, Kevin. 2013. "Steve Schmidt: CPAC 'Star Wars Bar Scene.'" *Politico.* www.politico.com. February 26.

Clift, Eleanor. 2012. "Why the Democrats Backed a Gay-Marriage Plank for the Party Convention." *Newsweek/Daily Beast.* July 31.

Clift, Eleanor. 2013. "How Obama and the Democrats Could Win on Gun Control—by Losing." *Daily Beast.* www.thedailybeast.com. January 21.

Clines, Francis X. 1996. "Spiro T. Agnew, Point Man for Nixon Who Resigned Vice Presidency, Dies at 77." *New York Times.* www.nytimes.com. September 19.

Clinton, Bill. 2013. "It's Time to Overturn DOMA." *Washington Post.* www.washingtonpost.com. March 7.

Clinton, William J. 1993. "Remarks Announcing the Nomination of Ruth Bader Ginsburg to Be a Supreme Court Associate Justice." At the *American Presidency Project,* established by Gerhard Peters and John T. Woolley. www.presidency.ucsb.edu. June 14.

CNBC. 2009. "Rick Santelli's Shout Heard 'round the World." www.cnbc.com. February 22.

CNN. 2000. "Sen. John McCain Attacks Pat Robertson, Jerry Falwell, Republican Establishment as Harming GOP Ideals." February 28.

CNN. 2007a . "The Death of Reverend Jerry Falwell." *CNN Larry King Live.* www.transcripts.cnn.com. May 15.

CNN. 2007b. "God's Warriors." Original air date August 23.

CNN. 2009. "Obama Overturns Bush Policy on Stem Cells." www.cnn.com. March 9.

CNN. 2010. "Palin Hits Campaign Trail for Anti-abortion Group." May 14.

CNN. 2012. "Political Ticker: Palin on Open Convention: Anything Is Possible." www.politicalticker.blogs.cnn.com. March 6.

Cohen, Jon, and Dan Balz. 2011. "Poll: Whites without College Degrees Especially Pessimistic about Economy." *Washington Post.* www.washingtonpost.com. February 22.

Cohen, Martin. 2010. Panel presentation, "The Tea Party and the Right: Fractures and Alliances within the Republican Party and other groups on the Right," at the conference "Fractures, Alliances and Mobilizations in the Age of Obama: Emerging Analyses of the 'Tea Party Movement.'" Center for the Comparative Study of Right-Wing Movements, University of California, Berkeley. October 22.

Cohen, Micah. 2012. "FiveThirtyEight: Signs of Shift among African-Americans on Same-Sex Marriage." *New York Times.* http://fivethirtyeight.blogs.nytimes.com. May 25.

Cohen, Nancy. 2012a. *Delirium: How the Sexual Counterrevolution Is Polarizing America.* Berkeley: Counterpoint Press.

Cohen, Nancy. 2012b. "Excerpt: Delirium: How the Sexual Counterrevolution Is Polarizing America." *Nervous Breakdown.* www.thenervousbreakdown.com. March 17.

Cohen, Nancy. 2012c. "3 Signs the National GOP Is over Its Birth Control Bender." www.nancylcohen.com. March 19.

Cohen, Tom. 2012. "Santorum Challenges Policy on Prenatal Testing." CNN. www.cnn.com. February 20.

Cohn, Jonathan. 2012. "Blue States are from Scandinavia, Red States are from Guatemala." *New Republic.* www.tnr.com. October 5.

Cohn, Nate. 2012. "The Conventions Didn't Fix Romney's Favorability Problem." *New Republic*. www.tnr.com. September 13.

Collins, Gail. 2012a. "March of Non-Mitts." *New York Times*. www.nytimes.com. January 5.

Collins, Gail. 2012b. *As Texas Goes: How the Lone Star State Hijacked the American Agenda*. New York: Norton.

Commission on Presidential Debates. 2012. "October 16, 2012 Debate Transcript." Washington, D.C.: Commission on Presidential Debates. www.debates.org. October 16.

Conason, Joe. 2008. "How Did That Realignment Work Out for You, Republicans?" *Salon*. www.salon.com. November 10.

Condon, George E., Jr. 2012. "Catholic Backlash against Obama Grows." *National Journal*. www.nationaljournal.com. February 1.

Congregation for the Doctrine of the Faith. 2012. "Doctrinal Assessment of the Leadership Conference of Women Religious." Vatican City: Vatican. April 18.

Corn, David. 2013. "Secret Tape: Top GOP Consultant Luntz Calls Limbaugh 'Problematic.'" *Mother Jones*. www.motherjones.com. April 25.

Coulter, Ann. 2014. "Gop Crafts Plan to Wreck the Country, Lose Voters." *Townhall. com*. www.townhall.com. January 29.

Cowan, Jon, and Evan Wolfson. 2010. "A GOP Surprise." *Los Angeles Times*. October 13, A21 at col. 1.

Craig, Barbara Hinkson, and David M. O'Brien. 1993. *Abortion and American Politics*. Chatham, N.J.: Chatham House.

Danforth, John. 2005. "In the Name of Politics." *New York Times*. www.nytimes.com. March 30.

Davey, Monica. 2010. "In Iowa, Other Issues Crowd Out Gay Marriage." *New York Times*. www.nytimes.com. June 7.

Davidson, Amy. 2012a. "A War on Nuns?" *New Yorker*. www.newyorker.com/news/amy-davidson/a-war-on-nuns. April 19.

Davidson, Amy. 2012b. "The War on Nuns: Two Women Go to Rome." *New Yorker*. www.newyorker.com/news/amy-davidson/the-war-on-nuns-two-women-go-to-rome. June 1.

Davis, Lanny J. 2008. "The Obama Realignment: This Could Be the Start of a Lasting Democratic Majority Like That Created by FDR." *Wall Street Journal*. http://online.wsj.com. November 6.

Decker, Cathleen. 2009. "Support for Gay Marriage Varies Widely among Racial and Ethnic Groups: The *Los Angeles Times* Poll." *Los Angeles Times*. June 20.

D'Emilio, John. 2000. "Cycles of Change, Questions of Strategy: The Gay and Lesbian Movement after Fifty Years." In Craig Rimmerman et al., eds., *The Politics of Gay Rights*. Chicago: University of Chicago Press.

Democracy Corps. 2009. "Rush Limbaugh Weighs Down Heavily on Republicans." www.democracycorps.com/National-Surveys/rush-limbaugh-weighs-down-heavily-on-republicans. March 11.

Democracy Corps. 2012. "The Role of the Rising American Electorate in the 2012 Election." www.democracycorps.com/National-Surveys/the-role-of-the-rising-american-electorate-in-the-2012-election. November 14.

Devlin, Sarah. 2012. "Gov. Nikki Haley on *The View*: 'Women Don't Care about Contraception.'" www.mediate.com. April 3.

Dewan, Shaila. 2010. "To Court Blacks, Foes of Abortion Make Racial Case." *New York Times*. www.nytimes.com. February 26.

Dickerson, John. 2012a. "Not Jeb Bush's GOP." *Slate*. www.slate.com. June 11.

Dickerson, John. 2012b. "Why Romney Is Still Struggling to Get on-Message." *Slate*. www.slate.com. July 5.

Dillon, Michelle. 2011. "What Is Core to American Catholics in 2011." *National Catholic Reporter*. www.ncronline.com. October 24.

Dionne, E. J., Jr. 2008a. *Souled Out: Reclaiming Faith and Politics after the Religious Right*. Princeton, N.J.: Princeton University Press.

Dionne, E. J., Jr. 2008b. "A Gamble for Obama . . . and a Risk for Rick Warren, Too," *Washington Post*. www.washingtonpost.com. December 23.

Dionne, E. J., Jr. 2010. "The Tea Party: Tempest in a Very Small Teapot." *Washington Post*. www.washingtonpost.com. September 23.

Dionne, E. J., Jr. 2012a. "Obama Does the Right Thing on Contraception." *Washington Post*. www.washingtonpost.com.. February 10.

Dionne, E. J., Jr. 2012b. "Contraception and the Cost of the Culture War." *Washington Post*. www.washingtonpost.com. February 12.

Dionne, E. J., Jr. 2012c. "What Romney Won on Super Tuesday." *Commonweal*. www.commonwealmagazine.org. March 7.

Dionne, E. J., Jr. 2012d. *Our Divided Political Heart: The Battle for the American Idea in an Age of Discontent*. New York: Bloomsbury.

Dionne, E. J., Jr. 2013. "The Tea Party's Ghost." *Commonweal*. February 22.

Dionne, E. J., Jr., and John C. Green. 2008. "The Religion and American Politics: More Secular, More Evangelical . . . or Both?" In Ruy Teixeira, ed., *Red, Blue and Purple America: The Future of Election Demographics*. Washington, D.C.: Brookings.

Dobson, James C. 2008. "Dr. Dobson: 'We Won't Be Silenced,'" *CitizenLink*. www.citizenlink.org. November 25.

Dobson, James C., and Focus on the Family Action. 2008. "2008 Values Voter Pledge." *CitizenLink*. www.citizenlink.org. February 5.

Dodds, Graham G. 2010. "Crusade or Charade? The Religious Right and the Culture Wars." Presented at the conference "Culture Wars in the United States: The Politics of Religious Conservatism in Obama's Time." Center for United States Studies, University of Quebec at Montreal. October 14.

Dombrink, John. 2005. "Red, Blue, and Purple: American Views on Personal Morality and the Law." *Dissent* 52, no. 2 (Spring): 87–92.

Dombrink, John. 2009a. "After Falwell: Shifts and Continuities in the Culture War and the Role of Religion in America." Presented at the Religion and Public Life Seminar, University of Southern California. April 3.

Dombrink, John. 2009b. "The Long Culture War? The Vitality of 'Wedge Issues' in the Obama Era." Presented at The Inside Edge Foundation for Education, Irvine, Calif. October 28.

Dombrink, John. 2010a. "After the Culture War? Shifts and Continuities in the Obama Era and Beyond." Presented at the Boisi Center for Religion and American Public Life, Boston College. February 17.

Dombrink, John. 2010b. "Crime, Morality, and Bioethics in America: The Religious Right and the 'Culture Wars.'" Presented at the Centre for Health Governance, Law and Ethics; the Sydney Institute of Criminology; and the Centre for Values, Ethics and Law in Medicine, University of Sydney. August 31.

Dombrink, John. 2010c. "After Falwell: Shifts and Continuities in American Religion and Culture Wars in the Obama Era." Presented at the Research Unit for the Study of Society, Law and Religion, University of Adelaide. September 1.

Dombrink, John. 2010d. "The American Culture Wars: Birthers and Tea Parties and Abortion . . . Oh my!" Presented at the Department of Criminal Justice, Texas Christian University, Fort Worth. September 16.

Dombrink, John. 2010e. "After the Culture War? Shifts and Continuities in American Religious Conservatism." Presented at the conference "Culture Wars in the United States: The Politics of Religious Conservatism in Obama's Time." Center for United States Studies, University of Quebec at Montreal. October 14.

Dombrink, John, and Daniel Hillyard. 2007. *Sin No More: From Abortion to Stem Cells, Understanding Crime, Law and Morality in America*. New York: NYU Press.

Dorning, Mike. 2012. "Obama Prospects Improve as Swing State Economies Improve." *Bloomberg*. www.bloomberg.com. May 22.

Dorrien, Gary. 2012. "The Reagan Era, Still Going." *Religion Dispatches*. www.religion-dispatches.org. March 7.

Douthat, Ross. 2010. "Why We Have a Culture War." *New York Times*. www.nytimes.com. September 21.

Douthat, Ross. 2012a. "Personal and Political." *New York Times Sunday Review*. www.nytimes.com. January 8, 12 at col. 1.

Douthat, Ross. 2012b. "The Persistence of the Culture War." *New York Times*. www.campaignstops.blogs.nytimes.com. February 8.

Douthat, Ross. 2012c. "The Future of the Santorum Coalition." *New York Times*. www.campaignstops.blogs.nytimes.com. March 7.

Douthat, Ross. 2012d. *Bad Religion: How We Became a Nation of Heretics*. New York: Free Press.

Douthat, Ross. 2012e. "Playing for 51 Percent." *New York Times*. www.campaignstops.blogs.nytimes.com. July 11.

Douthat, Ross. 2013. "Libertarian Populism and Its Critics." *New York Times*. http://douthat.blogs.nytimes.com. August 16.

Dowd, Maureen. 2012a. "The Grating Santorum." *New York Times Sunday Review*. www.nytimes.com. January 8, 12 at col. 1.

Dowd, Maureen. 2012b. "Rick's Religious Fanaticism." *New York Times*. www.nytimes. com. February 21.

Dowd, Maureen. 2012c. "Ghastly Outdated Party." *New York Times*. www.nytimes.com. March 26.

Dowd, Maureen. 2012d. "Father Doesn't Know Best." *New York Times*. www.nytimes. com. May 22.

Dowd, Maureen. 2012e. "Fight Really about Controlling Women, Not Birth." *New York Times*. www.nytimes.com. May 28.

Dowd, Maureen. 2012f. "When Cruelty Is Cute." *New York Times*. www.nytimes.com. August 14.

Drake, Bruce. 2011. "Obama's Second Year Widened the Partisan Divide on How He Is Seen." *Politics Daily*. February 6.

Draper, Robert. 2013a. "Can the Republicans be Saved from Obsolescence?" *New York Times Magazine*. www.nytimes.com. February 14.

Draper, Robert. 2013b. "Steve Schmidt Says Republican Campaigns Haven't Changed. But They Will," *New York Times*. www.nytimes.com. August 2.

Dreher, Rod. 2008. "GOP's Path to Victory Still Goes through God." *USA Today*. www. usatoday.com. December 1.

Drew, Elizabeth. 2013. "Are the Republicans beyond Saving?" *New York Review of Books*. www.nyrb.com. February 11.

Drudge, Matt. 2013. Tweets @Drudge. *Twitter*. https://twitter.com. September 3.

Drum, Kevin. 2010. "Tea Party: Old Whine in New Bottles." *Mother Jones*. October.

Drum, Kevin. 2012. "Planned Parenthood and the Culture Wars." *Mother Jones*. http:// motherjones.com. February 2.

D'Souza, Dinesh. 1984. *Falwell: Before the Millennium*. Chicago: Regnery Gateway.

Dubner, Stephen J. 2010. "Predicting the Midterm Elections: A Freakonomics Quorum." *New York Times*. www.nytimes.com. October 27.

DuBois, Joshua. 2013. *The President's Devotional: The Daily Readings That Inspired President Obama*. New York: HarperOne.

Duin, Julia. 2009. "D.C. Archdiocese Hedges on Communion for Sebelius." *Washington Times*. March 13.

Dworkin, Ronald. 2012. "A Bigger Victory than We Knew." *New York Review of Books*. www.nybooks.com. August 16.

Easley, Jonathan. 2012a. "Newt Gingrich: Bain Capital 'Undermined Capitalism,' Killed Jobs." *The Hill*. www.thehill.com. January 10.

Easley, Jonathan. 2012b. "Gallup: 2012 Election Had the Largest Gender Gap in Recorded History." *The Hill*. www.thehill.com. November 9.

Eastwood, Clint, dir. 2011. *J. Edgar*. Burbank, Calif.: Warner Bros. Pictures.

Eckholm, Erik. 2012a. "Evangelicals Step Up Efforts to Unite on an Alternative to Romney." *New York Times*. www.nytimes.com. January 7, A12 at col. 1.

Eckholm, Erik. 2012b. "One Man Guides the Fight against Gay Marriage." *New York Times*. www.nytimes.com. October 9.

Eckholm, Erik. 2013. "Arkansas Adopts a Ban on Abortions after 12 Weeks." *New York Times*, www.nytimes.com. March 6.

Edsall, Thomas. 2008. "Republican Purgatory: How Long Will It Last?" *Huffington Post*. www.huffingtonpost.com, December 10.

Edsall, Thomas B. 2012a. "White Working Chaos." *New York Times*. www.campaign-stops.blogs.nyt.com. June 25.

Edsall, Thomas B. 2012b. "Is Rush Limbaugh's Country Gone?" *New York Times*. www.campaignstops.blogs.nyt.com. November 18.

Edsall, Thomas. 2013a. "Can Republicans Change Their Spots?" *New York Times*. http://opinionator.blogs.nytimes.com. January 23.

Edsall, Thomas. 2013b. "The Republican Autopsy Report." *New York Times*. http://opinionator.blogs.nytimes.com. March 26.

Edsall, Thomas. 2013c. "A Republican Left Turn?" *New York Times*. http://opinionator.blogs.nytimes.com. March 28.

Edsall, Thomas. 2013d. "Should Republicans Just Focus on White Voters?" *New York Times*. http://opinionator.blogs.nytimes.com. July 3.

Edsall, Thomas Byrne. 2012. *The Age of Austerity: How Scarcity Will Remake American Politics*. New York: Doubleday.

Egan, Patrick J.. and Kenneth Sherrill. 2009. "California's Proposition 8: What Happened, and What Does the Future Hold?" San Francisco: Evelyn & Walter Haas, Jr. Fund. January 6.

Egan, Timothy. 2012. "Tribes of the Swing States." *New York Times*. http://opinionator.blogs.nytimes.com. July 12.

Eligon, John. 2012. "In Kansas, Conservatives Vilify Fellow Republicans." *New York Times*. www.nytimes.com. August 5.

Eligon, John, and Michael Schwirtz. 2012. "Senate Candidate Provokes Ire with 'Legitimate Rape' Comment." *New York Times*. www.nytimes.com. August 19.

Ellison, Christopher G., Gabriel A. Acevedo. and Aida I. Ramos-Wada. 2011. "Religion and Attitudes toward Same-Sex Marriage among U.S. Latinos." *Social Science Quarterly*, 92, no. 1 (March): 35–56.

Epstein, Reid J. 2013. "Obama Meets 47% Video Guy." *Politico*. www.politico.com. February 14.

Erdreich, Sarah. 2013. *Generation Roe: Inside the Future of the Pro-choice Movement*. New York: Seven Stories Press.

Erickson, Erick. 2012. "The Supreme Court Forces Us to Deal within the Political System." *RedState*. www.redstate.com, June 28.

Erickson, Erick. 2013. "We Will Have a Third Party." *RedState*. www.redstate.com. July 29.

Face the Nation. 2011. Transcript. *CBS News*. www.cbsnews.com. January 9.

Faith and Freedom Coalition. 2013. "Statement by Faith and Freedom Coalition Chairman Ralph Reed." www.ffcoalition.com. June 26.

Faith in Public Life. 2008. "The Young and the Faithful." Findings from the Faith and American Politics Survey. Washington, D.C.: Faith in Public Life, conducted by Public Religion Research. October 8.

Fallon, Jimmy. 2012. *Late Night with Jimmy Fallon.* NBC. June 20.

Farnam, T. W. 2012. "Money Gap May Not Matter So Much In November." *Washington Post.* www.washingtonpost.com. July 11.

Farrington, Brendan. 2014. "A Younger Generation of Republicans Split with Party on Gay Marriage, Pot and Social Issues." *Minneapolis StarTribune.* May 25.

Favreau, Jon. 2013. "Jon Favreau on the Destructive Rise of the No-Government Conservatives." *Daily Beast.* July 30.

Feldman, Noah. 2005. *Divided by God: America's Church-State Problem—and What We Should Do about It.* New York: Farrar, Straus & Giroux.

Feldmann, Linda. 2012. "Did Mitt Romney Suggest Eliminating FEMA?" *Christian Science Monitor.* www.csmonitor.com. October 30.

Feller, Ben. 2012. "Obama Criticizes GOP Candidate's Rape Remarks." *Huffington Post.* www.huffingtonpost.com. October 24.

Ferguson, Andrew. 2010. "Ride along with Mitch." *Weekly Standard* 15, no. 37 (June 14). www.weeklystandard.com.

Fineman, Howard. 2010. "What Went Wrong: A 'Pre-mortem' for the Democrats." *Newsweek.* September 12.

Finnegan, Michael. 2012. "Santorum Renews Attack on JFK's Speech on Church and State." *Los Angeles Times.* March 9.

Fiorina, Morris, Jeremy C. Pope, and Samuel J. Abrams. 2005. *Culture War? The Myth of a Polarized America.* New York: Longman.

Fish, Stanley. 2009. "Sarah Palin Is Coming to Town." *New York Times.* http://opinionator.blogs.nytimes.com. December 7.

Fish, Stanley. 2010. "Antaeus and the Tea Party." *New York Times.* www.nytimes.com. September 27.

Foley, Elise. 2011. "Mike Pence: Spending Deal 'Probably Not Good Enough' to Vote For." *Huffington Post.* www.huffingtonpost.com. April 10.

Fouhy, Beth. 2012. "2012 Ad Blitz: Big Money, Smaller Audience." Associated Press. www.yahoo.com. November 4.

FoxNews. 2013a. "Bill O'Reilly: The Culture War Goes Worldwide." *The O'Reilly Report.* www.foxnews.com. January 15.

FoxNews. 2013b. "Romney Relays Disappointment over Loss, Admits Mistakes, in First Sitdown since 2012 Election." www.foxnews.com. March 2.

Frank, Thomas. 2004. *What's the Matter with Kansas? How Conservatives Won the Heart of America.* New York: Metropolitan Books.

Frank, Thomas. 2012a. *Pity the Billionaire: The Hard-Times Swindle and the Unlikely Comeback of the Right.* New York: Metropolitan Books/Henry Holt.

Frank, Thomas. 2012b. "What's for the Tea Party Not to Like in Romney." *Los Angeles Times.* January 8.

Franzen, Jonathan. 2010. *Freedom.* New York: Farrar, Straus & Giroux.

Frassica, Matt. 2009. "At n+1 Conference, the Cat Got Douthat's Tongue on Topic of Gay Marriage." *New York Observer.* www.observer.com. October 21.

Friedman, Emily. 2012. "Mitt Romney Launches Fresh Attack on President Obama, Dubbing Him 'The Great Complainer.'" *ABC News.* www.abcnews.go.com. January 2.

Frum, David. 2009. "Why Rush Is Wrong." *Newsweek.* March 2.

Frum, David. 2013. "Why I Signed the Republican Brief Supporting Gay Marriage." *Daily Beast.* www.thedailybeast.com. February 27.

Gagnon, Frederick. 2012. "Introduction: Ceasefire or New Battle? The Politics of Culture Wars in Obama's Time." *Canadian Review of American Studies* 42, no. 3 (December): 261–273.

Gainor, Dan. 2012. "CNN's Crowley First Plays Umpire, then Joins Team Obama." *FoxNews.* www.foxnews.com. October 17.

Gallup 2014. "Marriage." www.gallup.com.

Galston, Bill, and Mark McKinnon. 2012. "The American People Deserve the Facts." *Real Clear Politics.* www.realclearpolitics.com. October 18.

Galston, William. 2010a. "The Politician of the Future Will Resemble . . . Ross Perot?" *New Republic.* www.tnr.com. March 15.

Galston, William. 2010b. "How Bad Is It Really for the Unemployed? My 'Aha' Moment." *New Republic.* www.tnr.com. May 26.

Galston, William. 2010c. "How Americans' Shifting Political Ideologies Threaten the Democrats." *New Republic.* www.tnr.com. July 28.

Galston, William. 2010d. "Can't Run on It, Can't Run Away from It." *New Republic.* www.tnr.com. September 21.

Galston, William. 2011. "Slice the Demographics Any Way You Want, But Obama Is in Trouble." *New Republic.* www.tnr.com. November 30.

Galston, William. 2012a. "Why Romney's Bain Problem Could Kill His Candidacy." *New Republic.* www.tnr.com. January 12.

Galston, William. 2012b. "Treading Water: Why the Obama Campaign Is Doing Worse than It Seems." *New Republic.* www.tnr.com, July 13.

Galston, William A. 2013. "The 2012 Election: What Happened, What Changed, What It Means." Brookings Institution. www.brookings.edu. January 4.

Gardner, Amy. 2010. "'Tea Party' Candidates Hurt by Lack of Organization in Movement. *Washington Post.* www.washingtonpost.com. June 12, A05.

Gardner, Amy. 2011a. "Activists Slowly Chip Away at Health-Care Law." *Washington Post.* www.washingtonpost.com. February 3.

Gardner, Amy. 2011b. "At CPAC Forum, Potential GOP Candidates Must Navigate Social-Fiscal Tension." *Washington Post.* www.washingtonpost.com. February 9.

Garofolo, Joe. 2011. "Rick Santorum: Obama's Health Care "Will Rob America of Its Soul." *San Francisco Chronicle.* www.sfgate.com. August 8.

Garrahan, Matthew. 2012. "Rich Donors Back Gay Marriage." *Financial Times.* www.ft.com. July 24.

Garrett, Major. 2010. "After the Wave." *National Journal.* www.nationaljournal.com. October 23.

Gast, Phil. 2012. "Obama Announces He Supports Same-Sex Marriage." CNN. www.cnn.com. May 9.

Gelman, Andrew, and Avi Feller. 2012. "Campaign Stops: Red versus Blue in a New Light." www.campaignstops.blogs.nytimes.com. *New York Times.* November 12.

Gerson, Michael, and Peter Wehner. 2013. "How to Save the Republican Party." *Commentary.* www.commentarymagazine.com. March.

Gibson, David. 2012. "American Nuns: Do They Have A Future?" Religion News Service. *Huffington Post.* www.huffingtonpost.com. August 9.

Gibson, James L. 2009. "Religion and Intolerance in Contemporary American Politics." Miller-McCune Center for Research, Media and Public Policy. www.miller-mccune.com. March 2.

Gilgoff, Dan. 2009. "Leaving Religion Behind: A Portrait of Nonreligious America." *U.S. News and World Report.* March 13.

Gillespie, Nick, Matt Welch, and Jim Epstein. 2012. "Sen. Jim DeMint: Why Republicans Must Become More Libertarian." *Reason.* February 7.

Gjelten, Tom. 2011. "Is China's Economy Already No. 1?" *Morning Edition.* NPR. www.npr.org. January 21.

Glueck, Katie. 2013. "GOP Youth 'Evolve' On Gay Marriage." *Politico.* www.politico.com. March 26.

Goldberg, Jonah. 2010. "Demography Isn't Political Destiny." *Los Angeles Times.* November 2.

Goldberg, Michelle. 2010. "Tea Party, Meet the Religious Right." *American Prospect.* January 19.

Goldberg, Michelle. 2012. "The War on Women Backfires." *Daily Beast.* www.thedailybeast.com. November 9.

Goodman, Rob, and Jimmy Soni. 2012. "The Culture War of National Security." Pacific Standard. www.psmag.com. November 13.

Goodstein, Laurie. 2013. "Hispanics Grow Cool to G.O.P., Poll Finds." *New York Times.* www.nytimes.com. September 27.

Gormley, Ken. 2010. *The Death of American Virtue: Clinton vs. Starr.* New York: Crown Publishers.

Gorski, Eric. 2010. "Health Care Overhaul Fight Exposes Catholic Rift." Associated Press, March 19.

Grad, Shelby. 2008. "70% of African Americans Backed Prop. 8, Exit Poll Finds." *Los Angeles Times.* http://latimesblogs.latimes.com. November 5.

Graham, Kate Childs. 2008. "Archbishop Calls Democrats 'Party of Death.'" *Religion Dispatches.* www.religiondispatches.org. October 2.

Green, John C. 2004. "The American Religious Landscape and Political Attitudes: A Baseline for 2004." Pew Charitable Trusts. September 10.

Green, John, and Anna Greenberg. 2008. *"Religion and the 2008 Election: Surprising Finds." USA Today.* December 8.

Green, John, Corwin Schmidt, and Lyman A. Kellstedt. 2005. "The American Religious Landscape and the 2004 Presidential Vote: Increased Polarization." Pew Forum on Religion and Public Life. February 3.

Green, J. P. 2011. "Progressives Voice Concerns about SOTU." *Democratic Strategist.* www.thedemocraticstrategist.org. January 27.

Green, J. P. 2012. "Maher: 'Hello 911? There's an Old Man Beating a Child on My TV.'" *Democratic Strategist.* www.thedemocraticstrategist.org. October 12.

Green, Lloyd. 2013. "Why Asian-Americans Have Turned Their Backs on the Republican Party." *Daily Beast.* www.thedailybeast.com. February 26.

Greenberg, Stan, James Carville, and Erica Seifert. 2012. "Getting to the Bold Policy Offer Winning Now Requires: Report on Democracy Corps National Survey on Presidential Narrative." Washington, D.C.: Democracy Corps. October 15.

Greenberg, Stanley, James Carville, Erica Seifert, and Dave Walker. 2011. "Seizing the New Progressive Common Ground." Washington, D.C.: Democracy Corps. November 10.

Greenberg, Stanley B. 2008. "Goodbye, Reagan Democrats." *New York Times.* www.nytimes.com. November 10.

Greenhouse, Linda. 2013. "The Next Abortion Case is Here." *New York Times.* www.opinionator.blogs.nytimes.com. September 4.

Gushee, David. 2009. "Mr. President, We Need More than Lip Service." *USA Today.* March 16.

Guttmacher Institute. 2012. "Guttmacher Statistic on Catholic Women's Contraceptive Use." Washington, D.C.: Guttmacher Institute. www.guttmacher.org. February 15.

Haberman, Maggie. 2012. "Foster Friess: In My Day, 'Gals' Put Aspirin 'between Their Knees' for Contraception." *Politico.* www.politico.com. February 16.

Haberman, Maggie. 2013. "RNC: Voters See GOP as 'Scary' and 'Out Of Touch.'" *Politico.* www.politico.com. March 18.

Haberman, Maggie, Jonathan Martin, and Glenn Thrush. 2012. "President Obama's Marriage Muddle." *Politico.* www.politico.com. May 8.

Haberman, Maggie, and Emily Schultheis. 2012. "GOP Steers Clear of Gay Marriage Issue." *Politico.* www.politico.com. August 6.

Hagan, Joe. 2011. "Goddangit, Baby, We're Making Good Time." *New York Magazine.* www.nymag.com. February 27.

Hagan, Joe. 2012. "Bush in the Wilderness." *New York Magazine.* www.nymag.com. October 14.

Hagerty, Barbara Bradley. 2010. "The Tea Party's Tension: Religion's Role in Politics." *All Things Considered.* NPR. www.npr.org. September 30.

Hagerty, Barbara Bradley. 2012. "Feeling under Siege, Catholic Leadership Shifts Right." *Morning Edition.* NPR. www.npr.org. July 4.

Haidt, Jonathan. 2012a. *The Righteous Mind: Why Good People Are Divided by Politics and Religion.* New York: Pantheon.

Haidt, Jonathan. 2012b. "Romney, Obama, and the New Culture War over Fairness." *Time.* www.ideas.time.org. October 8.

Haidt, Jonathan. 2013. "Of Freedom and Fairness." *Democracy: A Journal of Ideas*, no. 28 (Spring): 38–50. www.democracyjournal.org.

Haidt, Jonathan, and Marc C. Hetherington. 2012. "Look How Far We've Come Apart." *New York Times*. www.nytimes.com. September 18.

Haines, Errin. 2011. "Birther Bills Pop Up in Numerous States ahead of 2012." *Huffington Post*. www.huffingtonpost.com. March 2.

Halperin, Mark. 2012. "Between the Lines." *Time*. www.content.time.com. May 28.

Halperin, Mark, and John Heilemann. 2013. *Double Down: Game Change 2012*. New York: Penguin.

Halpin, John, and Karl Agne. 2009. "State of American Political Ideology, 2009: A National Study of Values and Beliefs." Washington, D.C.: Center for American Progress.

Halpin, John, and Ruy Teixeira. 2011. "The Path to 270: Demographics versus Economics in the 2012 Presidential Election." Washington, D.C.: Center for American Progress, www.americanprogress.org. November 22.

Harding, Susan. 2000. *The Book of Jerry Falwell: Fundamentalist Language and Politics*. Princeton, N.J.: Princeton University Press.

Harmon, Steven. 2012. "Golden State's Optimism Is Back, New Poll Says." *San Jose Mercury News*. December 6.

HarperCollins. 2013. "HarperOne to Publish the President's Devotional by Pastor Joshua Dubois, Former White House Staffer." Press release. New York: HarperCollins Publishers. www.harpercollins.com. February 14.

Harris, John F., and Jonathan Martin. 2012. "GOP Fears Rise over 2012 Tone, Message." *Politico*. www.politico.com. February 23.

Harris, Mark. 2011. "The Leo Tapes." *GQ*. September.

Harris Poll. 2010. "'Wingnuts' and President Obama." Harris Interactive. March 24.

Harsanyi, David. 2010. "Will D.C. Listen to the Tea Parties?" *Real Clear Politics*. www.realclearpolitics.com. April 16.

Heilemann, John. 2012a. "The Lost Party." *New York Magazine*. www.nymag.com. February 25

Heilemann, John. 2012b. "Hope: The Sequel." *New York Magazine*. www.nymag.com. May 27.

Heilemann, John. 2012c. "The Waitress-Mom War." *New York Magazine*. www.nymag.com. October 19.

Heilemann, John. 2012d. "After an Emotional Finale, Team Obama Fears a Split Decision." *New York Magazine*. www.nymag.com. November 6.

Heilemann, John, and Mark Halperin. 2010. *Game Change: Obama and the Clintons, McCain and Palin, and the Race of a Lifetime*. New York: Harper.

Helderman, Rosalind S., and Jon Cohen. 2012. "Romney's Favorability Ratings Stall." *Washington Post*. www.washingtonpost.com. August 8.

Hennessey, Kathleen. 2011. "'Tea Party' Freshmen Embrace Status Quo." *Los Angeles Times*. January 5.

Hennessey, Kathleen, and James Oliphant. 2010. "A Vanishing Coalition." *Los Angeles Times*. November 5, A1 at col. 3.

Hennessey, Kathleen, and Christi Parsons. 2012. "Birth-Control Fight Unlikely to Hurt Obama, His Strategists Say." *Los Angeles Times*. February 6.

Herbst, Susan. 2010. *Rude Democracy: Civility and Incivility in American Politics*. Philadelphia: Temple University Press.

Herbst, Susan. 2011. "Time to Agree on Media Standards?" *Washington Post*. www.washingtonpost.com. January 11.

Hetherington, Marc J., and Jonathan D. Weiler. 2009. *Authoritarianism and Polarization in American Politics*. New York: Cambridge University Press.

Hirshman, Linda. 2012. *Victory: The Triumphant Gay Revolution*. New York: HarperCollins.

Hirshman, Linda. 2013. "Roe v. Wade Is More Popular than Ever—a Fact the Supreme Court Is Unlikely to Ignore." *New Republic*. www.tnr.com. January 22.

Hitchens, Christopher. 2011. "Tea'd Off." *Vanity Fair*. January.

Hofstadter, Richard. 1965. *The Paranoid Style in American Politics and Other Essays*. New York: Knopf.

Hogue, Ilyse. 2014. "2014: The Year the Pro-choice Crowd Fights Back." *Politico*. www.politico.com. January 24.

Holland, Joshua. 2013. "Jacob Hacker on Obamacare's Rollout and Our Frail Democracy." Moyers & Company, www.billmoyers.com. November 27.

Huckabee, Mike. 2008. *Do the Right Thing: Inside the Movement That's Bringing Common Sense Back to America*. New York: Sentinel/Penguin.

Huckabee, Mike. 2013. Tweets @GovMikeHuckabee. *Twitter*. https://twitter.com. June 26.

Huffington Post. 2012a. "Pat Robertson on Homosexuality: It's Related to a Type of 'Demonic Possession.'" www.huffingtonpost.com. March 27.

Huffington Post. 2012b. "Daniel Jenky, Peoria Catholic Bishop, Compares Obama's Actions to Hitler's: IRS Complaint Filed over Comment." www.huffingtonpost.com. April 19.

Huffington Post. 2012c. "Congressman Calls Evolution Lie from 'Pit Of Hell.'" www.huffingtonpost.com. October 6.

Hulse, Carl. 2009. "In Lawmaker's Outburst, a Rare Breach of Protocol." *New York Times*. www.nytimes.com. September 9.

Hulse, Carl, and Kate Zernicke. 2011. "Bloodshed Puts New Focus on Vitriol in Politics." *New York Times*. www.nytimes.com. January 9, A1 at col. 3.

Human Rights Campaign. 2013. www.hrc.org.

Human Right Campaign Foundation. 2009. "At the Intersection: Race, Sexuality and Gender." Washington, D.C.

Hunt, Mary E. 2012. "Nuns on the Bus: 2700 Miles, Nine States, and a Rock Star DC Welcome." *Religion Dispatches*. www.religiondispatches.com. July 5.

Huntsman, Jon. 2013. "Marriage Equality Is a Conservative Cause." *American Conservative*. www.americanconservative.com. February.

Hymowitz, Kay S. 2011. "Sarah Palin and the Battle for Feminism." *City Journal* 21, no. 1 (Winter). http://www.city-journal.org/2011/21_1_palin.html.

Ingersoll, Julie. 2013. "Obama Inaugural Address Challenges Tea Party History." *Religion Dispatches*. www.religiondispatches.com. January 21.

Ingraham, Laura. 2013. "Laura Ingraham: Graham, McCain Are the Ones on the Fringe." *Real Clear Politics*. www.realclearpolitics.com. March 9.

Jackson, David. 2012. "Obama Takes Heat from Catholic Leaders." *USA Today*. February 1.

Joffe, Carole. 2005. "It's Not Just the Abortion, Stupid." *Dissent* 52, no. 1 (Winter): 91–96.

John and Ken Show. 2011a. KFI AM (radio). January 10.

John and Ken Show. 2011b. KFI AM (radio). January 12.

Johnson, Charles S. 2011. "Rep. Bachmann Blasts Obama, Democrats during GOP Dinner in Helena." *Missoulian*. February 5.

Joint Chiefs of Staff. 2010. "Testimony Regarding DoD 'Don't Ask, Don't Tell' Policy." Delivered by Secretary of Defense Robert M. Gates and Admiral Mike Mullen, chairman of the Joint Chiefs of Staff. Washington, D.C.: Dirksen Senate Office Building. www.jcs.mil. February 2.

Jones, Jeffrey M. 2009. "More Independents Lean GOP; Party Gap Smallest since '05." Gallup. www.gallup.com. September 30.

Jones, Jeffrey M. 2012a. "In U.S., Nearly Half Identify as Economically Conservative." Gallup. www.gallup.com. May 25.

Jones, Jeffrey M. 2012b. "Americans' Views of Obama More Polarized as Election Nears." Gallup. www.gallup.com. October 11.

Jones, Jeffrey M. 2014. "Conservative Lead on Social and Economic Ideology Shrinking." Gallup. www.gallup.com. May 28.

Jones, Robert P. 2014. "Pope Francis's Challenge to the Evangelical-Catholic Coalition." *Atlantic*. www.theatlantic.com. April 17.

Jones, Robert P., and Daniel Cox. 2010. "Religion and Same-Sex Marriage in California: A New Look at Attitudes and Values Two Years after Proposition 8." Washington, D.C.: Public Religion Research Institute. July 21.

Jonsson, Patrik. 2012. "Missouri Primary: Tea Party Win Sets Up Battle for Control of Senate." *Christian Science Monitor*. August 8.

Judis, John. 2008. "America the Liberal: The Democratic Majority: It Emerged!" *New Republic*. November 18.

Kabaservice, Geoffrey. 2012. *Rule and Ruin: The Downfall of Moderation and the Destruction of the Republican Party, from Eisenhower to the Tea Party*. New York: Oxford University Press.

Kapur, Sahil. 2012. "McCain: GOP Needs to Give Up on Contraception." *TPM*. www.talkingpointsmemo.com. March 18.

Keck, Kristi. 2010. "Tea Party Battles for 'Soul of This Country.'" CNN. www.cnn.com. April 15.

Keenan, Nancy. 2013. "Millennials Have the Power to Protect *Roe v. Wade*." CNN. www.cnn.com. January 22.

Keller, Bill. 2011. "Is the Tea Party Over?" *New York Times*. www.nytimes.com. October 9.

Kellman, Laurie 2011. "Anti-abortion Plans Pose Problem for Republicans." *Huffington Post*. www.huffingtonpost.com. March 5.

Kesler, Charles R. 2012. *I Am the Change: Barack Obama and the Crisis of Liberalism.* New York: Broadside Books.

Kilgore, Ed. 2009. "On 'Ending the Culture Wars.'" *Democratic Strategist.* www. thedemocraticstrategist.org. January 30.

Kilgore, Ed. 2011. "Culture Shock." *Democratic Strategist.* www.thedemocraticstrategist. org. February 21.

Kilgore, Ed. 2012a. "Reports of the Religious Right's Death Are Greatly Exaggerated." *New Republic.* www.tnr.com. January 19.

Kilgore, Ed. 2012b. "Political Animal: Did Obama Thread the Needle on Contraception Mandate?" *Washington Monthly.* February 12.

Kilgore, Ed. 2012c. "Political Animal: Santorum Folds." *Washington Monthly.* www. washingtonmonthly.com. April 10.

Kilgore, Ed 2012d. "Is Romney Campaign Incompetent?" *Democratic Strategist.* www. thedemocraticstrategist.org. March 20.

Kimmel, Michael. 2013. *Angry White Men: American Masculinity at the End of an Era.* New York: Nation Books.

King, Neil., Jr., and Naftali Bendavid. 2012. "Tea Party Seeks to Regroup." *Wall Street Journal.* http://online.wsj.com. November 22.

Kinsley, Michael. 2013. "Annihilate! Obama's Very Secret Plot to End the Republican Party." *New Republic.* www.tnr.com. February 27.

Kissling, Frances. 2011. "A Catholic House Divided over Reproductive Healthcare: Bishops Launch a New Campaign." *Religion Dispatches.* www.religiondispatches. com. October 9.

Kleefeld, Eric. 2009. "About That Dropped Gun In Arizona . . ." *TPM.* www.talking-pointsmemo.com. August 11.

Kleefeld, Eric. 2011. "Flashback: Giffords Opponent Had M16 Shooting Event. 'Help Remove Gabrielle Giffords from Office.'" *TPM.* www. talkingpointsmemo.com. January 8.

Kleiman, Mark A. R. 2013a. "Obama on Guns." *The Reality-Based Community.* www. samefacts.com. January 16.

Kleiman, Mark A. R. 2013b. "Wedge Politics." *The Reality Based Community.* www. samefacts.com. January 31.

Kleiman, Mark A. R. 2013c. "Mitt Romney Writes His Own Obituary." *The Reality-Based Community.* www.samefacts.com. March 3.

Klein, Ezra. 2013. "Transcript: President Obama 2013 Inaugural Address." *Washington Post.* www.washingtonpost.com. January 21.

Klein, Joe. 2011a. "Huckabucking." *Time.* www.time.com. March 10.

Klein, Joe. 2011b. "Obama's SOTU Success: Making Democrats the Party of Optimism." *Time.* www.time.com. January 27.

Klein, Joe. 2012. "In the Arena: Mitt Romney's Etch a Sketch Disaster." *Time.* www. swampland.time.com. March 22.

Kliff, Sarah. 2012. "Health Reform at 2: Why American Health Care Will Never Be the Same." Ezra Klein's WonkBlog. *Washington Post.* www.washingtonpost.com. March 24.

Klinenberg, Eric. 2012. *Going Solo: The Extraordinary Rise and Surprising Appeal of Living Alone*. New York: Penguin Press.

Kmiec, Douglas W. 2008. "For Obama but Against Abortion: Can a Catholic Vote for the Pro-choice Obama? Yes." *Los Angeles Times*. October 18.

Kohut, Andrew. 2010. "The Electorate Changes, and Politics Follow." *New York Times*. www.nytimes.com. April 16.

Kohut, Andrew. 2013. "WP Opinions: The Numbers Prove It: The GOP Is Estranged from America." *Washington Post*. www.washingtonpost.com. March 22.

Kondracke, Mort. 2006. "Moderates Fed Up with Polarization." *RollCall*. www.rollcall.com. November 9.

Koppelman, Alex. 2010. "Republican Party's 2010 Fundraising Strategy: Fear." *Slate*. March 3.

Kornacki, Steve. 2012a. "Rush Limbaugh and the Poisoning of the GOP Brand." *Salon*. www.salon.com. March 6.

Kornacki, Steve. 2012b. "Mitt's Primary Season Demons Return." *Salon*. www.salon.com. July 9.

Kornblut, Anne E. 2010. "'Soul-Searching' Obama Aides: Democrats' Midterm Election Losses a Wake-Up Call." *Washington Post*. www.washingtonpost.com. November 14.

Kosmin, Barry A., and Ariela Keysar. 2009. "American Religious Identification Survey (ARIS 2008): Summary Report." Hartford, Conn.: Trinity College. March.

KOSU News. 2010. "Two Views of the Tea Party's Appeal." *KOSU News in Politics*. Stillwater, Okla. February 6.

Kramer, Marcia. 2010. "Rep. Weiner: Palin Is Stoking Liberal Hate." CBS New York. WCBSTV.com. March 25.

Kraushaar. John. 2012. "Romney Campaign Declaring Cease Fire on Health Care." *National Journal*. http://decoded.nationaljournal.com. July 3.

Krauthammer, Charles. 2003. "Bush Dereangement Syndrome." *Townhall.com*. www.townhall.com. December 5.

Krauthammer, Charles. 2010. "Visigoths at the Gate?" *Washington Post*. www.washingtonpost.com. September 24.

Kristol, William. 2012. "A Note on Romney's Arrogant and Stupid Remarks." *Weekly Standard*. September 18.

Kroll, Andy. 2012. "Ralph Reed's Group: An Obama Victory Means 'He Can Complete America's Destruction.'" *Mother Jones*. www.motherjones.com. October 2.

Laarman, Peter. 2011. "Top 2011 Religion Stories That Weren't." *Religion Dispatches*. www.religiondispatches.com. December 27.

La Corte, Patrick Condonrachel [Patrick Condon and Rachel La Corte]. 2012. "In Gay Marriage Fight, Some Brands Take a Stand." *Bloomberg Businessweek News*. www.businessweek.com. July 27.

Lakoff, George. 2004. *Don't Think of an Elephant: Know Your Values and Frame the Debate*. White River Junction, Vt.: Chelsea Green.

Landsberg, Mitchell. 2010. "Nuns in U.S. Back Healthcare Bill despite Catholic Bishops' Opposition." *Los Angeles Times*. March 18.

Landsberg, Mitchell. 2012a. "Losing Faith in Nonpartisanship?" *Los Angeles Times.* June 13.

Landsberg, Mitchell. 2012b. "Tax or Penalty? Romney's Evolving Statements Irritate Conservatives." *Los Angeles Times.* July 5.

Landsberg, Mitchell. 2012c. "How Will Social and Religious Issues Factor into 2012 Election?" *Los Angeles Times.* July 26.

Latino Decisions. 2012. "New Poll: Obama Leads Romney among Latinos in Key 2012 Battleground States." www.latinodecisions.com. June 22.

Lauter, David. 2014. "Conservative Tide Continues to Ebb, Particularly on Social Issues." *Los Angeles Times.* May 28.

Leadership Conference of Women Religious. 2012. "Statement of the Leadership Conference of Women Religious regarding CDF Report." Silver Spring, Md.: Leadership Conference of Women Religious. http://www.lcwr.com. June 1.

Leadership Conference of Women Religious. 2013. "About LCWR." Silver Spring, Md.: Leadership Conference of Women Religious. http://www.lcwr.com.

Leal, David J., and Jerod Patterson. 2014. "House Divided? Evangelical Catholics, Mainstream Catholics, and Attitudes toward Immigration and Life Policies." *Forum* 11, no. 4:561–587.

Leighton, Kyle. 2012. "Why the Latino Vote Isn't Really Up for Grabs." *TPM.* www.talkingpointsmemo.com. April 24.

Leno, Jay. 2010. *The Tonight Show with Jay Leno.* NBC. July 12.

Leno, Jay. 2012a. *The Tonight Show with Jay Leno.* NBC. February 29.

Leno, Jay. 2012b. *The Tonight Show with Jay Leno.* NBC. October 8.

Leonard, Andrew. 2011. "The GOP's Risky Bet to Repeal Healthcare Reform." *Salon.* January 4.

Lepore, Jill. 2010. *The Whites of Their Eyes: The Tea Party's Revolution and the Battle over American History.* Princeton, N.J.: Princeton University Press.

Lepore, Jill. 2011. "Birthright: What's Next for Planned Parenthood?" *New Yorker.* www.newyorker.com. November 14.

Levendusky, Matthew. 2009. *The Partisan Sort: How Liberals Became Democrats and Conservatives Became Republicans.* Chicago: University of Chicago Press.

Levin, Mark R. 2012. *Ameritopia: The Unmaking of America.* New York: Threshold Editions/Simon & Schuster.

Levison, Andrew. 2010. "The Democrat's Major Problem Is Not the Tea Party Minority; It's the Non–Tea Party White Working Class." *Democratic Strategist.* www.thedemocraticstrategist.org. May 18.

Levison, Andrew. 2012. "A TDS Strategy Memo: The Surprising Size of 'White Working Class' America—Half of All White Men and 40 Percent of White Women Still Work in Basically Blue-Collar Jobs." *Democratic Strategist.* www.thedemocraticstrategist.org. September 6.

Levy, Ariel. 2013. "The Perfect Wife." *New Yorker.* www.newyorker.com. September 30.

Lilla, Mark. 2010. "The Tea Party Jacobins." *New York Review of Books.* May 27.

Limbaugh, Rush. 2009. "Rush's First Televised Address to the Nation: Conservative Political Action Conference (CPAC) Speech." *The Rush Limbaugh Show.* www.rushlimbaugh.com. February 28.

Limbaugh, Rush. 2012a. "Gingrich and Perry Blew It on Bain Attack (Update: Newt Admits He Made a Mistake)." *The Rush Limbaugh Show*. www.rushlimbaugh.com. January 11.

Limbaugh, Rush. 2012b. "Santorum Suspends: So What Now?" *Rush Limbaugh Show*. www.rushlimbaugh.com. April 10.

Limbaugh, Rush. 2012c. "Candy Crowley's Act of Journalistic Terrorism Failed to Help Obama on Libya," *The Rush Limbaugh Show*. www.rushlimbaugh.com. October 17.

Limbaugh, Rush. 2013. "How Will GOP Deal with Gay Marriage?" *The Rush Limbaugh Show*. www.rushlimbaugh.com. March 27.

Liptak, Adam. 2008. "California Supreme Court Overturns Gay Marriage Ban." *New York Times*. www.nytimes.com. May 18.

Liptak, Adam. 2010. "Tea-ing Up the Constitution." *New York Times*. www.nytimes.com. March 13.

Liptak, Adam. 2013. "Surprising Friend of Gay Rights in a High Place." *New York Times*. www.nytimes.com. September 1.

Lizza, Ryan. 2011. "G.O.P. Debate: A Booing Guide." *New Yorker*. September 23.

Lizza, Ryan. 2012a. "Fussbudget: How Paul Ryan Captured the G.O.P." *New Yorker*. August 6.

Lizza, Ryan. 2012b. "The Final Push." *New Yorker*. October 29.

Lochhead, Carolyn. 2012. "Same-Sex Marriage Foes Pitted Blacks, Latinos against Gays." *San Francisco Chronicle*. www.sfgate.com. March 27.

LoGiurato, Brett. 2012. "Mitt Romney: 'I Will Repeal Obamacare.'" *Business Insider*. www.businessinsider.com. June 28.

Los Angeles Times. 2007. "Editorial: Falwell's America." *Los Angeles Times*. May 16.

Los Angeles Times. 2009. "Big Racial, Ethnic Divide Remains in L.A. on Gay Marriage, Times Poll Finds." www.latimesblogs.latimes.com. June 19.

Los Angeles Times. n.d. "Database: Proposition 8: Who Gave in the Gay Marriage Battle?" http://projects.latimes.com/prop8.

Lott, Jeremy. 2012. "Is the Era of Big Religion Over?" *Real Clear Politics*. www.realclearpolitics.com. January 18.

Lowry, Rich. 2012. "The Corner: The Candidate of 'Eh.'" *National Review*. www.nationalreview.com. March 7.

Luntz, Frank. 2013. "Why Republicans Should Watch Their Language." *Washington Post*. www.washingtonpost.com. January 11.

Luo, Michael. 2008. "The Caucus: Catholics Turned to the Democrat." *New York Times*. thecaucus.blogs.nytimes.com. November 5.

MacGillis, Alec. 2012a. "How Lucky Is Obama in His Opponent?" *New Republic*. www.tnr.com. January 20.

MacGillis, Alec. 2012b. "On the Swiss-Yachting of Mitt Romney." *New Republic*. www.tnr.com. July 16.

MacGillis, Alec. 2012c. "The Right's (Possible) Coming Freak-Out." *New Republic*. www.tnr.com. November 4.

Madison, Lucy. 2012a. "Freedomworks: 'We're Not in the Tank for Romney at All.'" *CBS News.* www.cbsnews.com. March 21.

Madison, Lucy. 2012b. "Richard Mourdock: Even Pregnancy from Rape Something 'God Intended.'" *CBS News.* www.cbsnews.com. October 23.

Madrick, Jeff. 2012. "The Most Important Elections Since 1932?" *Commonweal.* www.commonweal.com. August 2.

Maher, Bill, writer and actor. 2008. *Religulous,* dir. Larry Charles. Documentary. Santa Monica, Calif.: Lionsgate.

Mali, Meghashyam. 2012. "Senior Obama Adviser: Romney Backers Trying to 'Purchase' Election." *The Hill.* www.thehill.com. July 10.

Malkin, Michelle. 2011. "Branding the Tucson Massacre: 'Together We Thrive' in White and Blue . . ." *Michelle Malkin.* www.michellemalkin.com. January 12.

Martin, Jonathan. 2011. "Obama Takes Opportunity Palin Missed." *Politico.* www.politico.com. January 13.

Martin, Jonathan. 2012a. "GOP Elites Eye 'Consensus' Candidate." *Politico.* www.politico.com. January 5.

Martin, Jonathan. 2012b. "GOP Discovers That Mitt Could Win." *Politico.* www.politico.com. May 23.

Martin, Jonathan. 2013. "Vote on Syria Sets Up Foreign Policy Clash between 2 Wings of G.O.P." *New York Times.* www.nytimes.com. September 2.

Martin, Jonathan, and John F. Harris. 2011. "She's Becoming Al Sharpton, Alaska Edition." *Politico.* www.politico.com. March 14.

Martin, Jonathan, John F. Harris, and Alexander Burns. 2012. "GOP Fears Rise over 2012 Tone, Message." *Politico.* www.politico.com. February 23.

Martin, Jonathan, and Carol E. Lee. 2009. "Crist Joins Obama to Sell Stimulus." *Politico.* www.politico.com. February 11.

Martinez, Jessica, and Michael Lipka. 2014. "Hispanic Millennials Are Less Religious than Older U.S. Hispanics." Washington, D.C.: Pew Research Center. May 8.

Mason Robert. 2004. *Richard Nixon and the Search for a New Majority.* Chapel Hill: University of North Carolina Press.

Mayer, Jane. 2010. "Back to the Seventies." *New Yorker.* September 27.

McAuliff, Michael 2012. "Richard Mourdock on Abortion: Pregnancy from Rape Is 'Something God Intended.'" *Huffington Post.* www.huffingtonpost.com. October 23.

McAuliff, Michael, and Sabrina Siddiqui. 2012. "Richard Mourdock Rape Comments May Be October Surprise to Help Dems, Obama." *Huffington Post.* www.huffingtonpost.com. October 24.

McCarthy, Daniel. 2012. "Why the Right Can't Win the Gay Marriage Fight." *American Conservative.* www.theamericanconservative.com. April 25.

McCrummen, Stephanie, and Jerry Markon. 2012. "Rick Santorum Has Embraced Spanish Priest behind Devout Catholic Group Opus Dei." *Washington Post.* www.washingtonpost.com. March 19.

McDonald, Greg. 2012. "Palin to Romney: 'Light Our Hair on Fire.'" *Newsmax.* www.newsmax.com. July 11.

McGurn, William. 2012. "The Wizard of Obama." *Wall Street Journal*. http://online.wsj. com. October 15.

McKenzie, William. 2008. "Can Obama Score among 'Values Voters'?" *Dallas Morning News*. August 26.

McKinley, Jesse, and Kirk Johnson. 2008. "Mormons Tipped Scale in Ban on Gay Marriage." *New York Times*. www.nytimes.com. November 14.

McManus, Doyle. 2010. "Year of the Conservative Woman." *Los Angeles Times*. June 10, A21 at col. 1.

McManus, Doyle. 2012. "Political Ads—an American Art Form." *Los Angeles Times*. July 12, A17 at col.1.

McManus, Doyle. 2013. "McManus: SCOTUS-Induced Chaos on Gay Marriage?" *Los Angeles Times*. www.latimes.com. March 31.

McMorris-Santoro, Evan. 2012a. "Karl Rove: Romney Blew It in London." *TPM*. www. talkingpointsmemo.com. July 27.

McMorris-Santoro, Evan. 2012b. "Things Are So Bad for Romney, Republicans Are Letting Him Tout RomneyCare." *TPM*. www.talkingpointsmemo.com. September 28.

McMorris-Santoro, Evan, and Jillian Rayfield. 2011. "Tucson Tea Party Leader: We Won't Change Our Rhetoric after Giffords Shooting." *TPM*. www.talkingpointsmemo.com. January 8.

McPike, Erin. 2012. "Is Libertarian Gary Johnson the Wild Card in Fall Election?" *Real Clear Politics*. www.realclearpolitics.com. June 15.

Mead, Walter Russell. 2010. "Do Soldiers Drink Tea?" *American Interest*. http://www. the-american-interest.com. February 21.

Mead, Walter Russell. 2011. "The Tea Party and American Foreign Policy: What Populism Means for Globalism." *Foreign Affairs* (March/April). www.foreignaffairs.com.

Meeker, James W., John Dombrink, and Gilbert Geis. 1985. "State Law and Local Ordinances in California Barring Discrimination on the Basis of Sexual Orientation." *University of Dayton Law Review* 10, no. 3 (Spring): 745–765.

Meet the Press. 2008. Transcript for August 24, 2008. MSNBC. www.msnbc.msn.com.

Meichtry, Stacy. 2013. "Pope Signals Openness to Gay Priests." *Wall Street Journal*. www.wsj.com. July 29.

Mellman, Mark. 2010. "The Public Attitude's Four Antis." *The Hill*. www.thehill.com. May 18.

Melzer, Scott. 2010. *Gun Crusaders: The NRA's Culture War*. New York: NYU Press.

Memmott, Mark. 2011. "The Two-Way: In Video: NPR Exec Slams Tea Party, Questions Need for Federal Funds." NPR. www.npr.org. March 9.

Mesko, Jennifer. 2008. "Gay Activists Erupt as Obama Invites Rick Warren to Pray." *Citizen Link*. December 18.

Meyer, David S. 2013. "Occupy v. the Tea Party and American Democracy." Presented at the Social-Legal Studies Workshop. University of California Irvine. November 1.

Miller, Jake. 2013. "Rove: 'I Could' See a 2016 GOP Candidate Supporting Same-Sex Marriage." *CBS News*. www.cbsnews.com. March 24.

Miller, Lisa. 2008. "The Silent Issue: Abortion Hasn't Been a Central Debate in the 2008 Campaign. But That Doesn't Mean That Its Opponents Feel Any Less Strongly about It." *Newsweek*. November 3.

Miller, Patricia. 2014. *Good Catholics: The Battle over Abortion in the Catholic Church.* Berkeley: University of California Press.

Mirkinson, Jack. 2012. "Rush Limbaugh: Sandra Fluke, Woman Denied Right to Speak at Contraception Hearing, a 'Slut.'" *Huffington Post*. www.huffingtonpost.com. February 29.

Moen, Matthew C. 1992. *The Transformation of the Christian Right*. Tuscaloosa: University of Alabama Press.

Mohler, Albert. 2013. "Losing Ever since *Roe?*—TIME Sounds the Siren for Abortion Rights." www.albertmohler.com. January 7.

Montgomery, Peter. 2012. "Growing Catholic Resistance to Bishops' Crusades." *Religion Dispatches*. www.religiondispatches.com. April 14.

Moore, Martha T. 2013. "Jeb Bush: GOP Must Embrace 'Inclusion and Acceptance.'" *USA Today*. March 15.

Moore, Russell. 2013. "A Prophetic Minority: Kingdom, Culture, and Mission in a New Era: The Inaugural Address of Russell D. Moore as President of the Ethics and Religious Liberty Commission of the Southern Baptist Convention." *Moore to the Point by Russell Moore*. www.russellmoore.com. September 10.

Moore, Russell. 2014. "The Prophetic Minority." The 13th Annual Prophetic Voices Lecture. Boisi Center for Religion and American Public Life, Boston College. April 2.

Morrison, Adele M. 2013. "It's [Not] a Black Thing: The Black/Gay Split over Same-Sex Marriage—a Critical [Race] Perspective." *Tulane Journal of Law and Sexuality* 1:22–53.

Morrison, Patt. 2005. "California's Life-and-Death Politics." *Los Angeles Times*. November 17.

Morrison, Patt. 2010. "Tea Time: Patt Morrison Asks Sal Russo." *Los Angeles Times*. October 2, A19 at col. 1.

Moses, Paul. 2014. "Study: Latino Catholics Joining the 'Nones.'" *Commonweal*. www.commonweal.com. May 7.

Moulitsas, Markos. 2011. Tweet @markos. *Twitter*. https://twitter.com. January 8.

Moynihan, Michael C. 2011. "The Extreme Rhetoric about Extreme Rhetoric (with Bonus Fake Sinclair Lewis Fascism Quote!)." *Reason*. www.reasoncom. January 12.

MSNBC. 2010. "After 'Shellacking,' Obama Laments Disconnect with Voters." www.msnbc.msn.com. November 3.

MSNBC. 2012a. *Andrea Mitchell Reports*. www.msnbc.msn.com. Broadcast, March 2.

MSNBC. 2012b. *Daily Rundown with Chuck Todd*. www.msnbc.msn.com. Broadcast. March 22.

Murray, Mark. 2013. "NBC/WSJ Poll: Majority, for First Time, Want Abortion to Be Legal." www.firstread.nbcnews.com. January 21.

Nakamura, David. 2012. "Obama Touts Gay Rights Record at Campaign Fundraiser." *Washington Post*. www.washingtonpost.com. February 10.

NARAL Pro-Choice America. 2009. "Emergency Alert: Stop Stupak's Last-Ditch Attempt." Choice Action Network e-mail. March 20.

Nather, David. 2012. "Why Dems Keep Stepping on Health Care Landmines." *Politico.* February 10.

National Federation of Independent Business et al. v. Sebelius. 2012. Ruling. 132 S.Ct 2566 (2012). June 28.

National Organization for Marriage. 2009. National Organization for Marriage Deposition Exhibit 12: "National Strategy for Winning the Marriage Battle." Dated U.S. District Court Maine. *National Organization for Marriage and American Principles in Action v. Walter F. McKee et al.* Civil no. 1:09-cv-0058.

National Organization for Marriage. 2013. "NOM Sharply Condemns US Supreme Court over Illegitimate Rulings Legislating from the Bench on Marriage and Rewarding Corrupt Politicians and Federal Judges on Prop 8 and DOMA." www.nomblog.com. June 26.

NBC News. 2008. "'Meet the Press' transcript for August 24, 2008." *Meet the Press.* www.nbcnews.com. August 24.

National Review. 2013. "The *Roe* of Marriage: Where Do We Go from the Supreme Court?" Interview with Maggie Gallagher. www.nationalreview.com. July 3.

New, Michael J. 2009. "The Case for Pro-life Optimism: Yes, Obama's Election Is a Setback, but Things Aren't So Bad as They Seem." *National Review.* www.nro.com. January 22.

Newport, Frank. 2011a. "Americans Say Reagan Is the Greatest U.S. President." Gallup. www.gallup.com. February 18.

Newport, Frank. 2011b. "For First Time, Majority of Americans Favor Gay Marriage." Gallup. www.gallup.com. May 20.

Newport, Frank. 2012. "Americans, Including Catholics, Say Birth Control Is Morally OK." Gallup. www.gallup.com. May 22.

New York Times. 2012a. "Editorial: Iowa Caucuses." www.nytimes.com. January 3.

New York Times. 2012b. "Editorial: Bigotry on the Ballot." www.nytimes.com. April 29.

New York Times. 2012c. "Editorial: Anti-abortionists on Trial." www.nytimes.com. July 25.

New York Times. 2012d. "Editorial: Desperate for Civility." www.nytimes.com. November 4.

Nicholas, Peter. 2010. "Independent Voters Deeply Dissatisfied with Obama, Poll Says." *Los Angeles Times.* September 20.

Nichols, John. 2011. "Palin Put a Gun Target on Giffords's District; Now a Colleague Says: 'Palin Needs to Look at Her Own Behavior.'" *Nation.* www.thenation.com. January 9.

Nixon, Richard M. 1969. "Nixon's Address to the Nation on the War in Vietnam." Washington, D.C.: White House. November 3.

Nocera, Joe. 2012. "Let the Debate Begin." *New York Times.* www.nytimes.com. August 14.

Nolan, Christopher, dir. 2008. *The Dark Knight.* Burbank, Calif.: Warner Bros. Pictures.

Noonan, Peggy. 2011. "The Divider vs. the Thinker." *Wall Street Journal.* http://online.wsj.com. October 29.

NPR. 2008a. Transcript of John McCain's concession speech. www.npr.org. November 8.

NPR. 2008b. "Rev. Richard Cizik on God and Global Warming." www.npr.org. December 2.

NPR. 2012. "Transcript: Gov. Chris Christie's Convention Speech." www.npr.org. August 28.

Obama, Barack. 1995. *Dreams from My Father*. New York: Times Books.

Obama, Barack. 2011a. "Transcript: Obama Speech Addresses Tragedy in Tucson." ABC News. January 12.

Obama, Barack. 2011b. "Obama: Reagan Saw That 'We Are All Patriots.'" *USA Today*. January 24.

Obama, Barack. 2011c. "President Obama: We Must Seek Agreement on Gun Reforms." *Arizona Daily Star*. March 13.

Obejas, Achy. 2013. "The Gay Old Party." *In These Times*. www.inthesetimes.com. April 16.

Olbermann, Keith. 2007. "Bush: Pathological Liar or Idiot-in-Chief?" *Countdown with Keith Olbermann*. MSNBC. www.nbcnews.com. December 6.

Oliphant, James. 2009. "Abortion Laws on Democrats' Back Burner." *Los Angeles Times*. February 10, A14 at col. 1.

The Onion. 2012a. "Romneymania Sweeps America." www.theonion.com. February 11.

The Onion. 2012b. "Obama Excited to Participate in First Debate." www.theonion.com. October 16.

Orange County Register. 2007. "Editorial: Falwell Leaves Movement That's Past Its Peak." May 16.

O'Reilly Factor. 2013. "Bill O'Reilly: The Culture War Goes Worldwide." www.foxnews. com. January 15.

Ornstein, Norman. 2012. "Not Your Father's Republican Party." *New York Times*. www. nytimes.com. January 4.

O'Toole, James. 2012. "Best Companies List Hits Gay Rights Milestone." CNN. www. money.cnn.com. January 20.

Packer, George. 2011. "It Doesn't Matter Why He Did It." *New Yorker*, www.newyorker. com. January 9.

Palin, Sarah. 2009. *Going Rogue: An American Life*. New York: HarperCollins.

Palin, Sarah. 2010. *America by Heart: Reflections on Family, Faith, and the Flag*. New York: HarperCollins.

Palin, Sarah. 2012. "Obama lied to the American people. Again. He said it wasn't a tax. Obama lies; freedom dies." Tweet @SarahPalinUSA. *Twitter*. https://twitter.com. June 28.

Pally, Marcia. 2011. "Campaign Stops: The New Evangelicals." *New York Times*. http:// campaignstops.blogs.nytimes.com. December 9.

Palmer, Anna, and Tarini Parni. 2013. "Republicans See Cash Opportunity in Gay Marriage Shift." *Politico*. www.politico.com. March 24.

Parker, Christopher S., and Matt A. Barreto. 2010. "Exploring the Sources and Consequences of Tea Party Support." Presented at the conference "Fractures, Alliances and Mobilizations in the Age of Obama: Emerging Analyses of the 'Tea Party

Movement.'" Center for the Comparative Study of Right-Wing Movements, University of California, Berkeley. October 22.

Parker, Christopher S., and Matt A. Barreto. 2013. *Change They Can't Believe In: The Tea Party and Reactionary Politics in America*. Princeton, N.J.: Princeton University Press.

Parker, Kathleen. 2008. "Giving Up on God." *Washington Post*. www.washingtonpost.com. November 18.

Paul VI. 1968. "On the regulation of birth, *Humanae vitae*." Encyclical letter of Pope Paul VI. Vatican City, July 25.

Pear, Robert. 2009. "Obama on Spot over a Benefit to Gay Couples." *New York Times*. www.nytimes.com. March 13.

Penalver, Eduardo. 2012. "Latinos and Immigration." *Commonweal*. www.comonweal.com. June 25.

Perlstein, Rick. 2001. *Before the Storm: Barry Goldwater and the Unmaking of the American Consensus*. New York: Hill & Wang.

Perlstein, Rick. 2008. *Nixonland: The Rise of a President and the Fracturing of America*. New York: Scribner.

Perlstein, Rick. 2010. "The Tea Parties Now." Keynote address. Presented at the conference "Fractures, Alliances and Mobilizations in the Age of Obama: Emerging Analyses of the 'Tea Party Movement.'" Center for the Comparative Study of Right-Wing Movements, University of California, Berkeley. October 22.

Perlstein, Rick. 2012a. "Why Mitt Romney's Mormonism Doesn't Matter." *Rolling Stone*. January 31.

Perlstein, Rick. 2012b. "Why Conservatives Are Still Crazy after All These Years." *Rolling Stone*. March 16.

Peters, Jeremy W., and Brian Stelter. 2012. "On Fox News, a Mistrust of Pro-Obama Numbers Lasts Late into the Night." *New York Times*. www.nytimes.com. November 6.

Peters, Thomas. 2010. "The GOP Is Abandoning the Fight for Family Values." *The Hill*. www.thehill.com. September 17.

Petrenko, Konstantin. 2009. "Godless America? Say Hello to the 'Apatheists.'" *Religion Dispatches*. www.religiondispatches.org. March 19.

Pew Forum on Religion and Pubic Life. 2008. "Voting Religiously." www.pewresearch.org. November 10.

Pew Forum on Religion and Public Life. 2007. "A Christian Right without Falwell." Interview with Dr. John C. Green. www.pewresearch.org. May 16.

Pew Forum on Religion and Public Life. 2009a. "A Look at Religious Voters in the 2008 Election." www.pewresearch.org. February 10.

Pew Forum on Religion and Public Life. 2009b. "In Mammon We Trust? Religions Agree Economy Is Issue Number One." www.pewresearch.org. March 4.

Pew Forum on Religion and Public Life. 2012. "'Nones' on the Rise: One-in-Five Adults Have No Religious Affiliation." www.pewresearch.org. October 9.

Pew Religion and Public Life Project. 2012a. "Latinos, Religion and Campaign 2012: Latino Catholics Strongly Favor Obama, Latino Evangelicals More Divided." www.pewforum.org. October 18.

Pew Religion and Public Life Project. 2012b. "How the Faithful Voted: 2012 Preliminary Analysis." www.pewforum.org. November 7.

Pew Religion and Public Life Project. 2014. "The Shifting Religious Identity of Latinos in the United States." www.pewforum.org. May 7.

Pew Research Center. 2006. "Less Opposition to Gay Marriage, Adoption and Military Service: Only 34% Favor South Dakota Abortion Ban." www.pewresearch.org. March 22.

Pew Research Center. 2011. "Tea Party: Better Known, Less Popular." www.pewresearch.org. April 8.

Pew Research Center. 2012a. "Partisan Polarization Surges in Bush, Obama Years: Trends in American Values: 1987–2012." www.pewresearch.org. June 4.

Pew Research Center. 2012b. "Obama Ahead with Stronger Support, Better Image and Lead on Most Issues." www.pewresearch.org. September 19.

Pew Research Center. 2013a. "*Roe v. Wade* at 40: Most Oppose Overturning Abortion Decision." www.pewresearch.org. January 16.

Pew Research Center. 2013b. "U.S. Catholics: Key Data from Pew Research." www.pewresearch.org. February 25.

Pew Research Center. 2013c. "Majority of U.S. Catholics Say Next Pope Should Allow Priests to Marry." www.pewresearch.org. February 28.

Pew Research Center. 2013d. "The Role of the Rising American Electorate in the 2012 Election." www.pewresearch.org. March 20.

Pew Research Center. 2013e. "In Gay Marriage Debate, Both Supporters and Opponents See Legal Recognition as 'Inevitable.'" www.pewresearch.org. June 6.

Pew Research Social and Demographic Trends. 2012. "The Big Generation Gap at the Polls Is Echoed in Attitudes on Budget Tradeoffs." www.pewsocialtrends.org. December 20.

Phillips, Kate. 2008. "The Caucus: Biden on Abortion Politics." http://thecaucus.blog.nytimes.org. September 7.

Phillips, Kevin. 2006. *American Theocracy: The Peril and Politics of Radical Religion, Oil and Borrowed Money in the 21st Century*. New York: Viking.

Polasky, Adam. 2012. "New Poll Shows Dramatic Shift in Maryland's Support for the Freedom to Marry." Freedom to Marry. www.freedomtomarry.org. May 29.

Politico. 2011a. "Tucson." www.politico.com. January 8.

Politico. 2011b. "Arizona Sheriff Slams Media 'Vitriol.'" www.politico.com. January 8.

Politico. 2011c. "On Congress: Broun: Obama Believes in 'Socialism.'" www.politico.com. January 25.

Politico. 2011d. "Video: Politico Playback: Jimmy Fallon on Bill O'Reilly Obama Interview." www.politico.com. February 8.

Ponnuru, Ramesh. 2010. "The Year of the (Pro-life) Woman." *New York Times*. www.nytimes.com. June 13.

Ponnuru, Ramesh. 2012. "Tea Party Rising." *National Review*. www.nro.com. May 8.

Porter, Ethan. 2010. "V-Day in the Culture Wars." *Democracy: A Journal of Ideas*, no. 17 (Summer). www.democracyjournal.org.

Portman, Rob. 2013. "Rob Portman Commentary: Gay Couples Also Deserve Chance to Get Married." *Columbus Dispatch.* www.dispatch.com. March 15.

Posner, Sarah. 2008. "Michele Bachmann's 'Normal People Values.'" *American Prospect.* http://prospect.org. October 20.

Posner, Sarah. 2010a. "The New 'Values Voters' Mantra." *Religion Dispatches.* www.religiondispatches.com. October 7.

Posner, Sarah. 2010b. "The Tea Party Illusion." *Religion Dispatches.* www.religiondispatches.com. November 2.

Posner, Sarah. 2012a. "The GOP's Race to the Dark Age." *Religion Dispatches.* www.religiondispatches.com. January 9.

Posner, Sarah. 2012b. "The Great Religious Realignment." *Religion Dispatches.* www.religiondispatches.com. November 7.

Posner, Sarah. 2013a. "6 Words Not in RNC Autopsy: Christian, Religion, Abortion, Marriage, Jesus, God." *Religion Dispatches.* www.religiondispatches.com. March 19.

Posner, Sarah. 2013b. "Are the Culture Wars Over? Look at the States." *Religion Dispatches.* www.religiondispatches.com. April 3.

Posner, Sarah. 2013c. "Myth Busted: The GOP Is through with the Religious Right." *Religion Dispatches.* www.religiondispatches.com. April 12.

Prager, Dennis. 2012. "Paul Ryan and the American Character." *Real Clear Politics.* www.realclearpolitics.com. August 14.

Preston, Julia. 2012. "The Caucus: Latinos Favor Obama by Wide Margin, Poll Finds." *New York Times.* www.thecaucus.blogs.nytimes.com. October 11.

Prothero, Stephen. 2012. "My Take: Welcome Back, Culture Wars (and Rick Santorum)." CNN. www.cnn.com. February 8.

Public Opinion Strategies. 2012. *NBC News/Wall Street Journal* poll. Alexandria, Va.: Public Opinion Strategies. March 5.

Public Policy Polling. 2012. "Subject: Maryland Same-Sex Marriage Referendum." www.publicpolicypolling.com. May 24.

Public Religion Research Institute. 2011. "Catholic Attitudes on Gay and Lesbian Issues: A Comprehensive Portrait from Recent Research." Report. http://publicreligion.org. March.

Public Religion Research Institute. 2012. "Religion, Values, and Experiences: Black and Hispanic American Attitudes on Abortion and Reproductive Issues." Survey. http://publicreligion.org.

Putnam, Robert D., and David E. Campbell. 2010. *American Grace: How Religion Divides and Unites Us.* New York: Simon & Schuster.

Quinnipiac. 2009. "Gays in the Military Should Be Allowed to Come Out, U.S. Voters tell Quinnipiac University National Poll." Quinnipiac, Conn.: Quinnipiac University. April 30.

Rankin, Russ. 2013. "Research: Same-Sex Marriage Is Civil Rights Issue, Americans Say." *LifeWay.* www.lifeway.com. March 12.

Rasmussen, Scott. 2013a. "Republican Establishment Declares War on GOP Voters." *Rasmussen Reports.* www.rasmussenreports.com. January 11.

Rasmussen, Scott. 2013b. "GOP Voters Give Rand Paul Much Higher Marks than Mc-Cain, Graham." *Rasmussen Reports*. www.rasmussenreports.com. March 14.

Rasmussen, Scott, and Douglas E. Schoen. 2010. "Tea Party Takes Seat at Political Table." *Politico*. www.politico.com. October 25.

Real Clear Politics. 2012a. "Krauthammer: Reagan Would Be "Very Comfortable" with the Tea Party." www.realclearpolitics.com. June 12.

Real Clear Politics. 2012b. "Sununu to CNN's O'Brien: 'Always Good to Come on the Groupie Channel.'" www.realclearpolitics.com. October 17.

Real Clear Politics. 2013. "Rand Paul: Country Is Ready for a 'Libertarian Republican Narrative.'" *Real Clear Politics*. www.realclearpolitics.com. February 17.

Real Time with Bill Maher. 2009. HBO. Broadcast, August 7.

Real Time with Bill Maher. 2013. HBO. Broadcast, March 2.

Redden, Molly. 2013. "Fetal-Heartbeat Abortion Laws Are Dangerous Even If Judges Reject Them." *New Republic*. www.tnr.com. March 28.

Rediff News. 2008. "Liberal California Shuts Door on Same Sex Marriages." www.rediff.com. November 6.

Red State. 2010. "The New Vocal Majority." Posting by nikitas3. www.redstate.com. March 31.

Reed, Jennifer. 2005. "Public Lesbian Number One." *Feminist Media Studies* 5, no. 1: 23–36.

Reeves, Richard. 2012. "It's about Sex and the '60s." *Truthdig*. www.truthdig.com. March 7.

Reich, Robert. 2010. "The 'Mad-as-Hell' Party Scores as the Anxious Class Stews." *Huffington Post*. www.huffingtonpost.com. May 18.

Remnick, David. 2010. *The Bridge: The Life and Rise of Barack Obama*. New York: Knopf.

Remnick, David. 2012. "Here Comes the Culture War!" *New Yorker*. www.newyorker.com. February 10.

Republican National Committee. 2013a. "Growth and Opportunity Project." http://go-project.gop.com. March 18.

Republican National Committee. 2013b. "Resolution for marriage and children." https://cdn.gop.com/docs/2013_Spring-Meeting_Resolutions.pdf. April 12.

Republican Party. 2012. "Republican Platform: We Believe in America." www.gop.com/platform.

Reyes, Raul. 2012. "Gay Marriage Not a Latino Wedge Issue." *USA Today*. June 1, 11A at col.1.

Rich, Frank. 2009. "The Culture Warriors Get Laid Off." *New York Times*. www.nytimes.com. March 15.

Rich, Frank. 2010. "Smoke the Bigots Out of the Closet." *New York Times*. www.nytimes.com. February 6.

Rich, Frank 2011. "The Tea Party Wags the Dog." *New York Times*. www.nytimes.com. January 29.

Rich, Frank. 2012a. "Stag Party." *New York Magazine*. www.nymag.com. March 24.

Rich, Frank. 2012b. "Mayberry R.I.P." *New York Magazine*. www.nymag.com. July 22.

Rich, Frank. 2012c. "My Embed in Red." *New York Magazine.* www.nymag.com. September 16.

Rich, Frank. 2012d. "The Tea Party Will Win in the End." *New York Magazine.* www.nymag,com. October 14.

Richards, Cecile. 2014. Speech by Cecile Richards, president of the Planned Parenthood Action Fund. Roe v. Wade Anniversary Celebration. Community Action Fund of Planned Parenthood, Orange and San Bernardino Counties, Newport Beach, Calif. January 29.

Richen, Yoruba. 2012. "The Black Vote for Gay Marriage." *New York Times.* www.nytimes.com. November 1.

Richen, Yoruba, dir. and prod. 2013. *The New Black.* San Francisco: California Newsreel.

Riley, Naomi Schaefer. 2013. "Russell Moore: From Moral Majority to 'Prophetic Minority.'" *Wall Street Journal.* http://online.wsj.com. August 16.

Roarty, Alex. 2012. "Santorum: Return of the Culture Warrior." *National Journal.* www.decoded.nationaljournal.com. February 10.

Roarty, Alex. 2014. "The Class War Inside the Republican Party." *Atlantic.* www.theatlantic.com. April 21.

Robbins, Danny. 2010. "Sarah Palin: Obama 'Most Pro-abortion President.'" *Huffington Post.* www.huffingtonpost.com. November 11.

Robert, Tom. 2011. "Fifth Survey of Catholics in America Released." *National Catholic Reporter.* www.ncr.com. October 11.

Roberts, Sam. 2010. "Study Finds Wider View of 'Family.'" *New York Times.* www.nytimes.com. September 15, A13, at col. 1.

Robillard, Kevin. 2013. "Hillary Clinton Announces Her Support for Gay Marriage." *Politico.* www.politico.com. March 18.

Robin, Corey. 2011. *The Reactionary Mind: Conservatism from Edmund Burke to Sarah Palin.* New York: Oxford University Press.

Rodgers, Daniel T. 2012. "'Moocher Class' Warfare." *Democracy* no. 24 (Spring). www.democracyjournal.org.

Rojas, Aurelio. 2008. "Anti-black Backlash over Prop. 8 'Appalls' Assembly Speaker." *Sacramento Bee.* www.smcclatchydc.com. November 19.

Romano, Andrew. 2010. "Newsweek Poll: Anger Unlikely to Be Deciding Factor in Midterms." *Newsweek.* October 1.

Romney, Mitt. 2011. *No Apology: Believe in America.* Paperback ed. New York: St. Martin's Griffin.

Ronan, Marian. 2012. "Rome vs. the Sisters." *Religion Dispatches.* www.religiondispatches.com. April 29.

Rosen, Ruth. 2010. Presentation on the panel, "New Forms of Activism on the Right: The Tea Party—Emergence of a Movement?"At the conference "Fractures, Alliances and Mobilizations in the Age of Obama: Emerging Analyses of the 'Tea Party Movement.'" Center for the Comparative Study of Right-Wing Movements, University of California. Berkeley. October 22.

Rosen, Ruth. 2012. "The Tea Party and Angry White Women." *Dissent* (Winter): 61–65.

Rosenthal, Andrew. 2012a. "Taking Note: The Iowa-Is-So-Important Phase Ends, the Iowa-Is-So-Over Phase Begins." *New York Times*. www.nytimes.com.

Rosenthal, Andrew. 2012b. "Taking Note: John Roberts Conspiracy Theories." *New York Times*. www.nytimes.com. July 2.

Rosenthal, Andrew. 2013. "Taking Note: G.O.P. Rebranding." *New York Times*. www.nytimes.com. January 25.

Rosenthal, Lawrence, and Christine Trost. 2012. *Steep: The Precipitous Rise of the Tea Party*. Berkeley: University of California Press.

Rove, Karl. 2009. "The President's Apology Tour." *Wall Street Journal*. http://online.wsj.com. October 28.

Rove, Karl. 2010a. *Courage and Consequence: My Life as a Conservative in the Fight*. New York: Threshold Editions/Simon & Schuster.

Rove, Karl. 2010b. "Signs of the Democratic Apocalypse." *Wall Street Journal*. http://online.wsj.com. October 27.

Roy, Avik. 2012. "Did Roberts Cave to Left-Wing Media Pressure?" *National Review*. www.nationalreview.com. July 1.

Rubin, Jennifer. 2007. "Romney and Huckabee: Club for Growth Comparisons." *Human Events*. http://beta.humanevents.com. August 24.

Ruffini, Patrick. 2009. "The Joe-the-Plumberization of the GOP." *The Next Right*. www.thenextright.com. February 25.

Ruprecht, Louis. 2010. "It's Not a Tea *Party*, Silly, It's a Rebellion; and It's Not Religious." *Religion Dispatches*. www.religiondispatches.org. May 27.

Rutenberg, Jim. 2012. "Spoiler Alert! G.O.P. Fighting Libertarian's Spot on the Ballot." *New York Times*. www.nytimes.com. October 14.

Saad, Lydia. 2009. "More Americans Pro-life' than 'Pro-choice' for First Time." Gallup. www.gallup.com. May 15.

Saad, Lydia. 2010. "At 52%, Palin's Unfavorable Score Hits a New High." Gallup. www.gallup.com. November 12.

Saad, Lydia. 2012. "U.S. Confidence in Organized Religion at Low Point." Gallup. www.gallup.com. July 12.

Sack, Kevin. 2010. "A Tough Race after Health Care Switch." *New York Times*. www.nytimes.com. September 11.

Saenz, Arlette. 2012. "Perry Likens Romney's Bain Capital to 'Vultures.'" *ABC News*. www.abcnews.go.com. January 10.

Sager, Rebecca. 2008. "Creating a New Place for Faith: The Reintegration of Religion into Democratic Politics." Unpublished. Los Angeles: Loyola Marymount University.

Sager, Rebecca. 2010. *Faith, Politics, and Power: The Politics of Faith-Based Initiatives*. New York: Oxford University Press.

Salam, Reihan. 2009. "The Last Culture Warrior." www.forbes.com. July 4.

Samuels, Dorothy. 2011. "The Landscape: Where Abortion Rights Are Disappearing." *New York Times*. www.nytimes.com. September 24.

Sanders, Sam. 2012. "It's All Politics: Luntz Warns GOP: 'A War Is about to Break Out within This Primary Field.'" NPR. www.npr.org. January 4.

Sanneh, Kelefa. 2012a. "Party Crasher." *New Yorker.* February 27.

Sanneh, Kelefa. 2012b. "An Insurgency in Texas." *New Yorker.* July 27.

Santarelli, Christopher. 2012. "'A Liberal, a Conservative and a Moderate Walk into a Bar' in New Santorum Radio Ad Hitting Romney, a LDS Member." *Blaze.* www. theblaze.com. March 19.

Saperstein, David. 2009. "On Faith: A Pro-life Position Most Religious People Embrace." www.washingtonpost.com. March 10.

Sargent, Greg. 2011a. "The Plum Line: For the GOP, There's No Putting The 'Repeal' Genie back in the Bottle. *Washington Post.* www.washingtonpost.com. February 3.

Sargent, Greg. 2011b. "The Right's Delusions of World-Historical Grandeur." *Washington Post.* www.washingtonpost.com. February 9.

Sargent, Greg. 2012. "Romney's GOP Critics Undermining His General Election Argument." *Washington Post.* www.washingtonpost.com. January 10.

Sargent, Greg. 2013. "How out of Touch Is Today's GOP?" *Washington Post.* www. washingtonpost.com. April 16.

Sarlin, Benjy. 2013. "6 Big Takeaways from the RNC's Incredible 2012 Autopsy." *TMP.* www.talkingpointsmemo.com. March 18.

Scheiber, Noam. 2012a. "47%" Was Bad for Romney; Ryan Has Been Deadly." *New Republic.* www.tnr.com. September 27.

Scheiber, Noam. 2012b. "Romney's Response to Sandy May Be the Campaign's Most Revealing Moment." *New Republic.* www.tnr.com. October 31.

Scherer, Michael. 2012. "Class War 2012: Why Both Parties Are Flying the Anti–Wall Street Banner." *Time.* http://swampland.time.com. February 2.

Schlesinger, Stephen. 2010. "The Party of Anger." *Huffington Post.* www.huffingtonpost. com. March 23.

Schmidt, Steve. 2009. "Steve Schmidt's Speech: The Full Text." *Atlantic.* www.theatlatic. com. April 17.

Schneider, Bill. 2011. "GOP Acts Out Revenge Fantasy." *Politico.* www.politico.com. February 22.

Schneider, Gregory L., ed. 2003. *Conservatism in America since 1930.* New York: NYU Press.

Schulz, Craig. 2010. "Rendell Rejects Tea Party as Legit Movement." *FoxNews.* www. foxnews.com. April 24.

Schultz, Daniel. 2010. "Why Do Evangelicals and Dems Want Immigration Reform? " *Religion Dispatches.* www.religiondispatches.com. July 6.

Scorsese, Martin, dir. 1976. *Taxi Driver.* Culver City, Calif.: Columbia Pictures.

Seelye, Katharine Q. 2009. "Top G.O.P. Consultant Endorses Gay Marriage." *New York Times.* www.nytimes.com. April 17.

Seidl, Jonathon M. 2011. "No Joke: Stephen Colbert Testifying before FEC to Defend His 'Super PAC.'" *Blaze.* www.theblaze.com. June 30.

Serwer, Adam. 2012. "You Can't Equate Your Sin with My Skin." *Mother Jones.* www. motherjones.com. September/October.

Shapiro, Walter. 2012. "Why Santorum's Not Going Away Anytime Soon." *New Republic*. www.tnr.com. February 8.

Shear, Michael D. 2012a. "For Romney's Trusted Adviser, 'Etch A Sketch' Comment Is a Rare Misstep." *New York Times*. www.nytimes.com. March 21.

Shear, Michael D. 2012b. "The Caucus: Ryan Surprised by Voters in 'Urban Areas.'" *New York Times*. www.nytimes.com. November 13.

Shear, Michael D. 2013. "The Caucus: Religious Groups Urge Deficit Reduction and Protection of the Poor." *New York Times*. www.nytimes.com. February 25.

Shen, Aviva. 2013. "5 Social Conservatives Threatening to Leave the GOP over Marriage Equality." *Think Progress*. www.thinkprogress.org. March 27.

Sheppard, Noel. 2012. "Palin: 'Doesn't Bode Well for Our President's Character to Not Speak Out against Maher's 'Dirty Money.'" *mrcNewsBusters*. newsbusters.org. March 9.

Sherman, Jake, and Meredith Shiner. 2010. "Bart Stupak Called 'Baby Killer' on House Floor." *Politico*. www.politico.com. March 22.

Shields, Jon A. 2009. "Life Support: Why Democrats Aren't Rushing to Overturn Bush's Abortion Restrictions." *New Republic*. March 2.

Shiner, Meredith. 2011. "Dems Budget Strategy: Blame the Tea Party." *Politico*. www.politico.com. March 29.

Shrum, Robert. 2013. "Washington's Endless Civil War." *Daily Beast*. www.thedailybeast.com. January 11.

Sidoti, Liz. 2010. "Analysis: GOP, Dems Compete for Populist Title." Associated Press. April 24.

Silk, Mark. 2013. "First the Nones, now the Spirituals." Religion News Service. http://marksilk.religionnews.com. September 26.

Silver, Nate. 2009a. "Americans Losing Their Faith in Faith . . . and Everything Else." *FiveThirtyEight*. www.fivethirtyeight.com. March 12.

Silver, Nate. 2009b. "Hispanics Back Gay Marriage at Same Rates as Whites." *FiveThirtyEight*. www.fivethirtyeight.com. May 26.

Silver, Nate. 2012a. "Reagan Count: Gingrich 55, Romney 6." *FiveThirtyEight*. www.fivethirtyeight.com. January 24.

Silver, Nate. 2012b. "Swing States and Elastic Voters." *FiveThirtyEight*. www.fivethirtyeight.com. May 21.

Silver, Nate. 2013. "Explaining the Senate's Surge in Support for Same-Sex Marriage." *FiveThirtyEight*. www.fivethirtyeight.com. April 4.

Skelton, George. 2010. "GOP Might Snub Reagan." *Los Angeles Times*. June 7, A2 at col 4.

Skocpol, Theda. 1996. *Boomerang: Health Care Reform and the Turn against Government*. New York: Norton.

Skocpol, Theda. 2012. *Obama and America's Political Future*. Cambridge, Mass.: Harvard University Press.

Skocpol, Theda. 2014. "They've Won by Leverage, Not Popularity," *New York Times*. www.nytimes.com. May 19.

Skocpol, Theda, and Vanessa Williamson. 2012. *The Tea Party and the Remaking of American Conservatism*. New York: Oxford University Press.

Skolnick, Arlene. 2005. "Rethinking the Politics of the Family: Part IV." *Dissent* (Summer): 63–64.

Smith, Aaron, and Maeve Duggan. 2012. "Online Political Videos and Campaign 2012." Washington, D.C. Pew Research and Internet Project. www.pewinternet.org. November 2.

Smith, Ben, and Byron Tau. 2011. "5 Things to watch at CPAC." *Politico*. www.politico.com. February 10.

Socarides, Richard. 2013. "Why Bill Clinton Signed the Defense of Marriage Act." *New Yorker*. www.newyorker.com. posted March 8.

Social Science Research Solutions. 2012. "LGBT Acceptance and Support: The Hispanic Perspective." www.nclr.org. April.

Soltis, Kristen. 2012. "One Approach, for Two Audiences." *New York Times*. www.nytimes.com. April 11.

Sonmez, Felicia. 2012. "Rick Perry Doubles Down on 'Vulture Capitalist' Criticism of Mitt Romney." *Washington Post*. www.washingtonpost.com. January 11.

Sorkin, Andrew Ross. 2012. "DealBook: The Election Won't Solve All Puzzles." *New York Times*. www.nytimes.com. November 6.

Spadaro, Anthony, S.J. 2013. "A Big Heart Open to God." *America: The National Catholic Review* 209, no. 8 (September 30).

Sparks, Frederick. 2012. "NOM Memo Reveals Strategy to 'Drive a Wedge between Blacks and Gays.'" *Free Thought Blogs*. www.freethoughtblogs.com. March 27.

Stanek, Steven. 2009. "American Faith Study Shows Secular Gain." *The National*. www.thenational.ae. March 11.

Starr, Paul. 2009. "Breaking the Grip of the Past." *American Prospect*. www.americanprospect.org. February 23.

Starr, Paul. 2010. "A 20-Year Tug-of-War." *American Prospect*. www.americanprospect.org. August 9.

Steenland, Sally. 2010. "Return of the Culture Wars: Tea Party's Social and Religious Agenda and How Progressives Can Respond." Center for American Progress. www.americanprogress.org. November 29.

Stein, Rob. 2007. "At the End of Life, a Racial Divide." *Washington Post*. www.washingtonpost.com. March 12.

Stein, Sam, and Ryan Grim. 2012. "Harry Reid: Bain Investor Told Me That Mitt Romney 'Didn't Pay Any Taxes For 10 Years.'" *Huffington Post*. www.huffingtonpost.com. July 31.

Steinfels, Margaret O'Brien. 2012. "A Losing Strategy: The U.S. Bishops' Campaign against the Contraception Mandate." www.comnonwealmagazine.org. April 23.

Steinfels, Peter, Mark Silk, Douglas Laycock, and Cathleen Kaveny. 2012. "The Bishops and Religious Liberty." www.commonwealmagazine.org. May 30.

Steinhauer, Jennifer. 2010. "Nevada Challenger Lifted by Tea Party Ardor." *New York Times*. www.nytimes.com. June 9.

Stephens, Bret. 2013. "The Robert Taft Republicans Return." *Wall Street Journal*. http://online.wsj.com. September 3.

Stevenson, Richard W. 2012. "The Caucus: Focus on Social Issues Could Shape Battle for Women." www.nytimes.com. February 24.

Stimson, James A. 2004. *Tides of Consent: How Public Opinion Shapes American Politics.* New York: Cambridge University Press.

Stoddard, A. B. 2013. "Rocky Reboot for GOP." *The Hill.* www.thehill.com. February 6.

Stolberg, Cheryl Gay. 2013a. "Young, Liberal and Open to Big Government." *New York Times.* www.nytimes.com. February 10.

Stolberg, Cheryl Gay. 2013b. "Republicans Sign Brief in Support of Gay Marriage." *New York Times.* www.nytimes.com. February 25.

Stolberg, Cheryl Gay. 2013c. "Strategist out of Closet and into Fray, This Time for Gay Marriage." *New York Times.* www.nytimes.com. February 25.

Sullivan, Amy. 2008a. *The Party Faithful: How and Why Democrats Are Closing the God Gap.* New York: Scribner.

Sullivan, Amy. 2008b. "How Catholics Are Judging Obama and the Democrats." *Time.* October 18.

Sullivan, Andrew. 2010. "The Daily Dish: The Tea-Partiers: Christianists, Not Libertarians." www.theatlantic.com. October 6.

Sullivan, Andrew. 2012a. "How Obama Set a Contraception Trap for the Right." *Newsweek.* February 13.

Sullivan, Andrew. 2012b. "The Daily Dish: The Twilight of Gay Wedge Issues?" *Atlantic.* www.theatlantic.com. November 6.

Sullivan, Andrew. 2013. "The Right And Marriage Equality: A Breakthrough." *The Dish.* http://dish.andrewsullivan.com. February 26.

Sullivan, Andy. 2012. "Santorum Left at the Altar by Fellow Catholics." Reuters. www.reuters.com. March 7.

Sweet, Lynn. 2012. "Election Could Come Down to What Women Want." *Chicago Sun-Times.* www.suntimes.com. October 13.

Taibbi, Matt. 2010. "Taibbi: The Tea Party Moron Complex." *Rolling Stone.* www.rollingstone.com. November 14.

Talbot, Margaret. 2012. "Taking Control." *New Yorker.* March 19.

Tanden, Neera. 2012. Neera Tanden fundraising letter. Center for American Progress. March 20.

Tanenhaus, Sam. 2009. "Conservatism Is Dead." *New Republic.* www.tnr.com. February 18.

Taylor, Paul. 2007. "Rev. Falwell's Moral Majority: Mission Accomplished?" Pew Research Center. www.pewresearch.org. May 17.

Teixeira, Ruy. 2009. "New Progressive America: Twenty Years of Demographic, Geographic, and Attitudinal Changes across the Country Herald a New Progressive Majority." Center for American Progress. www.americanprogress.org. March.

Teixeira, Ruy. 2010. "Demographic Change and the Future of the Parties." Center for American Progress Action Fund. www.americanprogressaction.org. June.

Teixeira, Ruy. 2012. "Public Opinion Snapshot: Public Supports Obama's Mini-DREAM Announcement." Center for American Progress. www.americanprogress.org. June 25.

Teixeira, Ruy, and John Halpin. 2010. "Job Loss and Liberal Apathy." *New Republic.* November 5.

Teshman, Brian. 2011. "Tea Party Nation: Gay Rights Will Doom America." *Right Wing Watch.* www.rightwingwatch.org. June 24.

Tesler, Michael, and David O. Sears. 2010. *Obama's Race: The 2008 Election and the Dream of a Post-racial America.* Chicago: University of Chicago Press.

Thompson, Krissah, and Amy Gardner. 2010. "Victories Give Force to Tea Party Movement." *Washington Post.* November 3.

Thrush, Glenn. 2012. "How Romney Lost Latinos." *Politico.* www.politico.com. March 14.

Tomasky, Michael. 2012. "Does Obama Even Want to Win the Election?" *Daily Beast.* www.dailybeast.com. October 7.

Toobin, Jeffrey. 2012a. "The Republicans' Lost Privacy." *New Yorker.* www.newyorker. com. January 12.

Toobin, Jeffrey. 2012b. "The G.O.P.'s Abortion Problem." *New Yorker.* www.newyorker. com. June 19.

Trende, Sean. 2012a. *The Lost Majority: Why the Future of Government Is Up for Grabs—and Who Will Take It.* New York: Palgrave Macmillan.

Trende, Sean. 2012b. "Why Neither Candidate Can Move the Polls." *Real Clear Politics.* www.realclearpolitics.com. July 12.

Trende, Sean. 2013a. "The Case of the Missing White Voters, Revisited." *Real Clear Politics.* www.realclearpolitics.com. June 21.

Trende, Sean. 2013b. "Does the GOP Has to Pass Immigration Reform?" *Real Clear Politics.* www.realclearpolitics.com. June 25.

Trende, Sean. 2013c. "The GOP and Hispanics: What the Future Holds." *Real Clear Politics.* www.realclearpolitics.com. June 28.

Trende, Sean. 2013d. "Demographics and the GOP, Part IV." *Real Clear Politics.* www. realclearpolitics.com. July 2.

Troy, Gil. 2012. "Culture Warriors Don't Win." *New York Times.* www.nytimes.com. April 26.

Tucker-Worgs, Tamelyn. 2013. "When Values and Interests Collide: Black Mega-churches, Same Sex Marriage and the 2012 Elections." Abstract of talk. Center for the Study of Religion, Ohio State University. April 22.

Tumolillo, M. Amedeo. 2011. "University of Arizona Sets Up Civility Institute." *New York Times.* www.nytimes.com. February 21.

Tumulty, Karen, and Nia-Malika Henderson. 2012. "Health-Care Ruling Motivates Romney Supporters." *Washington Post.* www.washingtonpost.com. June 28.

Tyrell, R. Emmett, Jr. 2010. "Out of the Wilderness." *American Spectator.* http://spectator.org. November 12.

United States v. Windsor. 2013.Opinion. 133 S.Ct. 2675 (2013).

U.S. Conference of Catholic Bishops. 2012. "Protecting Consciences." USCCB Nationwide Bulletin Insert. www.usccb.org. June.

U.S. Conference of Catholic Bishops. 2013a. "USCCB Chairman Commends Senate for Passage of Comprehensive Immigration Reform Legislation." www.usccb.org. June 28.

U.S. Conference of Catholic Bishops. 2013b. "Backgrounder, Papal Transition, 2013." Prepared by Office of Media Relations. Washington, D.C.: U.S. Conference of Catholic Bishops.

U.S. House of Representatives. 2011. H.R. 2 (112th Congress): Repealing the Job-Killing Health Care Law Act. Introduced January 11.Washington, D.C.: U.S. House of Representatives.

Vaisse, Justin. 2010. *Neoconservatism: The Biography of a Movement.* Cambridge, Mass.: Belknap Press of Harvard University Press.

Vanderhei, Jim, and Mike Allen. 2013. "The GOP, Fox Political Purge." *Politico.* www.politico.com. February 6.

Vega, James. 2010. "How Can Democrats Combat the 'Enthusiasm Gap' That Threatens to Cause Severe Democratic Losses This Fall?" *Democratic Strategist.* www.thedemocraticstrategist.org. June 27.

Viguerie, Richard. 2014. "The Establishment GOP Is Not the Political Home of Conservatives, and That Needs to Change." *Los Angeles Times.* April 30.

Vogel, Kenneth P., Alexander Burns, and Tarini Parti. 2013. "Karl Rove vs. Tea Party in Big Money Fight for GOP's Future." *Politico.* www.politico.com. January 7.

Von Drehle, David. 2010. "The Party Crashers: Behind the New Republican Revival." *Time.* www.time.com. October 28.

Von Drehle, David. 2012. "For Obama, Survival Is the New Winning." *Time.* www.time.com. November 12.

Waldman, Paul. 2010a. "Will the Right's Coalition Hold?" *American Prospect.* http://prospect.org. September 7.

Waldman, Paul. 2010b. "Tea Party Standard." *American Prospect.* http://prospect.org. September 21.

Waldman, Paul. 2012. "Are Conservatives Getting Crazier?" *American Prospect.* http://prospect.org. March 19.

Waldman, Steven. 2008. "Pastor Rick in the Political Spotlight." *Wall Street Journal.* http://online.wsj.com. December 18.

Wallace, Paul. 2011. "Top Ten Peacemakers in the Science-Religion Wars." *Religion Dispatches.* www.religiondispatches.com. December 18.

Wallis, Jim. 2005. *God's Politics: Why the Right Gets It Wrong and the Left Doesn't Get It.* San Francisco: HarperSan Francisco.

Wallsten, Peter. 2010. "Democrats Face Threat from Their Own Base." *Wall Street Journal.* http://online.wsj.com. May 19.

Wallsten. Peter. 2012. "Arizona Immigration Ruling Complicates Republicans' Strategy with Hispanics." *Washington Post.* www.washingtonpost.com. June 25.

Wall Street Journal. 2012a. "Review and Outlook: Romney's Tax Confusion." http://online.wsj.com. July 5.

Wall Street Journal. 2012b. "Editorial: Why Not Paul Ryan?" http://online.wsj.com. August 9.

Wall Street Journal. 2013. "Editorial: Rand Paul's Drone Rant." http://online.wsj.com. March 7.

Wall Street Journal. 2014. "Editorial: Jeb Bush's Immigration Heresy: The Former Florida Governor Makes More Sense than His Critics." http://online.wsj.com. April 8.

Walsh, Joan. 2012. "It's Not Mitt's Party," *Slate.* www.slate.com. June 22.

Walsh, Michael. 2012. "The Corner: Well, It Worked, Didn't It?" *National Review.* www.nationalreview.com. July 2.

Ward, Jon. 2012. "National Tea Party Groups Want on GOP Bandwagon but Face Chilly Reception." *Huffington Post.* www.huffingtonpost.com. June 22.

Warren, Mark. 2010. "Defiance." *Esquire.* www.esquire.com. December 13.

Warren, Rick. 2002. *The Purpose-Driven Life: What on Earth Am I Here For?* Grand Rapids, Mich.: Zondervan.

Washington Post. 2004. "Transcript: Illinois Senate Candidate Barack Obama." www.washingtonpost.com. July 27.

Weigel, David. 2011a. "Palin Spox: Targets on SarahPAC Map Were Actually 'Surveyors Symbols.'" *Slate.* www.slate.com. January 9.

Weigel, David. 2011b. "Pima County Sheriff Blames 'Paranoia about How Government Operates.'" *Slate.* www.slate.com. January 9.

Weigel, David. 2012a. "Maryland: A 36-Point Black Surge of Support for Gay Marriage." *Slate.* www.slate.com. May 24.

Weigel, David. 2012b. "Why the "Rape Thing" Haunts Republicans." *Slate.* www.slate.com. November 1.

Weinger, Mackenzie. 2012. "Karl Rove: Fox News Ohio Call 'Premature.'" *Politico.* www.politico.com. November 6.

Weisberg, Jacob. 2010. "The Right's New Left: The Tea Party Movement Has Two Defining Traits: Status Anxiety and Anarchism." *Slate.* September 19.

Weisberg, Jacob. 2011. "The Tea Party and the Tucson Tragedy." *Slate.* www.slate.com. January 10.

Weisman, Jon. 2013. "Ellen DeGeneres to Host Oscars." *Variety.* www.variety.com. August 2.

Weisman, Jonathan. 2011. "Hispanics Rise in Key States." *Wall Street Journal.* http://online.wsj.com. September 29.

Weisman, Jonathan. 2012. "Obama Backs Student in Furor with Limbaugh on Birth Control." *New York Times.* www.nytimes.com. March 2.

Welch, Chris. 2011. "Santorum: Obama Dividing Country to Win Election." www.cnn.com. December 22.

Wenner, Jan, and Eric Bates. 2010. "Roundtable: The GOP Victory—and Obama's Next Steps." *Rolling Stone.* www.rollingstone.com. December 10.

Werner, Erica. 2013. "Rand Paul Endorses Immigrant Path to Citizenship." Associated Press. March 19.

Westen, Drew. 2011."What Happened to Obama?" *New York Times.* www.nytimes.com. August 6.

Westen, Drew. 2012. "If Obama Loses The Election, Here's Why." *Washington Post.* www.washingtonpost.com. July 27.

Whitcomb, Dan. 2012. "Rush Limbaugh Apologizes to Law Student for 'Insulting' Comment." Reuters. www.mobile.reuters.com. March 4.

White House. 2013a. "Presidential Proclamation—Religious Freedom Day." www.whitehouse.gov. January 16.

White House. 2013b. "Remarks by the President at the Planned Parenthood Conference." www.whitehouse.gov. April 26.

Wilcox, Clyde. 2010. "The Christian Right and Civic Virtue." In Alan Wolfe and Ira Katznelson, eds., *Religion and Democracy in the United States: Danger or Opportunity?* New York: Russell Sage Foundation; Princeton, N.J.: Princeton University Press.

Wilentz, Sean. 2008. *The Age of Reagan: A History, 1974–2008.* New York: Harper.

Wilentz, Sean. 2010a. "Confounding Fathers: The Tea Party's Cold War Roots." *New Yorker.* October 18.

Wilentz, Sean. 2010b. "Live by the Movement, Die by the Movement." *New Republic.* www.tnr.com. November 9.

Will, George F. 2011. "Mike Huckabee, Newt Gingrich and the Spotlight-Chasing Candidates of 2012." *Washington Post.* www.washingtonpost.com. March 6.

Will, George F. 2012. "Why Americans Might Tolerate This Failed President." *Investors.com.* www.investors.com. October 1.

Williams, Rhys H. 2010. "Immigration and the Politics of Cultural Identity in Post Obama America." Presented at the conference "Culture Wars in the United States: The Politics of Religious Conservatism in Obama's Time." Center for United States Studies, University of Quebec at Montreal. October 14.

Winston, Diane. 2012. *The Oxford Handbook of Religion and the American News Media.* New York: Oxford University Press.

Winters, Michael Sean. 2012a. *God's Right Hand: How Jerry Falwell Made God a Republican and Baptized the American Right.* New York: HarperOne.

Winters, Michael Sean. 2012b. "How the Ghost of Jerry Falwell Conquered the Republican Party." *New Republic.* www.tnr.com. March 5.

Winters, Michael Sean. 2012c. "Please Let It Be Ryan." *New Republic.* www.tnr.com. August 9.

Wolfe, Alan. 2009. *The Future of Liberalism.* New York: Knopf.

Wolffe, Richard. 2010. *Renegade: The Making of a President.* New York: Crown.

Woodward, Bob. 2012. *The Price of Politics.* New York: Simon & Schuster.

Wuthnow, Robert. 2009. "Religion." In Peter H. Schuck and James Q. Wilson, eds., *Understanding America: The Anatomy of an Exceptional Nation.* New York: Public Affairs Books.

Yee, Vivian. 2013. "Dolan Says Catholic Church Should Be More Welcoming of Gay People." *New York Times.* www.nytimes.com. March 31.

Yepsen, David. 2011. "Iowa and the Future of the GOP." *Wall Street Journal.* http://online.wsj.com. December 24.

Younge, Gary. 2012. "Election 2012: The Return of 'Culture Wars.'" *Guardian*. www.theguardian.com. February 10.

YouTube. 2012. Rush Limbaugh show excerpts. https://www.youtube.com/watch?v=3k8yTvyG7nw. March 2.

Zernike, Kate. 2010. *Boiling Mad: Inside Tea Party America*. New York: Times Books.

Zernike, Kate. 2011. "Tea Party Gets Early Start on G.O.P. Targets for 2012." *New York Times*. www.nytimes.com. January 29.

Zernike, Kate, and Megan Thee-Brenan. 2010. "Poll Finds Tea Party Backers Wealthier and More Educated." *New York Times*. www.nytimes.com. April 14.

Zoellner, Tom. 2011. *A Safeway in Arizona*. New York: Viking.

ABOUT THE AUTHOR

John Dombrink is Professor of Criminology, Law, and Society at the University of California, Irvine. He is the co-author of *The Last Resort* (1990), *Dying Right* (2001), and *Sin No More* (2007).